anniversa
tion. A th
army, has
this book, ...nificant additions
to the other two parts (on the imperial
power, the organization and reserves of
the royal estates, and the other resources
of the crown). *Frankish Institutions under
Charlemagne* is based largely on original
sources and is the distillation of more
than forty years of research. Such a
comprehensive treatment of Carolingian
institutions has long been hoped for
from Professor Ganshof.

The author, who succeeded Henri
Pirenne in the chair of medieval history
at the University of Ghent, is known
throughout the world for his publica-
tions on medieval institutions. He is one
of twenty foreign members of the
Académie des Inscriptions et Belles-
Lettres, a section of the Institut de
France.

The American medievalist Bryce Lyon,
with his wife, has served as translator
and has written the Foreword, which
surveys interpretations of Charlemagne's
role in history in the light of Professor
Ganshof's work. Mr. Lyon is Barnaby
Conrad and Mary Critchfield Keeney
Professor of History at Brown University.

FRANKISH
INSTITUTIONS
UNDER
CHARLEMAGNE

FRANKISH
INSTITUTIONS
UNDER
CHARLEMAGNE

François Louis Ganshof

FOREWORD BY BRYCE LYON

TRANSLATED FROM THE FRENCH BY BRYCE AND MARY LYON

BROWN UNIVERSITY PRESS

PROVIDENCE, RHODE ISLAND 1968

Library of Congress Catalog Card Number: 68-29166

This book was designed by Richard Hendel.
The type was set in Perpetua and Janson types and
printed by the Crimson Printing Company on University Text.
The book was bound by the Stanhope Bindery.

Foreword

To men steeped in the history of the Western world the shadow of Charlemagne seems longer and his spell greater than that of Alexander the Great, Caesar, or Napoleon. Charlemagne and his accomplishments lie at the heart of the Western tradition. Like Alexander, with whom medieval men were fond of linking him, Charlemagne has become more of a historical legend than either Caesar or Napoleon. And yet, although more is known about Alexander than about Charlemagne, the sources for both are so meager that historians have been encouraged and tempted to speculate. Who would be so bold as to claim that he knows the historical Alexander or Charlemagne? The results of their labor may still be seen, but who knows completely how they were achieved or what the real objectives were.

In pursuit of the real Charlemagne historians have created many Charlemagnes. He has been used to justify the aspirations of many generations and nations. For each he has had a different image, an image created largely by historians to satisfy immediate needs and vindicate immediate goals. Literature has romanticized him, making of him what men wanted; art has given him many faces and personalities. But however depicted, he has become for all men of western

Europe a father figure. No one who has lived in western Europe or under the influence of its tradition has escaped the sweep of Charlemagne.

For over a thousand years German rulers and a succession of political regimes have invoked Charlemagne. At Rome in 962 when Otto the Great received the title *Imperator et Augustus* and renewed the Holy Roman Empire, he was only imitating Charlemagne. In 998 Otto the Great's grandson Otto III bedecked his seal with the majestic inscription *Renovatio imperii Romanorum*, and in 1000, not by accident, he made a pilgrimage to Aachen, had the tomb of Charlemagne opened, and then "did worship to him with bended thighs and knees." Throughout the Middle Ages the German kings and emperors associated their names with that of Charlemagne. When Frederick Barbarossa secured the canonization of Charlemagne in 1165, he thereby sanctified the imperial cause. By the thirteenth century, although the Holy Roman Empire was no longer a viable political organization, being already more fiction than fact, the memory and appeal of Charlemagne endured. Illuminated manuscripts continued to portray him as the mighty ruler and protector of Western Christendom. Indeed, in 1510, on the eve of the Reformation that was to shatter further the loose conglomeration of states that was Germany, Albrecht Dürer could paint Charlemagne as a symbol of German imperial majesty. In the now famous painting done for Nuremberg, Charlemagne is garbed in the imperial mantle and on his head is the imperial crown worn by all the emperors since Otto the Great. At the top right-hand corner of the painting Dürer inscribed his view of Charlemagne: "Das ist des heilgen grossen keiser karels habitus."

In the dreary centuries that followed, the memory of Charlemagne's achievements blurred but never disappeared from the historical consciousness of Germany. To the humble he became a savior who would someday return to free Germany from oppression and unify her into a great state. To the German intellectuals and political leaders he became a symbol in their attempt to re-create a great Germany. During the reunification of Germany in the years before 1870 Charlemagne was a favorite subject for historical writing. Eager to buttress Bismarck's program of unification, German historians turned to Charlemagne for precedent and justification. After the shocking defeat of Napoleon III's armies King William I of Prussia assumed the imperial title of Kaiser in the Hall of Mirrors at Versailles on 18 January 1871. The Second German Reich came into being. From then until 1914 German historians rediscovered and praised the *Germanentum* and military spirit of Charlemagne. Still later, in the 1930's, some German historians exaggerated the essential German qualities of Charlemagne, while others, under the influence of the ideology of the Nazi Third Reich, regarded him as the executioner of the only true Germans, the pagan Saxons, and as the ruler who corrupted the Franks and other German tribes by forcing them to embrace Christian faith and Roman culture.

Charlemagne's role in French history is also prominent. Able to claim descent from Charlemagne, the Capetian kings could also associate themselves with his glory. Philip Augustus certainly did so upon departing for the Third Crusade. In France, too, Charlemagne was a familiar figure in illuminated manuscripts. The history of Charlemagne was retold in the brilliantly colored glass of the cathedral at Chartres. French chroniclers, manipulating and fabricating historical facts, managed to prove that the French kings descended from Clovis by way of Charlemagne; indeed, this is what lawyers and historians were writing in the seventeenth century when Louis XIV was seeking historical and legal arguments to justify French expansion into Germany and to make himself more than just an emperor of the French. Nor was Napoleon loath to associate Charlemagne with his triumphs; proclaimed "Emperor of the French" in 1804, he was hailed as a "reborn Charlemagne." Even while presiding over the death of the Holy Roman Empire in 1806, Napoleon claimed rule over a vast new European empire that he considered a far worthier successor to Charlemagne's creation.

After the French Revolution and the era of Napoleon it was natural that historians should differ sharply over the impact of Charlemagne on France and Western Europe. Opposed to Guizot's famous and laudatory portrayal was Michelet's hostile evaluation of Charlemagne as the dupe and servant of the church. As historians widened their investigations of Charlemagne, creating a vast body of scholarly writing, our knowledge of him increased, and different interpretations of his significance arose. As a result, there is no agreement as to whether there was a Carolingian renaissance, whether the economy of western Europe revived under Charlemagne or dropped to its lowest point, whether Charlemagne saved the papacy and the church or placed them in humiliating dependence, whether Charlemagne planned to create an empire, or whether his support of feudalism led to the disintegration of the Carolingian empire.

On one point all historians agree: Charlemagne's significance will continue to be debated, but he will remain a great figure in the history of western Europe. This was evident during the summer of 1965 when a memorable exhibition devoted to Charlemagne was held at the town hall and the cloister of the cathedral at Aachen under the auspices of the Council of Europe. There, twelve hundred years ago, Charlemagne's father Pepin III made his first sojourn; there, for almost twenty years, Charlemagne had his palace; and there, in 1965, the eight-hundredth anniversary of Charlemagne's canonization was commemorated. More dramatically than most such events, the exhibition symbolized the transformation of western Europe since 1945. Charlemagne and his empire served as the exemplar for the growing European unity. Acquiring still another dimension, Charlemagne emerged as a great European citizen. Proud is the European who today wins the Prize of Charlemagne "for outstanding services to the cause of European unity."

The organizing committee of the exhibition, conscious that works of art and archeological remains give but an incomplete picture of Charlemagne and his achievements, decided to publish four volumes of studies by eminent scholars on every aspect of the age of Charlemagne. More than eighty scholars contributed studies to the four volumes. Among the more important studies the two by Professor François L. Ganshof on the impact of Charlemagne on Frankish institutions and law are extremely valuable, not only because they are written by the *doyen* of medievalists specializing in Carolingian history, but also because they concern the area where Charlemagne indisputably left his sharpest imprint.

The history called western European began with Charlemagne and his empire; yet, in 843, within thirty years after his death, the Carolingian empire was disintegrating and being replaced by the small political units characteristic of European history to the present time. While Charlemagne's empire disappeared, the political, military, and legal institutions that emerged during his long rule survived and became the foundation for the institutions of the successor states. It is impossible to understand European notions of royal and imperial power, kingship, central and local administrative institutions, legal concepts and procedures, respect for law, the inquest, the relation of church and state, or feudalism and seignorialism without knowing about their development under Charlemagne. The institutional history of Europe, even that of the United States, goes back to the age of Charlemagne. One who knows nothing about a Carolingian assembly, council, or court cannot understand modern European diets, parliaments, cabinets, ministers, administrative procedures, or church-state relations.

It therefore seemed both appropriate and pertinent to translate into English the studies by Professor Ganshof and to issue them together in a volume easily available to scholar and student. The publication of this book is, in a sense, the achievement of what scholars have hoped Professor Ganshof would do: write a volume on Charlemagne and his influence on institutions. In the two studies that appeared in *Karl der Grosse:* Volume I, *Persönlichkeit und Geschichte*, Professor Ganshof did not discuss the imperial power of Charlemagne, the organization and revenues of the royal estates, coinage, or military institutions because these subjects had been dealt with by scholars in other studies. To provide the present volume with a more comprehensive treatment of institutional development under Charlemagne, Professor Ganshof has added sections on these subjects and has, in fact, written a separate study on military institutions.

While this is not the place for detailed comment on the studies that follow, it seems fitting to note here what have come to be recognized as salient features in Professor Ganshof's historical research and writing. As a student of Henri Pirenne, who was probably the most distinguished medievalist of the late nineteenth and early twentieth centuries, and of Ferdinand Lot, whose works epitomize exact and critical historical scholarship, Professor Ganshof was trained in a rigorous school of history whose approach to research stemmed from the methodology of such scholars as Ranke, Waitz, Monod, and Giry. Under Pirenne one learned to write history from the primary sources, being constantly admonished not to draw conclusions or to advance theses unsupported by the evidence. What distinguished Pirenne from his generation of historians, however, was his ability to discover theses and themes in the sources and to sense the importance of providing historical syntheses and advancing fresh but sound interpretations. Anyone familar with the work of Professor Ganshof can recognize the influence of Pirenne. What Ganshof admired and what most impressed him was Pirenne's objectivity and impartiality. In a sensitive evaluation of Pirenne as master and historian he has written: "Pirenne was a man of great integrity; for him, devotion to scholarship was the historian's intellectual integrity, while objectivity was his moral integrity." (*Henri Pirenne: Le maître—l'historien* [Brussels, 1936], p. 27. This short brochure appeared originally as an article in the review *Le Flambeau*, XVIII [1935].)

This respect for evidence and objectivity is apparent in the chapters that follow. Unlike Inama-Sternegg, Dopsch, Fichtenau, Lord Bryce, Dawson, or various intellectual historians with elaborate theories on Charlemagne and his work, Professor Ganshof seldom speculates or theorizes. He selects with such care and describes with such clarity all that the pertinent records say about institutions under Charlemagne, that what results is a much firmer understanding of institutional development than can be obtained from books in which speculation prevails. For each observation and conclusion Professor Ganshof cites the evidence; so intimately does he know the sources that, contrary to most historians who have despaired of ever knowing the real Charlemagne or of determining his actual influence on the institutions and on the cultural and spiritual life of early medieval Europe, he indisputably shows the active role of Charlemagne and produces a realistic portrait of his accomplishments.

These pages, a distillation of Professor Ganshof's profound knowledge of the Carolingian period, distinguish him as a historian more in the tradition of Ranke and Waitz than in that which has emerged since World War I and includes such eminent scholars as Marc Bloch, Huizinga, and Dawson, historians concerned primarily with the mood and collective thought of society in different historical periods. Though this latter approach to medieval history has been in vogue and has provided new insights to the Middle Ages, the reader of this book by Professor Ganshof will be reminded that there is no substitute for knowledge unembellished with intriguing and suggestive theory. So difficult and tantalizing are the Carolingian sources that speculation, if not precluded, must at least follow an attempt to know what the sources actually say. This is the primary task of the historian working in the Carolingian period, and in this respect Professor Ganshof has not forgotten words he wrote over thirty years ago: "Two dangers menace the discipline of history . . . the taste for easy work and the tendency to make history partisan." (From *Henri Pirenne: Le maître—l'historien*, p. 27.)

I am grateful to those who have assisted in the publication of this translation. My greatest debt, however, is to Professor Ganshof for his patient co-operation and kindly, invaluable advice. He gave his consent to the proposal to translate the two studies that appeared in *Karl der Grosse*, wrote new sections to make the book more comprehensive, and meticulously checked the translation. What shortcomings and errors there may be are not his responsibility.

This is also the place to acknowledge the part of my wife. As always she has revised and typed the manuscript, but this time she has done even more. She has been responsible for much of the translation. It is fitting that her name appear with mine on the title page, not only because her contribution equals or surpasses mine, but also because we were delighted to work together on a book by Professor Ganshof, whose long friendship we treasure and whose scholarship we admire.

BRYCE LYON

Brown University

Acknowledgment

The publication of this book is due to the initiative of Professor Bryce Lyon. It was he who had the idea of translating my work on Charlemagne from French into English and who, with the collaboration of his wife, has produced a most accurate translation that involved on several occasions toilsome research. They more than once suggested alterations that improved both the form of the work and also its substance. I wish to express here my warmest gratitude to both of them.

F. L. G.

Contents

PART I

"Cette question, comme toutes celles que
renferme encore l'histoire, ne pouvait se résoudre
que par la lecture directe des documents et
l'observation attentive des faits."
—FUSTEL DE COULANGES,
Les transformations de la royauté
à l'époque carolingienne
(Paris, 1892), p. vii, n. 1.

"Bei Karls Begriff 'Ordnung' handelt es
sich um jene ganz natürliche Ordnung, die auf
einem Bauernhof, in einer königlichen Pfalz,
im ganzen Reich, unter den Völkern und zwischen
Kirche und Staat herrschen muss und die immer
wieder ins richtige Gleichgewicht zu bringen
die Hauptaufgabe des Herrschers ist."
—P. E. SCHRAMM, *Karl der Grosse.*
Denkart und Grundauffassungen, in *Orden pour le Mérite*
für Wissenschaften und Künste.
Reden und Gedenkworte, V (1962), 151.

"L'idéal de l'Empire chrétien, Charlemagne lui-même,
ont été trahis par les hommes."
—R. FOLZ,
Le couronnement impérial de Charlemagne
(Paris, 1964), p. 193.

Charlemagne and the Institutions of the Frankish Monarchy

This is not a comprehensive survey of the institutions of the Frankish monarchy under the reign of Charlemagne[1] but an attempt to show the influence that Charlemagne exercised over these institutions and, in some measure, the use he made of them. It is a discussion of central and local institutions, both administrative and financial, as well as such important developments as royal and imperial power, immunity, and vassalage. Military and judicial institutions are treated in Parts II and III.

Charlemagne's Influence on Frankish Institutions

Charlemagne influenced the institutions in the territories under his authority—the Frankish kingdom (*Regnum Francorum*) and the Lombard kingdom (*Regnum Langobardorum*). In the Frankish kingdom—the one that concerns us here—his influence was felt in each of the large regions known to men of that time: the lands between the Loire and the Rhine; the lands to the south of the Loire; and the lands to the east of the Rhine,[2] including Saxony, which came under the power of Charlemagne after its conquest, and Bavaria, which came to Charlemagne after the fall of its last "national" duke, Tassilo III, in 788. The instrument chosen above all others to mold the institutions was the capitulary, a decree first agreed upon and then orally promulgated, divided into articles (*capitula*), and used by the Carolingian rulers to publish legislative or administrative measures. These decrees were given such traditional names as *constitutio, decretum,* and *edictum,* or those by which they have come to be known—*capitulum, capitulare.*[3]

Among these capitularies are some that reveal Charlemagne as exercising a particularly strong influence on the institutions. These were extensive decrees dealing with various matters that were generally published at a time of crisis, most often at the close of a great assembly, and throughout them the force of religious preoccupation is obvious. Their immediate goal was twofold: on the one hand, to return to the correct application of traditional rules, which unfortunately had been abandoned, and on the other hand, to apply these rules and adapt them to new situations, which in many cases resulted in the creation of new regulations. The first capitulary of this type, the Capitulary of Herstal, was published in 779 and is the oldest decree known by the name *capitulare.* It climaxed a period of very serious political crisis: the disastrous expedition to Spain in 778; the violent Saxon reaction that in the same year menaced Cologne; and the fear of anti-Frankish movements in Aquitaine and Septimania. Prepared in the assembly gathered in the palace of Herstal on the Meuse and promulgated by the king, this capitulary amended or reorganized the most important sectors of public life by introducing substantial reforms.[4] Described with some exaggeration as "la charte constitutive que donne Charlemagne à tous les territoires de l'ancien royaume franc,"[5] it dealt notably with the functioning of several institutions and with ecclesiastical as well as with administrative and judicial matters, two domains closely intertwined in the structure of the Carolingian monarchy. It would seem that Charlemagne and his councilors interpreted the crisis of 778 as a sign from Heaven to extirpate scandalous abuses and to make justice reign.

Little is known about the circumstances surrounding the preparation of a second great capitulary published by Charlemagne in 789 and commonly called the *Admonitio generalis* or of two lesser capitularies that seem to have been published at the same time— one containing instructions for the *missi dominici*, the other containing instructions destined for some *missi* sent into Aquitaine.[6] Of the *Admonitio*, which deals primarily with ecclesiastical matters, more than two-thirds consists of canonical texts derived from the Dionysio-Hadriana,[7] but it also contains dispositions of a mixed nature concerning institutions. Among other things expressed and supported by biblical citations, it contains a fundamental rule of the Carolingian system of government, that there ought to be peace and concord—that is, confident collaboration—between ecclesiastical authorities and secular officials of royal power.[8] Later, under various forms, this rule was often repeated, and though we know that it often failed when applied, its authority as a directing principle for the functioning of institutions remained firm. In regard to the instructions for the *missi*, certain ones are exclusively ecclesiastical, even monastic, in character, while others are directly related to the state and its organs. The *missi* sent out in 789 were, by order of Charlemagne, to conduct for the first time a general swearing of an oath of fidelity to the king.[9]

A third great capitulary, published in 794 at the conclusion of the council convoked and presided over by the king at Frankfurt,[10] followed another period of crisis. In 792 Pepin the Hunchback, the favorite bastard of the king, directed a dangerous conspiracy against him; in the same year and also in 793 the Saxons, thought to be subdued, again revolted; operations against the Avars had to be halted; and the harvests were bad.[11] There were, in addition, such grave religious preoccupations as the Adoptionist heresy of Felix, bishop of Urgel, which imperiled the orthodox conception of the Trinity, and the re-establishment in the East of the worship of icons by a Byzantine council that pretended to be ecumenical.[12] That the Capitulary of Frankfurt should deal particularly with ecclesiastical matters is therefore natural; and yet there were some articles, evidently prepared in sessions at which laymen were also present, that ruled on problems of both a spiritual and secular nature, such as the exercise of jurisdiction over clerks or the establishment of the price of bread and of grains used for bread; and other articles contained important administrative dispositions concerning, in particular, weights and measures, and money.[13]

The fourth great capitulary that should be cited was published at Aachen in March 802.[14] It was not a political crisis that immediately preceded and provoked its formulation, but a psychological crisis within Charlemagne himself. His imperial coronation at Rome on 25 December 800, which had initiated for him a series of problems, some more grave than others but all of which he considered important, had rendered more acute and more agonizing the awareness of his responsibilities before God—an awareness that took immediate and definite form in the knowledge that he was the recognized holder of a universal power destined to protect and promote the Christian religion and the church;[15] and that, as such, he was responsible not only for his own acts but also for the attitudes or the acts of his subjects, particularly the ecclesiastical and secular officials exercising his authority.[16] From this sense of responsibility arose a clearer view of the contrast between what ought to be and what was in the Frankish state. This fourth capitulary—very comprehensive and displaying in some passages, it appears, the personal reactions of Charlemagne[17]—arose from discussions of Charlemagne with his councilors and from deliberations of a great assembly convoked for the reform of church and state. It presents a program of imperial government of church and state in the empire[18] and contains numerous purely ecclesiastical dispositions and many others of an administrative and judicial, even indeed of a political, nature, such as articles defining a new and more exacting concept of the fidelity owed to the emperor.[19]

The public institutions were the object of reform, for does not the rapport between what is and what ought to be depend upon their operation? In addition, other institutional measures followed. Some of the *missi*, bearers of the capitulary, were sent throughout the empire, not only to supervise the execution of measures already decreed, but to inform the emperor of the existing state of affairs and to prepare new reforms to be established at an assembly that was to convene in October at Aachen.[20] Besides the Programmatic Capitulary there is preserved the *Capitulare missorum*, the instructions to the *missi*.[21]

The last of the great capitularies, it would seem, was that published by Charlemagne toward the end of 805 at the palace of Thionville on the Moselle, where he resided at the time. Like the Capitulary of Herstal of 779, it concerned ecclesiastical and secular matters, notably the functioning of numerous institutions.[22] Although in the form of a *capitulare missorum*—that is, instructions addressed to the *missi dominici*—the Capitulary of Thionville, like that of Herstal, can be regarded as a "capitulary of reform." [23] Its preparation, about which little is known, must surely have been connected with serious deficiencies in the functioning of the institutions, as well as with the state of uncertainty and uneasiness shared by the emperor and his entourage regarding the succession to the throne and the profound troubles it might engender.[24] The great endeavor to end scandalous abuses that this capitulary represents appeared to the emperor and his councilors as a necessary condition for God to inspire them in their design to regulate the succession to the throne, a regulation that came in 806.[25]

Sometimes other capitularies or certain dispositions of some of them supplemented the content of the major capitularies when their intent was unclear. Thus, from assemblies meeting at Aachen in October 802 and undoubtedly from commissions that had carried on their activities, at least four such capitularies emerged to clarify and supplement the Programmatic Capitulary of March 802: two from 803, one completing all the national laws in force in the empire and the other revising the Ripuarian law; a third of 802, or more probably of 803, containing some articles intended to assure the execution of dispositions that, in the Programmatic Capitulary, were decreed in a manner too general to be completely effective; and finally a *capitulare missorum* of 803.[26] To these should be added two capitularies for Bavaria, one that revised the law of the Bavarians,[27] and another, dating from the beginning of 806, of which only a fragment is preserved, that, it appears, reinforced the authority of several dispositions of the Capitulary of Thionville by incorporating them into the national laws.[28]

While these great capitularies and the dispositions that completed them played a primary role in the power wielded by Charlemagne over the institutions of the Frankish monarchy, other capitularies, much more numerous though less extensive and published amid circumstances less solemn or less dramatic, also played an important role. The dispositions that merit being fully qualified as "legislative" are rare.[29] Their articles less often have the customary form for legislative or regulatory dispositions than that used for administrative decisions aimed at a group of given cases and entailing prohibitions or orders to officials or to subjects of the king to act in a certain way and to conduct themselves in a certain manner. That these prohibitions and orders were frequently repeated suggests that they were often not obeyed,[30] but constant repetition probably proved effective at times.

Some very important decisions made by Charlemagne in the domain of institutions do not appear in the capitularies. We do not have an article of a capitulary by which Charlemagne created the *scabini* (French, *échevins*; German, *Schöffen*)—permanent judges at the county court (*mallus*)—and yet we encounter the *scabini* in some capitularies where there is a question of their duties or of their appointment.[31] Although in the military domain we do not have an article of a capitulary decreeing that in case of war a certain number of the "economically weak" will be grouped in order to equip one of them who himself will have to serve, in 806, 807, and 808 we find measures for executing such an arrangement.[32] Either the capitularies containing these articles have perished or such dispositions were never drawn up in the form of articles. Also, Charlemagne might have taken a general decision and had it made known verbally, although only particular decisions were published in a capitulary after having been verbally promulgated.[33]

It was not enough simply to publish the capitularies. To insure that the dispositions they contained relating to institutions and to other domains were executed, local action was necessary. Despite scanty information in the sources regarding this action, three facts emerge. There was, first, action by the king himself, whose custom of moving about and residing in various parts of the kingdom enabled him to meet with the ecclesiastical and secular authorities and to give them verbal instructions. This action certainly became less important and effective when Charlemagne, in the last years of his reign, rarely moved about the realm.[34] A second and important action was exercised by the *missi dominici*, royal commissioners who were sent into all parts of the territory, one of whose chief duties was to make known the content of the capitularies and to supervise their execution.[35] There was, finally, the permanent action exercised by the regional officials, who were responsible for the normal functioning and regulation of the institutions.

Royal and Imperial Power

Royal power was acquired by Charlemagne at the death of his father on 24 September 768. Like his brother Carloman II, he received a part of the *Regnum Francorum* by right of succession. According to customary law, Pepin III had divided the kingdom between his two sons several days before his death. On 9 October at Noyon, Charlemagne was recognized by the great men who were to be dependent upon him, and for the second time he received the royal unction from the bishops present. Indeed, with his father and brother at Saint-Denis in 754 he had already received the unction from Pope Stephen II that assured him the qualities of king and of *patricius Romanorum*. In December 771, upon the death of his brother, he annexed his brother's part of the Frankish kingdom, thus reconstituting the unity of the *Regnum*. Three years later, in 774, after the victorious end of the Italian campaign, he subjected the Lombard kingdom to his authority and took the title of King of the Lombards. From 16 June of this same year his title was, as a rule, very general: *Carolus gratia Dei rex Francorum et Langobardorum atque patricius Romanorum.*[36]

On 25 December 800 at Rome, after an assembly had decided on 23 December to re-establish an emperor in the person of Charlemagne, Pope Leo III crowned him, and the "Roman people" shouted the acclamation that made him a Roman emperor.[37] He exercised imperial power at Rome and even in what one commonly calls the Papal States. From 29 May 801 his new title became permanent: *Karolus serenissimus augustus a Deo coronatus magnus pacificus imperator Romanum gubernans imperium, qui et per misericordiam Dei rex Francorum atque Langobardorum.*[38]

In spite of the profound impression that the acquisition of imperial dignity made on Charlemagne and in spite of his efforts to grasp the exact import of the *nomen imperatoris*—that is, of his new title and the realities it could involve[39]—he was too clairvoyant not to know that royal power was the only solid foundation of his authority. The imperial power permitted the king to exercise certain of his prerogatives with greater force and in a broader manner, at the same time creating for him the task of giving a special orientation to these prerogatives; but that is all. It has been said that the imperial power of Charlemagne was expressed by an intensification of his royal power.[40] This opinion seems to be correct.

This intensification and these orientations were manifested in several domains. Since, according to an opinion widespread among the clerics, the essential task of the emperor was to protect the faith and the church,[41] measures were taken and reforms accomplished with the idea of obliging each person "to keep himself fully in the service of God." [42] And so that the emperor could take these measures and realize these reforms, the idea of fidelity toward him was rendered more exacting and the oath of fidelity sworn to him, more rigorous.[43] With the same objective, the institution of the *missi dominici* underwent changes aimed at rendering their work and particularly their jurisdiction more regular and more effective.[44] Since the emperor was the successor of Roman Christian emperors who had been legislators, Charlemagne henceforth engaged in legislative activity with less caution, even in the realm of private law;[45] like the Roman emperors, he ordered that judgment should be made in accordance with the written text of the laws when one existed.[46] Some very important matters are involved here that concern measures or groups of measures having individual significance even when several of them were combined in a single programmatic capitulary.[47] Imperial power was not substituted for royal power. There was not even a profound transformation of royal power or fundamental reform of it. It is also striking that after the accession to imperial dignity the chief of the Frankish state was still designated in the text of the capitularies by the term *rex* as well as *imperator*. Let us, then, now discuss the royal power of Charlemagne.

Although essentially this power[48] was like that of his father, certain elements were accentuated and in some measure transformed. Charlemagne placed a strong emphasis on his *bannum*, his power to command or to prohibit and to punish any transgression of his orders or prohibitions.[49] Some of these orders and prohibitions he proclaimed permanently by making them rules of law aimed at the maintenance of public peace and the protection of the weak. They forbade the harming of churches, widows, orphans, or the "economically weak"; they prohibited rape, group assaults on a house, and arson; or they sought to procure more dependable military service for the king.[50] These eight examples are the best known and Charlemagne frequently called attention to their obligatory force and permanent character in his capitularies, even introducing dispositions concerning them into Saxony after its conquest and into the former duchy of Bavaria after it had been assimilated into the other parts of the realm.[51] But the *bannum* was not limited to any one area; Charlemagne used it, for example, to forbid the sale of slaves to territories outside the realm, to forbid incestuous unions,[52] and to give, in individual cases, orders that it would be dangerous to disobey.[53] A particularly heavy fine of sixty shillings punished all violations,[54] and it could be made even heavier.[55] After his accession to the empire, Charlemagne made transgression of the *bannum* a case of infidelity, a move that permitted the application of arbitrary penalties.[56]

Charlemagne accorded particularly great importance to the religious aspect of his power. Not only was he a veritable master of the church in his states,[57] but above all he could act with authority in the mixed domains of church and realm, of church and subjects of the king. Both a manifestation of his faith and an application of this religious aspect of his power are evident in his orders relating to public calamities; in orders to the clergy to celebrate masses, to chant the offices, to address supplications to God, to observe rigorous fasts, and to join in charitable activities; and in orders to the faithful to pray and to supplement their prayers as much as possible with charitable acts.[58] Motivating these orders was a sense of both right and duty or, in other words, a sense of power bestowed upon him by God. This power, he affirmed, permitted him to correct whatever ought to be corrected in the religious life of the clergy and the faithful; upon the exercise of this power and the manner in which its decrees were obeyed depended the preservation of his kingdom by God.[59] The rule of close co-operation between ecclesiastical and secular authorities, promulgated, as we have seen, in 789[60] and often repeated later[61] but poorly observed,[62] has this same religious aspect of the royal power for its juridical foundation. And after the coronation of 800—when Charlemagne solemnly stated in his program of imperial government that his subjects, both clerics and laymen, ought to rule their lives according to divine precepts and according to standards suitable to their estate, and when he correlated the attitude of each of his subjects, whether cleric or layman, in the service of God and the accomplishment of His will with the fidelity owed to the emperor—it was always by virtue of this same power that he imposed these rules.[63]

To the traditional elements of his power Charlemagne added the swearing of an oath of fidelity by all his subjects.[64] Such an oath had existed under the Merovingians, but it had fallen into desuetude. The duty of fidelity[65] to the king was no innovation: it had been an obligation of all the subjects in the Frankish monarchy regardless of any individual ties, and infidelity toward the king was punished by death.[66] What was novel was the oath. Although it was perhaps after the conspiracy of Hardrad in 785 that Charlemagne decided to impose the oath on his subjects, the general swearing of an oath apparently first occurred in 789, and we have the formula of the oath then sworn. The fact that after their arrest several conspirators in the plot of Pepin the Hunchback in 792 made a vain attempt to assert in their defense that they had never sworn the oath of fidelity to the king indicates that the swearing of the oath was not very effective. In 793 a new general swearing of the oath was prescribed and carefully organized. All male subjects of the king had to swear the new oath upon reaching the age of twelve.[67] The concept of fidelity was fundamentally negative: to do nothing that would endanger him to whom fidelity was owed. In 802 Charlemagne recalled that this was the usual interpretation of the fidelity owed to the king— not placing in peril the life of the sovereign, not introducing enemies into the realm, not witnessing with complacence the infidelity of another, and not refraining from denouncing it.[68]

After the coronation of December 800 a basic element in the program of imperial government was a change in the oath of fidelity.[69] Charlemagne decided in 802 that all subjects would not only have to swear fidelity to him as emperor, but that even the concept of fidelity should be enlarged. The *missi dominici*, charged as in 789 and 793 with the procedure of the swearing of the oath, had to explain to all that the traditional concept was inadequate and that to be faithful to the emperor implied numerous other elements—such as to serve God and to do His will, not to take from the emperor his lands or his serfs, to abstain from malicious acts against churches, to abstain from injury to *miserabiles per- sonae* (widows, orphans, and the poor), to abstain from despoiling the benefices held from the emperor, to obey without ruse the order to join the army, to obey without restraint the imperial *bannum*, to pay rents and other levies or debts owed to the em- peror, and in pleas of justice not to protect the guilty.[70] Even the formula of the oath also changed; it became almost identical to that of the oath of vassals.[71] Naturally the new oath did not make all subjects vassals of the king since it did not include the *commendatio per manus,*[72] but from those who swore it, a more complete devotion was expected, more like that expected from the vassals, in order to agree better with the new and more exacting concept of fidelity.[73] This new concept had little or no impact. In 805, 806, and 811 Charlemagne ordered that those who had been too young in 802 to swear the oath and those who had never sworn it for other reasons should do so, and he charged the *missi* with the execution of this order.[74]

The oath of fidelity was not intended to create the duty of fidelity to the king or to the emperor, since this duty already existed, but vigorously to confirm this duty. Whoever violated his oath committed perjury for which he could be punished and, in addition, placed himself in a state of mortal sin. Moreover, the oath of fidelity created a bond of man to man that was more in tune with the spirit of the times, little developed intellectually, than the duty of fidelity of the subject, which, being general, was consequently more abstract. In reality the result was contrary to what the emperor and his councilors expected because the oath of fidelity sanctioned the false idea that the royal authority was based on the oath of the subject, a situation that promoted the birth of a contractual concept of power that eventually contributed greatly to destroying the authority of the monarch.

Among the elements of royal power one that existed before Charlemagne and that he frequently referred to and often used was the *gratia*. The intrinsic meaning of this word is difficult to grasp;[75] moreover, it was perhaps not even precise in the minds of Charlemagne's contemporaries, even those capable of some intellectual effort. In the *gratia regis* may be seen the benevolence of the king, the possession and enjoyment of which was essential in a state based solely on royal power. *Gratia* was the source of all favors, such as offices, benefices, and various gifts and privileges. Moreover, in his writs[76] and even in certain of his diplomas issued in solemn form[77] Charlemagne exhorted his officials, both ecclesiastical and secular, to comply with his orders or his decisions if they wished to keep his *gratia*.[78] There are also comparable admonitions in the capitularies.[79] For a bishop, a count, a subordinate official, and a royal vassal, disgrace, or loss of *gratia*, was a catastrophe. Not only was one cut off from the palace and deprived of receiving the favors available and so sought after by everyone of importance in the realm, but also, in the frequent conflicts[80] at this time among holders of high offices or of other posts, one was certain of being considered guilty. The loss of *gratia* could amount to the loss of *honores*, that is to say, of the offices and endowments that constituted their principal attraction.[81] The lost *gratia* could be restored either by a gratuitous act of mercy or because Charlemagne, in consequence of a judgment or of some favorable circumstance, considered the loss unjust.[82] These remarks are intended to offer some idea of the role of *gratia* in the relations between Charlemagne and his officials.

Sometimes a clause of a diploma for a religious institution or for an individual would stipulate that the beneficiary should enjoy his goods and his rights with the *gratia* of God and of the king.[83] In regard to the divine *gratia*, Charlemagne could only wish for it and implore it; the royal *gratia*, however, signified that the institution or the individual could count on the benevolence of the monarch and could therefore hope for landed donations, privileges, and sympathetic consideration of ambitions and requests.

At the beginning of his reign we know that Charlemagne experienced difficulty in imposing his will over the great men of his realm,[84] but was there some legal limit to the royal and imperial power of Charlemagne? It does not seem so. In spite of the fact that in some capitularies and other documents there is mention of a *consensus* given by the great ecclesiastics and laymen united in the diet or in some more limited assembly—a *consensus* generally expressed by an appropriate form of the verb *consentire* or by other terms rendering the same idea[85]—this does not imply a consent that one was free to give or to refuse.[86] *Consentire* was both to give a compulsory recognition of a disposition, whether a general rule or particular measure, as being consistent with the law and also to pledge oneself to comply with it; it was one aspect of the subject's duty of obeying the royal *bannum*.[87]

There is no reason to admit a different interpretation for the *consensus* given to dispositions modifying the national laws (*leges*) by the great men of the region and by the members of the regional courts.[88] What was demanded of them was something totally different from consent freely given. After taking note of new dispositions and hearing a commentary on them, they had to acknowledge publicly that such dispositions constituted the law and that they were bound to employ it. *Consensus*, far from limiting the power of Charlemagne, constituted a supplementary, though doubtless ineffective, guarantee of obedience to his decisions.

How was the imperial and royal power to be transferred after the death of Charlemagne? This problem keenly preoccupied Charlemagne, his entourage, and certainly his sons—Charles; Pepin, king of Italy; and Louis, king of Aquitaine.[89] On 6 February 806 at Thionville, upon the conclusion of an assembly of the great men, Charlemagne settled the matter of his succession,[90] not by a disposition safeguarding the unity of the empire, but on the contrary, by a division among his three sons of the territories under his authority, thus conforming to Frankish tradition and expressly discarding all other solutions. There was no question concerning the transmission of imperial power.[91] Very likely it no longer had for Charlemagne the same prestige that it had around 802/3, and he perhaps considered it a personal dignity that was not transferable. He imposed upon his sons a series of rules in an attempt to make peace and concord rule among them. He imposed on them collectively the fundamental task of assuring the protection of the church,[92] which was, it has been said,[93] in the eyes of many the essential task of the emperor. It can therefore be said that, in default of a titular holder of the imperial power, the imperial idea was not wholly absent from the regulation.[94] Pepin died in 810 and Charles in 811; the regulation anticipated was thus not applied.

The succession could henceforth be regulated by a division between Louis, Charlemagne's only surviving son, and Bernard, the son of Pepin and king of Italy since 812.[95] But Charlemagne and doubtless certain influential members of the assembly who counseled him were again more strongly under the influence of the imperial and unitary idea. If anyone had suggested a new plan of division—and it is not known if this happened—it was obviously discarded. In September 813 at Aachen, Charlemagne crowned his only surviving son, Louis, and had him acclaimed as emperor by the great men present without any ecclesiastical act.[96] When Charlemagne died on 28 January 814, Louis, already emperor, succeeded him, therefore, by right.

Central Institutions

Under Charlemagne, as under his predecessors, the central institutions of the realm were simply the king's entourage. *Palatium* was used frequently to designate both the residence of the king in an abstract sense and his entourage.[97] In a concrete sense *palatium* or *palatium publicum* ("royal palace") referred to this or that residence in particular.[98] Like his father and brother and the Merovingian kings before them, Charlemagne was an itinerant sovereign.[99] At certain times, when he was not on a campaign, he resided more frequently and for longer periods at some *palatia* than at others. While he preferred Herstal on the Meuse up to 784 and Worms on the Rhine up to 791, there were many other palaces, domains, and towns where he sojourned. In 794 Charlemagne made the palace of Aachen, which until then he had rarely frequented, not his sole residence, but nevertheless the place where he lived by preference. Except for rare sojourns in other palaces, the beginning of a campaign against the king of Denmark in 810, a tour of military and naval inspection along the coasts of the North Sea and the English Channel in 811, and occasional weeks spent at the chase in the Ardennes, Charlemagne lived permanently at Aachen from 807 to 814.[100]

This creation of a residence and consequently of a center of government, in some sense fixed and permanent, is a new and important step. While it naturally favored the regular exercise of power, it did not, apparently, render it more effective, for added to the fact that since 802 the emperor had multiplied the cases submitted to his decision or to the judgment of the palace court, the palace was now more accessible to the crowd of petitioners and litigants, who created obstruction and disorder.[101] The fact, moreover, that the sovereign left this residence less, and in the end only rarely, reduced and later eliminated the action exercised by him personally during his sojourns or appearances in the various regions of his realm, with the result that the royal or imperial authority was weakened, and abuses and discord were facilitated.[102]

The immediate entourage of the king included the heads of the household staff of the palace. Foremost was the seneschal (*seneschalcus;* literally, "old servant"), already so designated at the time of Pepin III, who, because his responsibility was to supervise the provisioning of the palace, particularly the king's table, was some-

times called *regiae mensae praepositus.* The butler (*buticularius*),
or chief of the cupbearers (*magister pincernarum*), existed under
the Merovingians but at that time was not known by the first of
these titles. The chamberlain (*camerarius*), whose duties included
the care of the living quarters and the treasury, and whose title
was also new, does not seem to have had under Charlemagne the
pre-eminence that he acquired under Louis the Pious and his successors. The constable (*comes stabuli*), responsible for the mounts
and the transport so important for an itinerant court, had, it appears, no new functions or title.[103] Each chief had a staff at his
command. There were marshals (*marescalci*), who assisted the
constable; lower officials of the treasury (*sacellarii*), who were
under the authority of the chamberlain; and ushers (*ostiarii*),
although it is not known who was in charge of them at this time.[104]
There is evidence that at least two of these chiefs acquired new
and important duties under Charlemagne. Some administrators
of the royal domains (*domestici*),[105] who during part of Charlemagne's reign were perhaps still at the palace as before, were
dispensed with at a certain point and their functions assigned at
least partially to the seneschal and the butler, a move probably
explained as an attempt to reconcile the production of the domains
with the needs of the palace. The seneschal and butler,[106] and
perhaps also the chamberlain,[107] were, in turn, now placed under
the direct authority of the queen. The conferment of these new
domanial functions to the seneschal and the butler did not, however,
prevent Charlemagne from naming, perhaps temporarily, a general
administrator of the domains.[108] The count palatine (*comes palatii*), who assisted and at this time occasionally replaced the king
at the palace court, will be discussed in the framework of judicial
institutions.[109] It seems that some of the important household
functions that have been discussed may have had more than one
head. Charlemagne used the eminent dignitaries of the palace for
other tasks also; to some of them he entrusted high military commands or, more rarely, diplomatic missions.[110]

Although there had always been clerics to perform the religious service at the court of the Frankish king, they became more important under the first Carolingians by virtue of their numbers and duties. Already under Pepin III they had formed a body and had been called *capellani* ("chaplains"), no doubt because the principal place of their activity, the oratory of the palace, was called *capella* ("chapel") where among numerous relics was preserved the most famous of all—the cloak (*capa*) of St. Martin. Under Charlemagne the body of clerics of the palace itself was termed *capella*, and the number of its members was increased. To this community Pepin III had named as head Fulrad, the abbot of Saint-Denis, whom Charlemagne retained, appointing later as his successors, first, Archbishop Angilram, bishop of Metz, and then Hildebold, archbishop of Cologne. Each was designated *capellanus palacii nostri* ("chaplain of our palace") and was regarded as an extremely important personage.[111]

Under Charlemagne the chaplains were expected to commend themselves to the king and undoubtedly to swear an oath of fidelity to him, an act which ranged them among the royal vassals.[112] Their *servitium*, however, was not exclusively ecclesiastical; they were used by the king in other positions that the extent of their learning, superior to that of laymen, enabled them to carry out effectively, such as being *missi dominici* or performing diplomatic missions.[113] Because of their intellectual aptitude Charlemagne, continuing the tradition of the first Carolingians, employed certain chaplains to draw up and write his diplomas. As such, they were styled *notarii*, or perhaps *cancellarii*. At the beginning of his reign Charlemagne had given them a chief who, like them, belonged to the chapel and who was described in a capitulary of 808 as *cancellarius noster* ("our chancellor").[114] Without doubt he was subordinate to the chief of the *capella*.[115]

The importance of the formulation and publication of the royal and imperial diplomas made the office where these clerks were located[116] a department somewhat flexible in organization and procedure, but one that held an essential place in the realm. It did not, apparently, absorb all the activities of writing at the palace.

Outside its jurisdiction were the diplomas established after judgment of the palace court, the capitularies, although with some exceptions, and the correspondence of the sovereign.[117] Probably in many cases clerks of the chapel performed this work. Also at the palace were *vassi dominici* ("royal vassals") of whom little is known except that they were evidently free men who had commended themselves to the king and had sworn an oath of fidelity to him but, contrary to other royal vassals, did not ordinarily receive a benefice and had to be content, at least temporarily, with direct maintenance or a prebend. For this reason they were considered poor vassals and were occasionally open to bribery. In regard to the military character of Carolingian vassalage, it should be pointed out that although the vassals constituted a permanent troop of cavalry at the disposition of the king, they were, however, assigned other services; Charlemagne employed them, for example, as *missi dominici*.[118] During his reign there were also some royal vassals "beneficed," that is, having received a benefice, who performed, at least temporarily, some duty at the palace.[119] The king also had a troop of bodyguards.

A mysterious institution that played a role in the preparation of capitularies and probably was consulted on all questions of importance[120] was the council (*consilium*).[121] Not much is known about its composition. Charlemagne summoned to it those whose opinions he sought, with the choice seemingly governed by the circumstances and the nature of the affairs. Certainly the members of the immediate entourage of the sovereign—the household chiefs of the palace, the chaplain of the palace, the royal chancellor, and a few intimates[122]—must have been more or less permanent councilors (*consiliarii*), but it would be rash to say more, and even all this is highly conjectural.

Although distinction is sometimes difficult, the council should not be confused with what one usually calls the assemblies, to which previous reference has been made[123] and which must now be discussed as one of the central institutions of the monarchy. Although the assemblies existed prior to and under the first Carolingians, notably under Pepin III, they were transformed in the course of time and were no longer, under Charlemagne, completely what they had been at the time of his father. What needs emphasis first is that they should not be regarded as popular assemblies. When the sources give us information on their composition, it is easy to see that they had an aristocratic character,[124] including, besides the royal entourage, counts, often bishops and abbots, and probably important royal vassals.[125]

Each year, it seems, there was a session of an assembly[126] to which the sources give such various names as *synodus, conventus, generalis conventus* or *generalis populi sui conventus*, and *placitum*, often accompanied by the possessive *suum* or *nostrum*, or even *placitum generale*.[127] It shall be called here an ordinary assembly or an ordinary diet. This assembly was closely bound to the mustering of the army, being convened most often during the concentration of the army before a campaign, more rarely after a campaign, and sometimes during an inspection of troops not followed by operations.[128] In the last years of Charlemagne's reign the assembly sometimes was separated from the gathering of the army and met at Aachen.[129] The name *magiscampus* ("field of May") was given to the ordinary diet when it preceded military operations;[130] actually it met in May only from time to time.[131] Besides the ordinary diet there was sometimes another assembly held the same year at a different time and place.[132] When the sources give this assembly a name it is one of those mentioned above. Some of these extraordinary assemblies or diets had numerous participants;[133] others undoubtedly had a smaller number of persons and would in this case be considered a session of the enlarged council. Some assemblies or extraordinary diets, such as that of Herstal in 779 and those of Aachen in 802 and 813,[134] were extremely important for the governing of the *Regnum* or the empire and for the life itself of the institutions.

Some sources, more explicit than others, give the intimate procedural details of certain of these ordinary and extraordinary assemblies. The king or emperor, who convoked the assembly, presided over it and set the daily agenda.[135] A list of points to be discussed was agreed upon, probably in the council, and put into writing.[136] If necessary, the ecclesiastics and laymen sat separately in order to deliberate on questions relevant to their respective competence. The ecclesiastical section could have the characteristics of a council and even of a great council like that of Frankfurt in 794.[137] The important persons who normally sat in the assembly were in any case those who that year were in the army or, in the case of extraordinary assemblies, those who had been convoked and had obeyed the summons.[138] There were never, it seems, assemblies at which all the bishops and counts were present. Sometimes men of lower status were attached to the bishops and counts in the role of technicians.[139] The power of the assembly did not go beyond that of an advisory body; even when it gave its *consensus*,[140] the assembly only played a consultative role.[141] It would be erroneous to conclude, however, that this role was secondary because certainly the opinions of men having authority, experience, and occasionally some knowledge strongly influenced the decisions taken after the deliberations. But it was the king who made the decisions, and it was therefore his will that was conveyed in the published capitularies or the instructions given to the *missi*.[142]

The *Missi Dominici*

Although occasionally the Merovingians used *missi* and the Carolingians used the *missi de palatio discurrentes* ("*missi* who journeyed away from the palace"), it was Charlemagne who made a regular institution of the royal *missi*—indeed one of the most important institutions in the *Regnum Francorum*.[143] The *missus dominicus* was a commissioner whom the king used in order to make his personal action felt in a specified region. The king himself appointed the *missus*, gave him instructions, always oral and sometimes also written in the form of a *capitulare missorum*, and delegated to him a very large share of his own power. The *missus* acted on the spot in using this delegated royal power: *per verbum nostrum, ex nostri nominis auctoritate, ex parte domni imperatoris, ad vicem nostram*, as the sources express it.[144] To say it was the king who acted in the person of his *missi* would not be an exaggeration.[145]

The *missi dominici* fall into two categories, not according to the nature of their power, which was the same in both cases, but according to their mission. The *missus ad hoc*, sometimes called a "special" *missus*, was charged with a specific mission, for example, to inquire into an injustice that had been pointed out to the monarch and, if one existed, to put an end to it or to inquire into a definite usurpation of the rights of the king and to end it. This special mandate could be given to a single *missus* or to two *missi*, but rarely to a larger group.[146]

Much more important were the *missi* called "ordinary," who received a general mandate from the king.[147] The king sent them into a specified region where they were to execute his orders and make justice reign (*iustitias facere*).[148] With this objective the *missi* had to inquire into injustices and abuses; end them by their personal action or by the decisions of judicial assizes over which they presided; make a report to the chief of the state concerning the injustices and abuses they had been unable to remedy; make known to the population (actually to the notable men) the dispositions of new capitularies, especially those containing their instructions; and make, if warranted, a report to the monarch on the lacunae and imperfections of the legal or regulatory dispositions in force.[149] The capitularies contain numerous dispositions regarding the co-operation the counts should give the *missi*;[150] the publication of new dispositions and commentaries the *missi* had to make;[151] the control the *missi* ought to exercise over the behavior of territorial officials; the *missi*'s power of reform, which carried with it the right to remove inferior officials and the duty of proposing to the king measures against counts guilty of grave mistakes;[152] the exploitation of the royal domains, particularly those granted in benefice;[153] the manner in which former capitularies were enforced;[154] and the behavior of the *missi* themselves.[155] The competence of the *missi* extended, moreover, to certain aspects of ordinary administration of the realm, such as the collection of various revenues, notably fines, and particularly the *heribannum* owed by those who escaped military service. The *missi* were also responsible for making preparations for a campaign of the army, and in certain cases they had to make appointments.[156] The jurisdiction they exercised will be discussed in the framework of judicial institutions[157] (see Part III). Besides their ordinary duties the *missi* could undertake more specialized missions; it is known, for instance, that they executed the taking of oaths of fidelity to the king or to the emperor.[158] However, it is impossible in this short study to enumerate all the functions of the *missi*.

Charlemagne took or confirmed certain measures assuring the *missi* protection and seeking to procure lodging and food for them.[159] The importance attached to their reports and to the other documents they had to keep[160] rendered the presence of a scribe indispensable.[161] The *missi* had to submit uncertain cases to the king.[162] The ordinary *missi*, it seems, generally worked in groups of two, and occasionally three,[163] but rarely in larger groups. Their consignment to missions appears to date no later than 779.[164] Although it cannot be affirmed that before 802 the ordinary *missi* were sent out every year or that each time they were sent out they covered the whole territory of the kingdom, in many cases this was true. This probably occurred after the reform assembly of Herstal in 779 and certainly during the general swearing of oaths of fidelity in 789 and 792/93, and perhaps also in other years.[165]

During the assembly of March 802, at which a program of imperial government was elaborated,[166] Charlemagne initiated an important reform of the institution of the *missi dominici*. Until then the monarch had occasionally selected as *missi*—both *ad hoc* as well as ordinary—persons of high rank such as bishops or counts, but this was not, it seems, the general custom. Usually these positions had been filled by *vassi dominici* in permanent service at the palace, who, having only slender resources, were susceptible to bribery and corruption.[167] Alerted by the warnings of enlightened persons, conscious of his increased responsibilities before God in his status as emperor, and determined to procure for the *miserabiles personae* the means of asserting their rights, Charlemagne reorganized his personnel, summoning in 802 archbishops, bishops, abbots, and counts—persons of high rank and of sufficient means as to have no "need" of being corrupted.[168] These persons, most often grouped by two, one an ecclesiastic and the other a layman, generally received a *missaticum* or *legatio,* that is, a province of inspection and action[169] in the neighborhood of the place or district where they normally exercised their authority.[170] The sending each year of ordinary *missi* on missions throughout the realm[171] and the selection of these *missi* from among men of rank, superior officials, both ecclesiastic and lay, seems to have become the rule.[172] This selection, moreover, obliged the emperor to limit the duration of their service in the capacity of *missi*.[173] It is possible that the *missatica* may have acquired a certain stability and that the nomination of their holders may have taken on a permanent character.[174] If toward the end of Charlemagne's reign the zeal and perhaps the honesty of the *missi* left something to be desired,[175] the establishment of the *missi,* the work of Charlemagne and his councilors, had at least contributed to maintaining in the Frankish monarchy a minimum of cohesion, regularity, and security.

Territorial Officials

Charlemagne made few innovations in that which concerned the permanent exercise of power in the various parts of the territory. As under his Merovingian and Carolingian predecessors, the territorial official par excellence of his authority was the count (*comes* or *comis* in Latin; probably *grafio* in the Frankish vernacular), frequently given in the texts the traditional predicate *vir inluster*.[176] It is certain that Charlemagne freely appointed the counts, probably for life, removed them when this seemed necessary, and dismissed them when they committed grave mistakes.[177]

If counts were chosen from the *fiscalini*, that is, from the serfs of the royal domains, this was exceptional.[178] Normally they seem to have been chosen from the Frankish aristocracy and particularly, as they were under Charles Martel and Pepin III, from Austrasian aristocratic families. The counts belonging to certain of these families, at times allied by marriage or related to the royal house, created veritable dynasties.[179] In addition to the Frankish group other aristocratic groups, such as the Alamannian, Bavarian, Saxon, and Gothic, were represented among the counts, although not nearly so liberally.[180] Perhaps some royal vassals were able to rise to comital offices.[181] The texts separate *comites fortiores* from *comites mediocres*, a distinction indicating an obvious difference in wealth, for the counts often had their own landed patrimonies, which could be quite extensive.[182]

To designate the comital office the texts used such general terms as *honor* and *ministerium*,[183] the latter term applying equally to the territory the count administered. Also used in the territorial sense were *comitatus* ("county") and, although rarely, *grafia*, a Germanic word somewhat latinized.[184] A county normally corresponded to a *pagus* (Germanic forms, *gawi*, *gowe*; modern German, *Gau*),[185] a territorial circumscription having its origin in a "city" or subdivision of a city in lands that had been strongly Romanized, or in a natural region or territory inhabited by part of a tribe in the lands of Germanic settlement. There were exceptions, however, especially in conquered regions like Saxony[186] and regions like Bavaria that had been recently subjected to the common law of the *Regnum*. Elsewhere it even happened that *pagus* and *comitatus* did not coincide and that a *pagus* was divided into several counties.[187] There were likewise cases in which a count had more than one *pagus*, or county, under his authority.[188] These two phenomena seem still not to have been common at the time of Charlemagne. Under his reign, during the greatest extension of the *Regnum Francorum*, it seems that the number of counts discharging this office rose to about four hundred,[189] a number that included neither Italy nor the territories constituting protectorates like Brittany and Pannonia that were not satisfactorily subjugated.

The counts, territorial officials of royal power, had as their task to enforce the rights of the monarch. The *missi dominici* reminded them that they ought to be the defenders of the *iustitiae domni imperatoris*[190] and therefore among other things ought to prevent usurpations of the domains or, if this had occurred, to proceed to the confiscation of landed properties to the profit of the crown.[191] A permanent deputy of the king, the count held from him his authority (also called *comitatus*), which included the power to command, to prohibit, and to punish transgressions—in other words, the *bannum*. But only in exceptional cases did his orders and prohibitions have as a sanction the royal fine of sixty shillings; normally the transgression of the comital *bannum* was punished by a fine of fifteen shillings, one-fourth of the royal *bannum*.[192]

The most absorbing and important function of the count, after that of safeguarding the rights of the king, was incontestably the maintenance of order, of the public peace. Throughout Charlemagne's reign the capitularies contained dispositions relating to the extremely wide and varied police powers conferred upon the count,[193] complemented in a certain measure by his judicial duties (see Part III)[194] and also by his fiscal duties, which derived from his obligation to maintain the rights of the king.[195] The count also had some military duties; for instance, it was his responsibility to summon under arms the free men for military service, to make certain they had the necessary arms, to take the measures required for provisioning and baggage, and when necessary, to take a command himself.[196] Also incumbent upon him was a series of ordinary and sometimes extraordinary administrative tasks, such as collaborating with the *missi dominici* in the organization of the taking of the oath of fidelity.[197] In his county the count normally appointed the subordinate officials of justice and the *scabini*, and it was his responsibility to control the manner in which they fulfilled their functions; in this regard the count's authority seemed to produce the same effect as that of the *missi*.[198] The monarch never ceased reminding the counts of a fundamental rule of his system of government—the necessity for agreement and for trusting collaboration between secular and ecclesiastical officials, particularly between counts and bishops.[199] Alarmed at the serious deficiencies he noted in this respect, Charlemagne insisted upon the necessity of holding to this rule, and he ordered that uncertain cases of conflict be submitted to him.[200] Besides some subordinate officials and a chancellor or notary (see Part III), the counts had at their command only a few servants (*iuniores*) and vassals to aid them in the exercise of their duties, assistance that did not amount to much.[201] The counts could call upon no real administrative staff.

Charlemagne did not remunerate the counts any more than his predecessors had. In their own counties the counts were entitled to one-third (*tertia*) of the purely penal fines and of the *fredus*, that is, the portion of the compositions paid to the king; probably they also received one-third of the tolls.[202] Attached to the office was an endowment in domains later called *comitatus*, but under Charlemagne it was designated *ministerium*. Because it was held in benefice it could also be called *beneficium*, like the other benefices the counts held from the king.[203] Examples of counts as lay abbots are rare under Charlemagne.[204]

In addition to the functions they had to fulfill in their county, the counts had to perform many other tasks at the will of the king. They had to attend the ordinary diets and sometimes the extraordinary assemblies,[205] and they had to go to the palace for other reasons.[206] They were used as ordinary or *ad hoc missi*,[207] as military chiefs,[208] and as ambassadors,[209] all of which occasioned a count's absence from his county. Toward the end of Charlemagne's reign the functions of an ordinary *missus* alone occupied the counts performing them for at least four months a year.[210] Certain counts, whose advice and military or political services were greatly valued by the emperor, spent at least half of the year outside their counties, leaving administration, the police, and justice to deputies or inferior officials, or entrusting these tasks in part to a neighboring count in addition to his own responsibilities,[211] a situation scarcely favorable to a satisfactory exercise of power. In addition, some counts were negligent in the exercise of their functions, preferring to hunt rather than to render justice,[212] while others let themselves be bribed and favored, administratively or judicially, powerful persons or friends. Still others used their power to exploit those whom they administered, particularly men of modest circumstances upon whom they exerted formidable pressure to compel them to surrender the ownership of their lands. Other abuses also flourished, with churches and the *miserabiles personae* being the principal victims.[213] The repetition of warnings, prohibitions, and threats of sanctions show that these oppressive wrongs occurred frequently. The absences of the counts, the failure to discharge their responsibilities of which many were guilty, and the lack of an administrative staff and sufficient subordinate personnel largely contributed to rendering the comital institution inefficient. This Charlemagne understood, and it was in large measure to rectify these weaknesses that he strengthened the institution of the *missi dominici*.[214]

Although subjected to the control of the *missi*, the counts were no less under the immediate control of the monarch. Because Charlemagne distrusted intermediate levels of power, in 788 he ended the existence of Bavaria, the last national duchy still surviving, and the country was henceforth simply administered by counts, like other parts of the territory.[215] Only rarely did Charlemagne make exceptions to this rule. In 781 he established Italy and Aquitaine as kingdoms, put his son Pepin at the head of Italy (and later, in 812, his grandson Bernard), and gave his son Louis the throne of Aquitaine. This concession to tradition and to the very deep-rooted autonomous tendencies in these two countries appeared to him indispensable. Moreover, his sons enjoyed only a strongly limited power of decision; Charlemagne directly intervened in the administration of Aquitaine and, occasionally, in that of Italy.[216] To be sure, there was a certain concession to Bavarian autonomy in the appointment of the brother of Queen Hildegarde, Count Gerold, who was part Frank and part Alamannian, and after him the Frankish count Audulf as *praefectus* in Bavaria—that is, as titular holder of a superior power—but this was at first merely a matter of a military command against the Avars and the Slavs, and only later involved an authority over these conquered and partially subjugated peoples.[217] As for the "duchy" of Maine—entrusted by Charlemagne in 790 to his eldest son Charles, called the Young— it was perhaps the nearness of the Bretons that inspired the king to create this high, but probably ephemeral, command.[218] The members of the dynasty, when invested with a superior authority over some parts of the territory, ought to be regarded as high officials of government.[219]

Although some texts cite dukes (*duces*) among the holders of territorial authority and place them on a more elevated level than the counts, this has little significance in view of the traditional and doubtless anachronistic character of the formulae in certain diplomas and the possible allusions to some duchies existing in the Italian kingdom.[220] Might not *dux* be a title held by a count governing in a frontier zone, a county of vast dimensions, and probably having a certain authority over neighboring counts, at least in military affairs? This is probably why the count of Toulouse, at first Chorso and then William ("Saint Guilhem"), who had to face the Gascons and the Saracens, was given the title *dux*.[221] Other counts, however, having a march (*marca*), that is, a frontier zone to defend,[222] and exerting in all probability superior authority over the neighboring counts, were not so called in the contemporary texts; the title is not, for example, applied in the *Royal Annals* to the count at the head of the march of Brittany, of which the *pagus* of Nantes seems to have been the most important component.[223] There was not, it seems, a uniform system of titles.[224] Nor is there much information for the epoch of Charlemagne regarding the commands that existed in the marches.[225]

In any case, exclusive of the king's sons, all the holders of superior authority were counts. On the other hand, the officials to whom we now turn occupied a rank in the hierarchy inferior to that of the counts. Under Charlemagne these officials were, first, the *vicarii* and *centenarii,* who were frequently cited in the contemporary texts[226] and who were under the authority of the counts, whose orders they received and had to execute.[227] Originally the offices of *centenarius* and *vicarius* were completely separate; their functions were probably combined under the first Carolingians, but certainly at least before Charlemagne's accession to the throne. During his reign *centenarius* and *vicarius* were simply two names for the same official.[228] Both, moreover, appear in the enumerations of the holders of power found in the address or the notification of royal or imperial diplomas.[229] Actually, *centenarius* was used more in the Germanic regions and *vicarius* more in the Romance countries, but this division was far from absolute.

Because as a rule the *pagus* was divided into *centenae* or *vicariae, centenarii* and *vicarii* had territorial authority.[230] Probably Charlemagne introduced this division into certain regions where it had not existed before.[231] The functions of these lesser officials, like those of their chief the count, constituted a public charge, a *ministerium.*[232] These functions, in the framework of the subdivision headed by these officials, were of the same order as those of the count: police, administration, summons to arms, supervision of the domains, collection of the royal revenues, and jurisdiction.[233] Generally the count named his own subordinate officials; and to insure that he chose men endowed with the necessary moral qualities, as he was supposed to, Charlemagne charged him to make this choice in the presence of the *populus,* that is, the prominent men of the *centena* or *vicaria,* for which it was necessary to appoint an administrator. The count also had the right to dismiss any *vicarius* or *centenarius* who was not satisfactory.[234] *Centenarii* or *vicarii* were under the control of the *missi dominici,* who were constantly admonished by Charlemagne to dismiss officials who behaved in a dishonest or negligent manner and to name trustworthy men in their place.[235] The abuses of which many of these lesser officials were guilty were analogous to those committed by the counts and were perhaps even more serious.[236] In the eyes of the monarch the necessity of repressing these abuses was the more urgent because the frequent absences of the count placed the exercise of public power in many counties in the hands of lesser officials for several months a year.[237] The institution of the *centenarius* and of the *vicarius* had either already existed or had been introduced into Alamannia and Bavaria by Charlemagne.[238] In these regions there was also a *scultetus* or *sculdahis* who, it seems, should be regarded as an executive official rather than as a holder of territorial authority.[239]

Certain counts felt it necessary to have at their command one or more assistants to whom they could delegate all of their authority throughout their county during their absences, or a part of their authority for the accomplishment of specific tasks. These assistants appeared as early as the last years of the eighth century under the title *missi comitis*,[240] a term that could also designate every deputy of the count, even one charged temporarily with a single mission.[241] In the south of Gaul the word *vicedomini* was applied to these assistants of the count,[242] but its use remained very limited, probably because of the possible confusion with another *vicedominus*, the administrator of the possessions of the church.[243] In the last years of Charlemagne's reign it seems that the use of assistants became institutionalized.[244] The assistant became a separate official and took the name *vicecomes*, meaning one who acted *ad vicem comitis*, that is, in place of the count; he appeared, moreover, to have become a permanent deputy provided with full powers.[245] Like that of the count, his name is sometimes even embellished in the texts with the predicate *vir inluster*. Although the expression *missus comitis* is still found,[246] *vicecomes* ("viscount") eventually replaced it.

There is here, then, an institution, probably created from the initiative of regional officials, that the monarch was content to introduce gradually into the institutional framework. The viscount is found only in the western parts of the *Regnum Francorum* where his position developed during the course of the ninth century.[247]

Royal Resources

An attempt to give some idea of Charlemagne's role in the institutions of the Frankish monarchy requires an examination of the resources the monarch had at his command. There were, first, the casual resources—those procured by war. There may have been some enslavement of prisoners during the first phase of the Saxon wars to provide manual labor for the royal domains, but, if so, this practice does not seem to have been continued.[248] A more important source of wealth was the booty taken from the enemy, part of which was certainly reserved for the king. Information about this revenue, however, is scanty and limited to a few instances, like the one in 796 when the fabulous treasures accumulated by the chiefs of the Avars were carried to the palace at Aachen.[249] The tributes, which in theory appeared to be regular revenues, were in reality quite different. Those assessed on the Bretons were not paid regularly despite two campaigns Charlemagne mounted against them.[250] As for those owed by the duke of Benevento, which amounted to several thousand gold shillings, several military interventions were also necessary to obtain payment, which most likely remained incomplete.[251]

The most important revenues were those that came from the royal landed estates, particularly the royal domains. It is essential at this point to discuss these estates, at least as sources of revenue.[252] Although the royal domains were called *fisci*,[253] they were frequently designated only by the more general name of *villae*. Expressions like *villa regis* and *villa regia* clearly stated to whom the domain belonged. The name *fisci* often continued to be given to royal domains when they were conceded in benefice or in endowment of office and even when they were given to churches or to laymen in full ownership.

The origins of the royal domains as they existed at the time of Charlemagne could be quite diverse—for example, family possessions of the Carolingians, vestiges of the landed patrimony of the Merovingians, confiscated possessions, and possessions acquired by conquest. Sometimes the first category is distinguished from the others by calling it patrimonial domains (German, *Hausgut*), and the others, domains of the Crown (German, *Krongut* or *Reichsgut*). But this distinction is quite ineffectual since the administration and utilization of these possessions was generally the same.[254] It should also be noted that the king considered himself the owner of possessions that were abandoned or without apparent owners.[255]

We are relatively well informed about the royal domains. An excellent source is the *Capitulare de villis* published by Charlemagne between 771 and 800, although probably a little before 800.[256] This great ordinance contained measures to eradicate the abuses and especially the misappropriations rampant in the exploitation of the *fisci* and dispositions for a program of better administration that were intended to assure more satisfactory production.[257] A series of these dispositions reappeared in a capitulary of 802/3.[258] The *Capitulare de villis* was applicable throughout all of the *Regnum Francorum*[259] but was aimed only at those royal domains whose production constituted immediate revenue for the king.[260]

There are, indeed, other sources concerning the royal domains. Several times Charlemagne ordered the *missi* to establish detailed inventory statements (*brevia*) of his landed fortune.[261] These statements were to include, on the one hand, what had been given in benefice to bishops, abbots, abbesses,[262] counts, or royal vassals,[263] and on the other hand, *fisci* not granted out. What the king was seeking, which was important politically, was a knowledge of his landed capital by *missaticum*. Since, however, only the elements not granted out procured revenue for the king, it is to them exclusively that we shall now turn.

There are several descriptions of *fisci* not granted out that seem to be based on a uniform model. Perhaps they were composed with the help of extracts from the inventory statements mentioned above, but it is also possible that they may have been inventory statements taken on the spot by the *missi* in execution of orders contained in a subsequent capitulary that has been lost. In any case, these descriptions referred to a group of *fisci dominici*[264] situated in what is today the north of France (Nord and Pas-de-Calais departments). They have been preserved, along with descriptions of ecclesiastical domains, in a type of formulary reserved for the establishment of such statements, the *Brevium exempla ad describendas res ecclesiasticas et fiscales*. The statements of the *fisci* inventoried and sometimes briefly described the buildings, the provisions destined for sowing or consumption, and the cattle. These are not *polyptyques* because they included no mention of the lands or the manner of their exploitation. Whoever composed the models for these descriptions used the *Capitulare de villis*. Quite probably they dated from the end of Charlemagne's reign or the beginning of the reign of Louis the Pious.[265] However, it should not be thought that these statements were actually established for all the *fisci* and that the descriptions had the same uniformity everywhere as those preserved in the *Brevia*.[266] Sometimes the legal records, royal or imperial diplomas, and private charters also enlighten us on the landed property of the Carolingians.

The domains responsible for the maintenance of the court, which for a long time was itinerant, were situated in various regions of the empire, but were unequally distributed. Saxony, Raetia, and Brittany seem to have been provided with hardly any, while Aquitaine and Alamannia had only a very limited number. The regions that seem to have been the most numerously endowed were the northwest of France; the west of Belgium; the basins of the Oise, the Aisne, and the Marne; the basins of the Meuse and the Moselle, the middle Rhine, the low Rhine, and the Main; and Bavaria. However, this observation makes no definitive claim.[267] A numerical estimate from our actual state of knowledge would risk creating a false impression.

Thanks to the descriptions in the *Brevium exempla*[268] and to certain charters, the structure of some of the *fisci* providing maintenance for the king and his entourage is relatively well known. Among the *fisci* described in the *Brevia* are the domain of Annappes (Nord), which appears under its own name, and according to identifications made, the domains of Cysoing, Somain-en-Ostrevant (both Nord), and Vitry-en-Artois (Pas-de-Calais).[269] To the first of these *fisci* cited were attached three *mansioniles*, or small dependent domains, of which Annappes was the *caput fisci*, or the *villa capitanea* ("chief domain"), a situation analogous to that encountered in the *Capitulare de villis*, in which the *mansioniles* are contrasted to the *villae capitaneae*.[270] According to reasonable estimates the dimensions of these *fisci* are: Annappes, 2,063 hectares, plus the *mansioniles* of Gruson, 311 hectares, Noyelles-lez-Seclin, 238 hectares, and Wattiesart, 200–300 hectares—a total of 2,800–2,900 hectares; Cysoing, 1,867 hectares; Somain-en-Ostrevant, 1,368–1,406 hectares; Vitry-en-Artois, 1,855 hectares. These figures are, however, approximate.[271] The four *fisci* in question constituted a group called a *ministerium* having its center at Annappes.[272] It seems that belonging to it was a detached element—a wine-producing domain situated at Triel on the Seine (Seine-et-Oise).[273] From charters we learn about the *fiscus* of Tournai in western Belgium, which, like Annappes, was a *caput fisci* with a dependent domain, that of Marquain.[274] It is impossible to give a true evaluation of this *fiscus*.[275] Other examples could easily be cited; and from certain cases[276] it is obvious that the *fisci* and the *mansioniles* were bipartite domains comprising a center of exploitation (*curtis*), a reserve, and some holdings.

Although what has been said about the fiscal *ministeria*—and the structure of some *fisci* and *ministeria* is valid for many of them—there was much variation. Some groups of landed elements assigned to the royal *servitium* presented quite a different structure. In this respect, characteristics peculiar to a region, the age of the properties and their cultivation, the transformations undergone by these properties, their particular use, and other factors played a decisive role. Extensive woodlands (*silvae*) were attached to certain *fisci;* they could even constitute the major part of a *fiscus*, as was the case, for example, of the *fiscus* of Theux in eastern Belgium, east of the Meuse. The woods of the *fisci* were generally set entirely or partially in a forest (*forestis*), that is, in a hunting preserve, and *forestarii* had the task of keeping them in this natural state.[277]

The administration and exploitation of a *fiscus*, or of a *ministerium* comprising several *fisci*, were in the hands of stewards, who could be of a rather high rank. They were called *iudices*, as in the *Capitulare de villis*, or *actores*, as in various charters relating either to a *ministerium* like that of Aachen or to *fisci* like those of Theux or Frankfort on the Main.[278] The administrator of the *ministerium* of Annappes and its environs was called *maior*,[279] which is rather surprising in view of the fact that in the *Capitulare de villis* the *maior* is a subordinate of the *iudex* and, under his orders, only administers a *villa*, which is but a part of a *ministerium* or a *fiscus*.[280] There are even instances in which the steward of a domain assigned to the royal *servitium* was called *villicus*.[281] It must be admitted that the names of these offices were used with a certain lack of precision. Moreover, these and other names were only Latin terms belonging exclusively to a written language; we do not know the Germanic or pre-Romance terms of the spoken language of which they were translations. The stewards of the *ministeria* and the *fisci* probably had at their disposal a clerk capable at least of writing. As has been said, the stewards of the domains were subject to the control of the *missi*.[282]

At the palace there were certain persons responsible for giving the stewards and *missi* instructions so that the administration and exploitation of the domains would be done in conformance with prescribed rules and needs, so that errors would be corrected, so that threats to the integrity of the domains would be eliminated, and so that production would be oriented toward a given goal, most often an immediate one. Naturally it was also their duty to take note of documents coming from the *fisci* or concerning them. These persons were the *domestici*, as long as there were any; the queen, when there was one; and the seneschal, the butler, and the constable.[283] Although Count Richard, who was charged with the general administration of the royal domains about 794, seems to have had some knowledge and experience in this respect, it would be difficult to define his competence in comparison with that of the queen and the heads of the great household services. It is not known up to what date he exercised his duties or whether he was replaced.[284] Some clerks were probably put, perhaps temporarily, at the disposition of the officials noted above. But this anomalous group cannot be considered a central administration.

Exploitation of the *fisci* was oriented toward the most abundant production possible.[285] The whole of what was produced in a year—the *conlaboratus*—included, first, agricultural commodities and the increase of animals from breeding and, second, other elements, among which could be money from quitrents or from sales. By the terms of the *Capitulare de villis* this aggregate had to be divided into four parts, naturally unequal in importance and size: that necessary for the royal *servitium* and the army; that needed for sowing; that destined for consumption on the premises, in other words, furnished to prebendaries or put at the disposition of the working quarters of the women (*gynaeceum*); and, last, that kept in storage to await royal instructions either to put it in reserve or to sell it.[286] Some statements (*brevia*) had to be put in writing and sent to the palace indicating, first, what had been delivered or reserved for the service of the king and the army; second, what had been disposed of or, in other words, consumed on the premises; and, third, what had been kept, that is, that part destined for sowing and that reserved for the royal decision.[287] Money was supposed to be delivered to the palace on Palm Sunday.[288] Special dispositions ordered certain other deliveries or written information to be furnished.[289] The *Brevium exempla* reflects in part this same situation. It contains, in the description of the commodities on hand at the center of various *fisci*, the distribution of the principal elements of the *conlaboratus* for two years: what was reserved and was on the domain, what had been set apart for sowing, and what had been portioned out on the domain.[290] This seems to indicate that the prescriptions contained in the *Capitulare de villis* were to some extent fulfilled. It is nevertheless better not to have too many illusions concerning the regularity or the complete and general character of this operation.

Like all the Carolingians, Charlemagne depended on the *fisci* of his *indominicatum* for his subsistence and that of his entourage. It is important to try to understand in what way he was able to make maximum use of the products of the *fisci*. In 794 Charlemagne discovered the decay of the Aquitanian *indominicatum*, which was supposed to provide the subsistence for his son, the young king Louis the Pious. He ordered two *missi*, Willebert, very likely a cleric of his chapel, and Count Richard, the administrator of his domains,[291] to reorganize this patrimony. The most important result was to guarantee to the king of Aquitaine four winter residences, to each of which were attached certain domains capable of providing food and other necessary resources. A circuit was established among these residences so that each one and the domains supporting it were called upon to serve the king only once every three years.[292]

These measures taken in Aquitaine on the initiative of Count Richard evidently copied what was done in the parts of the kingdom subject directly to Charlemagne, who also had *palatia* or other residences where he spent the winter months, which were generally not devoted to military campaigns.[293] It should be noted that the winter *palatium* (German, *Winterpfalz*) where the king was to sojourn was designated several months in advance. It had to be ascertained by an examination of reports of the *missi* and statements drawn up by the stewards that everything was in good order in the palace and that the domain attached to it, as well as the neighboring or more remote *fisci*, would be able to furnish the king and the court with sufficient food and other supplies. A circuit, particularly a four-year circuit, was evidently excluded in territories that were too vast.[294] Nevertheless the *fisci* could be called upon to serve with some regularity.[295]

Similar service by the *fisci* of the region or neighboring regions was also assured to the king in those of his palaces or other residences where he stayed on the eve of military expeditions. The forms of this service could be different[296] from those supplying the service owed to the king in his winter residences. It is believed that *servitium* was occasionally furnished to the king by his domains even if he resided temporarily in an abbey or an episcopal palace.[297] In addition to these revenues from the royal domains were those from the hunting preserves and from metal and salt mines.[298]

Another group of resources can be called "profits derived from the exercise of power," among which should be cited, first, the profits from coinage.[299] Charlemagne, completing the work of Pepin III, not only made the silver penny the only real money,[300] but he also made coinage what it had ceased to be: a royal monopoly and a function of the state. He determined the types of money,[301] their weight and format, decreed the list of monetary workshops, and toward the end of his reign, with the aim of preventing the flourishing activity of counterfeiters, forbade the striking of money except *in palatio nostro*.[302] The capitularies listed in detail the penalties against those who refused to accept the new coins that Charlemagne had ordered to be struck and substituted for previously issued coins.[303]

The profits of justice were another important source of revenue. The king had the right to the *fredus*, that is, to a part of the fines and compositions equal to one-third of the total amount, according to Frankish law, or to a fixed sum in other Germanic laws.[304] Charlemagne frequently reminded the *missi* and the counts that the *fredus* had to be paid to him,[305] obviously after deduction of the *tertia* of the count.[306] And when, by an article of a capitulary, he ordered the repression of a determined violation, he anticipated his *fredus* as equal to one-third in addition to the two-thirds owed to the damaged party.[307] As for purely penal fines, particularly the royal *bannum* amounting to sixty shillings,[308] Charlemagne definitely accorded them a special importance in that he increased his orders to the *missi* and to the counts to see to their exact collection and their payment into the treasury. He particularly had in mind the *heribannum*, a fine of sixty shillings levied upon the free man who did not obey the call to arms.[309] From the amounts owed to the monarch should be subtracted, at least after 811, the one-third apportioned to the counts, although they did not have the right to collect the *heribannum*, this being reserved to the *missi* or to *heribannitores*.[310] There was evidently some leakage, for part of the fines certainly did not reach the treasury. Moreover, the sums payable were diminished by what was owed by insolvent debtors or by those whom the emperor had pardoned.[311] Nevertheless, in order not to crush men of moderate resources under the weight of the heavy army fine, at the beginning of 805 Charlemagne instituted reduced tariffs for them.[312] The *bannum* was payable in kind, in precious metals, in movable goods of value, and in animals, but not in lands or in serfs of an inferior status (*mancipia*); nor could women and children be deprived of their clothes.[313]

The confiscation of goods pronounced as an accessory penalty or by what we would call today an administrative measure sometimes also constituted a source of revenue for Charlemagne.[314] The same may be said of the presents offered by the ambassadors of sovereigns or foreign peoples, which were normally rare objects of great value, often made from precious metal.[315]

Several other sources of revenue can be grouped together by virtue of the fact that they have some analogy to direct taxes and yet cannot be considered such. Charlemagne frequently ordered the *missi* and the counts to investigate and to enforce payment of personal or real rents owed to him. In the capitularies these were termed *census regalis* or *census noster*. In 802, when he broadened the concept of fidelity owed to him, Charlemagne made the regular payment of royal rents an aspect of this fidelity.[316] The rents were nevertheless obviously difficult to collect.[317] Perhaps they were vestiges of ancient Roman taxes that had disappeared before the end of the seventh century but still survived here and there as customary dues.[318] Some scholars see them, just as they see the payments (*tributum, stuofa, osterstuofa, medem*) owed to the king by some inhabitants of certain completely Germanic parts of the *Regnum*, as a totally different thing—a rent for the occupation of royal lands by men of diverse origin, who nevertheless owed their status of *Franci liberi* (German, *Königsfreien*)[319] to royal protection and to service due to the king. This interpretation, although probably valid for certain parts of the territory, appears to have no general applicability.

The *inferenda*, a tax in western Gaul payable originally in head of cattle, was in force under Charlemagne but was then paid in money; it was, however, not very important.[320] In this same group of revenues were the gifts (*annua dona*), originally voluntary, made annually to the king. They had become real taxes owed by the members of the aristocracy and by ecclesiastical establishments. Charlemagne attached importance to their payment, which was often made in kind, notably in horses and arms.[321] Mention should also be made here of the successions in escheat and the goods of those freed by charter who died intestate.[322] These resources were even more uncertain than the royal rents.

The last group of resources can be described as indirect taxes. First, under Charlemagne and his successors, as well as under his Merovingian and Carolingian predecessors, there was the toll (*teloneum*), a royal tax on the circulation of merchandise and on its sale at the market.[323] It was not levied on persons or on the products transported from one property owned by an individual or an ecclesiastical establishment to another.[324] The existence of the toll is attested to at the time of Charlemagne in all of the

Regnum Francorum. Collection stations were situated on the frontiers (including maritime ports) and in the interior in such places as cities (*civitates*) and other fortified agglomerations (*castra, castella*), where a market was held, at river ports, along certain routes, or where a bridge permitted an easy crossing.[325] Normally the count was responsible for the toll in his county, although he was assisted by his subordinate officials and had at his command toll collectors (*telonearii*), who were charged with the actual work. The count had to turn over to the king whatever he collected, probably after deducting a share amounting perhaps to a third.[326]

Although Charlemagne maintained the rule that the toll could be collected only where it traditionally had been,[327] it seems he permitted exceptions, such as new offices established where help was furnished to debtors; where a bridge, a ford, or a passage was laid out across a river or a marsh; where mooring facilities were installed; and where a market was newly organized.[328] Some offices were particularly important, such as that of the port of Duurstede in Frisia on the lower course of the Rhine near its mouth, that of the port of Quentowic on the English Channel at the mouth of the Canche, and those of the *clusae*, that is, places where the principal Alpine passes emptied onto the Lombard plain. The collection of the toll at Quentowic and at other ports of the English Channel and its environs was placed under the authority of a *procurator*. In these three great offices the rate of the toll was 10 per cent ad valorem.[329]

At the time of Charlemagne the toll constituted an important source of revenue for the king, but it should be noted that fraud and above all the numerous privileges granted principally to ecclesiastical establishments greatly reduced the yield.[330] No doubt these privileges were sometimes abused by a count or by his toll collectors,[331] and one can be sure that these violations were committed, not for the profit of the treasury, but for those guilty of the violation. Likewise when a count or a subordinate official unlawfully created new offices for the collection of the toll, it was he and not the monarch who benefited. It is probable that some counts and their subordinates quite simply diverted part of the sums they collected for the king or had pretended to collect for him. Besides the toll there were certain complementary taxes on the means of transport (*rotaticum, saumaticum*), such as for passage over a bridge (*pontaticum*), on the right of moorage (*ripaticum*), and for the use of a port (*portaticum*). These taxes were handled like the toll.[332]

The profit from all the royal revenues not intended for special appropriation was paid into the royal treasury (*fiscus, camera*). It included not merely minted money or precious metal that could be minted but objects of value, some of which were reducible to coined metal, and others, like cloth and books, which were not.[333] It is known that the *camerarius* had charge of the treasury,[334] but whether there was an accounting, even elementary, of assets, receipts, and expenditures is not known and seems improbable. The treasury was an instrument of government that Charlemagne used for foreign relations.[335] It was never employed to remunerate officials, but it played an essential role in the acts of munificence in favor of the church and the faithful servants of the monarchy.[336]

Privileges—Particularly Immunity

One of the peculiar characteristics of the institutional system of the Frankish monarchy is the place held by the privilege, which should be construed as certain legal rights derogatory to the common law and more favorable than it to the individual or ecclesiastical establishment profiting from the privilege. One of several factors that explains the spreading of the privilege was the inadequate protection guaranteed to persons and possessions by the irregular and ineffective action of officials. Despite Charlemagne's efforts to improve this state of affairs he had little success. Like his predecessors and successors, Charlemagne was generous in the distribution or the confirmation of certain privileges.

The inadequate protection just mentioned accounted for the privilege of *mundbyrd* (*mundeburdis, tuitio, defensio*), a special protection accorded by the king to various individuals or ecclesiastical establishments. Although there are few texts giving information on the granting of this privilege by Charlemagne, there is no doubt that it was accorded to some individuals[337] and also to some monastic establishments. Unquestionably, the royal abbeys possessed this privilege, and abbeys such as Lorsch, Hersfeld, and Aniane had been given to the king in order to be able to enjoy it.[338] Some abbeys had received the privilege by special concession,[339] after having commended themselves to the king as if they were individuals. The individual or ecclesiastical establishment enjoying the privilege was protected from any harm by the interdiction of the king, and if harm was done it involved the condemnation of the guilty party to a fine of sixty shillings for disobedience of the *bannum*.[340] Even more important was the privilege of jurisdiction, which meant that the individual or the establishment admitted into the royal *mundbyrd* had the right to be judged by the palace court.[341] While those admitted *qualitate qua* into the royal *mundbyrd* (such as churches, widows and orphans, the poor, and certain categories of persons going to and from the palace) were protected by the *bannum*,[342] only churches, widows, and orphans obtained the privilege of jurisdiction.[343] It is certain that the rule was not always observed and that the protection was not always effective.

One group of privileges concerned the toll, which has already been discussed.[344] Following the example of the Merovingians and his father Pepin III, Charlemagne confirmed the transfer of, or himself surrendered to some ecclesiastical establishments, the right to collect the toll in a certain place or region. The surrender could be absolute or limited either in time or in relation to the proceeds from the tax. However, these transfers or confirmations of transfer were not frequent.[345] On the contrary, the privileges

of exemption from toll or the confirmations of such privileges issued by Charlemagne were considerably more numerous. Sometimes
an ecclesiastical establishment obtained a total exemption;[346] in
other cases the exemption was limited to a certain number of
boats or, if on land, wagons per year.[347] Some exemptions were
granted to individuals for particular reasons[348] or to a specific
group of persons, such as pilgrims.[349] All surrenders of toll and
all franchises of toll pertained equally to the complementary taxes.
Although the motive that led Charlemagne to confirm or concede
these privileges was evidently piety, perhaps in certain cases the
concern to assure himself of the support of some powerful person
also played a role. For a church these privileges facilitated provisioning and substantially favored the sale of products from its
domains and the purchase of commodities its domains did not
produce.[350]

Under Charlemagne by far the most important and most widely
prevalent privilege in all of the *Regnum Francorum* was that of
immunity.[351] While the general characteristics of this institution
remained the same as under the Merovingians and the first Carolingians, Charlemagne introduced into its operation an important
series of reforms. For instance, the privileged system of the *emunitas* (more rarely, *immunitas*),[352] although occasionally accorded
to some specified estates, was granted much more often to a church
or to an abbey for all of its patrimony. The royal diplomas of
donation or confirmation of donation of estates with the grant
or confirmation of immunity[353] are much less numerous than
those of concession or confirmation of immunity to an entire
ecclesiastical patrimony.[354] Perhaps laymen could be beneficiaries
of this privilege, but this must have been exceptional;[355] the contemporary sources present the immunity as a system of favor
applying to estates of the church.

The fundamental provisions of the immunity at the time of
Charlemagne remained what they had been:[356] to prohibit royal
officials from entering immune lands to carry out acts of authority;
to free holders of immunity from taxes, rents, and the furnishing of

provisions; and, frequently, to relinquish to the holder of immunity all the revenues to which the treasury would have had the right, notably the *fredus* (that part of the fines owed to the king).[357] The freedom from taxes in many cases was extended to the toll, which formerly was not generally included.[358] As in the Merovingian period and under Pepin III or Carloman II, the privilege had a perpetual force.[359]

The existence of numerous domains barred to royal officials constituted a danger for the public peace because these domains risked becoming, and indeed frequently did become, zones where brigands took refuge and from which they emerged only in order to commit new crimes. Charlemagne thus ordered the holders of immunities to turn over to the count brigands and other criminals who had taken refuge in these privileged islets, and sanctions were provided against those who would not respond to the comital summons.[360] In 803 new dispositions making sanctions more severe and authorizing the count to enter the immune lands were even inserted in a capitulary intended to complement all the national laws. Group resistance to the count's action could condemn the recalcitrant holder of immunity to a heavy fine of six hundred shillings.[361] Henceforth, the same enormous fine also punished unjustified violations of the privilege.[362] There is doubt, however, as to the effectiveness of this double fine, which almost no one could pay.

Another important reform of Charlemagne was the creation of the permanent advocate (*advocatus;* French, *avoué;* German, *Vogt*). Unlike the *vidame* (*vicedominus*), who was the ecclesiastical administrator of church possessions, the permanent advocate was always a layman. Unlike the *advocatus ad hoc,* who often represented a church or another party in justice or in the accomplishment of extrajudicial acts,[363] the permanent advocate represented the church or abbey possessing immunity, not only in justice and in the accomplishment of extrajudicial acts, but also vis-à-vis the public power, notably in seeing that the inhabitants of the lands under immunity accomplished their military obligations.[364] The permanent advocate was created, it seems, prior to 792/93.[365]

The advocate was appointed by the holder of immunity in the presence of the count and notable men of the county or, more likely, by the count acting on the proposal of the holder of immunity in the presence of notable men. This seems to imply the existence of an advocate in each county where the ecclesiastical establishment had estates. Religious and moral virtues as well as ownership of land in the county were required of the advocate.[366] The *missi dominici*, who controlled the advocates, could in the case of grave misconduct remove them and name new holders to the office.[367] The rank of the advocates in the hierarchy corresponded to that of the subordinate royal officials.[368] An official serving both the holder of immunity and the king, the advocate was considered a holder of a public charge, a *ministerium*.[369] From the time of Charlemagne and probably by his will, the advocate was normally the president of the court of immunity,[370] the *audientia privata*.[371] While the competence of this court was probably more inclusive than that of the domanial courts of lords, who were without immunity,[372] it probably did not extend to the most serious infractions or to trials relating to personal status or landed property. These cases were reserved for the *mallus*, presided over by the count or viscount.[373] One can be somewhat skeptical as to the actual respect for these rules of competence. There is no doubt that the advocates, like the holders of immunity themselves, sometimes abused their power and acted as fomenters of disorder in the state.[374]

Although the privilege of immunity had probably been accorded to churches and monasteries other than the ecclesiastical establishments for which some diplomas are preserved, it cannot be said that immunity constituted the normal regime for all important churches; this was certainly not the case under Charlemagne. If he generously distributed or confirmed the privilege, he did so, apparently, with a new preoccupation: to make the institution serve to improve the administration of the kingdom, at least from the time when the institution of the permanent advocate was introduced. The domains of immunity were withdrawn, in what concerned the current jurisdiction and administration, from the competence of the count. To concede the immunity was to lighten the already heavy tasks of this royal official and to hope that he would better consecrate himself to those tasks remaining to him. The domains with immunity no longer depended completely upon the count's power, which he had sometimes used arbitrarily. They were entirely withdrawn from the competence of subordinate officials, too often negligent, tyrannical, greedy, and mercenary. It was thought that the advocates would ameliorate the situation by exercising their prerogatives, that the inhabitants of the islets of immunity would be less oppressed and would be more punctual in fulfilling their duties to the king. But this was not always the case.

The Introduction of Vassalage

Vassalage and the benefice are the main components of the complex development often called Carolingian feudalism, a development that cannot be ignored by whoever studies the institutions, the law, and society in the eighth and ninth centuries of the Frankish monarchy. We do not intend here to examine the institution of feudalism[375] but rather to see how Charlemagne, even more than his father and brother, used vassalage and the benefice in the organization of the state and in the functioning of public institutions.[376]

This is indicated, above all, by the development given to royal vassalage. The vassals of the king (*vassi* or *vassalli dominici*, *vassi* or *vassalli regis* or *imperatoris*, *vassi* or *vassalli nostri*), like those of the churches, the counts, and the individual lords, performed the two acts by which one entered into the vassalage of another: commendation (*commendatio*), which consisted of placing one's clasped hands between the lord's, and the swearing of an oath of fidelity to this lord. But with royal vassals the fact that their lord was the king placed them higher than other vassals in the social hierarchy.[377] The king used them in all branches of his service. They sat as assistant judges at the palace court and at the judicial assizes of the *missi*;[378] they could be charged to accomplish extrajudicial acts on behalf of the king;[379] and they were employed as *missi dominici*, a function that appears to have been reserved, until 802, primarily for royal vassals in service at the palace.[380] As a general rule, these royal vassals were supported directly by the monarch or were entitled to a prebend. Certain of them belonged to the permanent personnel of the itinerant court,[381] while others lived at one or another of the royal residences. These vassals, not landed—that is, not holding land from the king—were generally held in low esteem.[382] They were always inferior to the landed vassals, those who had received a piece of land or lands in benefice from the king.[383] The *beneficium* of the vassal was a tenure for which no rent was paid but which enabled the vassal to support himself and perform his service.[384] Charlemagne increased the number of landed vassals in order to have at his command loyal elements, well armed and mounted, in the various parts of the *Regnum Francorum*. In certain parts of the territory where his authority seemed less certain, these vassals appear to have constituted a kind of military colony.[385] The benefices were formed from lands belonging to the monarch [386] or from lands of the church.[387] Certain landed vassals had to serve periodically at the palace.[388]

If the nonlanded royal vassals appeared to be poor, among those with lands there were certainly great differences in resources. Undoubtedly many had only a modest benefice, while others had several extremely important ones in addition sometimes to their alods.[389] Large benefices permitted landed royal vassals to concede, in their turn, a part of these lands in subbenefices to their own vassals.

There is good reason to acknowledge that Charlemagne developed a practice, going back at least to his father, of persuading his officials—that is, the counts—to enter into his vassalage with the clear aim of doubling their public duties by obligations arising from the relations of man to man, relations more meaningful to men of limited intellectual development. There are no texts existing prior to the reign of Louis the Pious in which counts are termed *vassi* or *vassalli*, but there are texts relating to *beneficia* held by counts, which undoubtedly were tenures by vassalage.[390] It is not possible to say whether or in what measure this custom became general. The counts, in their turn, could have vassals and could grant them lands. These *vassi comitis* were also responsible for service to the king; they could be called for service as judgment-finders at the *mallus* (the court of the county over which their lord presided), and they could be used as a police force in the county.[391]

The vassals of the lords, whether ecclesiastics or laymen, could be called to arms for service to the king.[392] Military service constituted for all the vassalage—royal, comital, episcopal, abbatial or private, landed or without land—its principal *raison d'être*. Charlemagne promulgated several dispositions intended to make this service more effective. While vassals normally joined the army under the command of their lord, subvassals of the king had to join the contingent of the county commanded by the count if their lord, a royal vassal himself, was retained for service within the county. A royal vassal in each county had to assemble and direct the wagons carrying baggage and provisions.[393] Whoever held at least twelve manses of land in ownership or whoever—as a vassal of the king, a count, a church, or another lord—held them in benefice owed service not only on horseback but with complete armament including a *brunia* (a leather jacket with scale-like pieces of metal sewn on it).[394] It could happen that in case of war all the landed vassals in a given region might be called to arms, while only a portion of the other elements of the contingent would be mobilized.[395] The importance of vassalage, and particularly royal vassalage, was so great in the eyes of Charlemagne that he enjoined the *missi* to see that the *vassi dominici* always lived on good terms among themselves as well as with ecclesiastical and secular authorities.[396] Stemming from this same preoccupation of Charlemagne was the disposition aimed at assuring each royal vassal the assistance of other royal vassals when he was in a struggle with hostile forces.[397] The development of vassalic relations in the general framework of institutions, such as was realized by Charlemagne, introduced an element with a contractual basis that was soon to alter and then transform the nature and functioning of these institutions.

Writing in the Administration of the *Regnum Francorum*

This exposition would lack an essential element if it did not include some mention of the role of writing in the administration of the state.[398] Although at the end of the seventh and at the beginning of the eighth century this role had become insignificant, the use of writing in administrative matters reappeared under Pepin III, although not to a great extent. It was Charlemagne who restored it to real importance.[399]

Among the written documents that have been preserved are some drawn up at the palace for the use of the monarch himself, notably *aide-mémoires* concerning questions that would be discussed at a diet or at some restricted assembly. It is surprising that any of these have been preserved.[400] In a second group are documents dispatched from the palace. In an administrative class none are more important than the written instructions delivered to the *missi dominici*, which were soon called *capitulare missorum*. These instructions, as has been said previously, were always oral.[401] It was the order given verbally by the king that conferred the obligatory force to the disposition taken, and not the written form of the capitulary, which was simply a means of publication.[402] The *capitulare missorum* served before all as a memorandum to the *missi*. This explains why the articles of these texts were so often drawn up in a very concise manner and why they were even sometimes in the form of suggestions or simple headings.[403] Other instructions of similar import were delivered to the bishops or counts not invested with the authority of *missi*, who returned to their bishopric or county after a diet or another assembly.[404] Also deserving mention are the written instructions confided to envoys in service outside the realm.[405] Charlemagne sometimes dispatched circulars to ecclesiastical or lay authorities,[406] but it is not known exactly how the necessary copies were set up or how they arrived at their destination.

The principal administrative documents emanating from the palace having been cited, it is now important to indicate certain ones that were addressed to the king and that, with rare exceptions, have not been preserved. The importance of the reports required from the *missi*, notably those they prepared after inquests into particular cases,[407] has been pointed out already. Some reports with supporting lists of figures or names (*brevia*) were instituted by the *missi* charged, in 792/93, with the general swearing of oaths of fidelity to the king. These lists were compiled with the collaboration of the counts.[408] The same procedure was almost certainly followed also in 802, at the time of the swearing of the oath to the emperor and, later, during complementary swearings of the oath.[409]

Among the written records to be drawn up, beginning in 802/3 there were reports of an undoubtedly general nature that the *missi* had to draft on the information (*de adnuntiatione*) given by them to regional authorities and subjects of the emperor and on their actual interventions (*de opere*).[410] They had to report to the emperor the mistakes committed by ecclesiastical and secular officials, especially the counts.[411] They had to furnish a list of names when they appointed *scabini*, advocates, and *notarii*.[412] When they had to notify the counts, the subordinate officials, and the *scabini* of their *missaticum* of a capitulary modifying any of the national laws, they had to supply the palace with a copy signed by all these persons.[413] The very complete reports have already been mentioned that were demanded on the subject of imperial domains—the *fisci*—and notably but not exclusively those given in benefice.[414] Sometimes the *missi* were expected to prepare numerical lists of the nonnative elements of the population in each *missaticum*.[415] All this involved a first stage of reports and lists drawn up by the counts for each *pagus*. The stewards at the head of the royal or imperial domains (*fisci*) were expected to send periodic, detailed reports on production to the palace.[416] Charlemagne even required at a stipulated time that statements of the linen and wool furnished to the women working in the women's quarters of the *fisci* and of the garments fashioned by them[417] be sent to his *camera*.[418] It is not known to what degree all these orders were carried out.

There was a place at the palace where records were stored, the *archivum palatii*.[419] Nothing is known about its organization except that it was probably under the authority of the imperial chancellor. It included at least a part of the documents sent to the king and some copies or minutes of documents expedited in his name, notably capitularies.[420] Probably the counts also had some archives.[421] The keeping of records, however, was incomplete and unsystematic.[422]

Despite its imperfections and its frequent ineffectiveness, the wide use of written records introduced by Charlemagne in the administration of the *Regnum Francorum* is an important event in the history of institutions. Beyond its immediate effects it contributed to the formation and development of the political and social structure that left its imprint on the lands that belonged to the Carolingian empire.

PART II

"La guerre est pour les Francs une institution nationale. . . .
Les annalistes relèvent comme des années exceptionnelles celles où l'on
ne s'est point battu. Chaque année par conséquent, tout sujet de l'Empire
peut être requis de prendre les armes au premier appel."
—L. HALPHEN,
Charlemagne et l'empire carolingien (2nd ed.; Paris, 1949), p. 167.

Charlemagne's Army

The large role that the Frankish army played during his reign is indicated by the fact that Charlemagne united to the territories inherited from his father Pepin III and his brother Carloman II many others that he conquered and annexed, as well as some over which he established authority that was limited or unstable. The military institutions must therefore be discussed at some length.[1] The sources are relatively abundant for certain aspects of the history of these institutions, but less so for others.[2]

Recruitment of the Army

One of the most important objectives of the *bannum* (the power of the king to command, prohibit, and punish)[3] was that all the subjects of the king, even peoples recently subjugated such as the Saxons,[4] owed him military service. This service was general only in case of enemy invasion of the territory of the *Regnum* and only in the region where invasion was feared. Orders were given, for example, for the defense of Saxony in 806 when it was thought that there would be an immediate invasion by the Sorbs.[5] This general call to arms was named *lantweri*[6] and was introduced into Italy.[7]

Who was normally called to arms when a military expedition was to take place during the reign of Pepin III and the greater part of Charlemagne's reign is not precisely known. Some formulas, however—such as *ut omnes . . . veniant hostiliter* (792/93), "that all should go to the army"; *ut omnes pleniter bene parati sint* (802), "that all should be ready and fully equipped"; and *ut comiti . . . unumquemque hominem . . . in hostem pergere bannire studeat* (803), "that the count should order every man to join the army"[8]—create no illusion: it was never possible to mobilize all the free men.

Beginning in 806 certain dispositions of capitularies or other legal records, most of which dealt with military expeditions to be undertaken, furnish precise information about who was called to arms. Those called were: in 806 in Frisia all the royal landed vassals and other men known as *caballarii*, who very likely were free men of comfortable circumstances serving on horseback; in 807, between the Seine and the Loire, all the landed vassals; in 808 all the landed vassals and owners of land amounting to at least four manses; in 811 all the landed vassals; and in 818/19, under Louis the Pious, all the vassals.[9] This reveals the importance of the whole vassalic element, and not just that of the royal vassalage, in the composition of the army.[10] This should not be interpreted, however, to mean that the army was ever composed exclusively of vassals.[11] If most of the texts make no mention of nonlanded vassals, it is probably because the bond, exclusively personal, that united them to their lord placed them in a dependence so strong that they accompanied him on a campaign without the king having to so order.[12] From the reign of Pepin III, but principally under Charlemagne, royal and nonroyal vassals in regions menaced or adjacent to menaced regions were landed.[13] This facilitated their mobilization.

As to other elements of the free population liable to military service, in 806 a strict system of regulation was applied, obviously adopted earlier, although it is impossible even to suggest a date. Under this system there were a certain number of others who helped to equip a man who had to join the army. In 806 in Frisia this number was set at six helpers for one who joined, but in Saxony the number varied according to the distance between Saxony and the presumed theater of operations. If the march was toward Spain or the country of the Avars, the number was five helpers for one who joined; if toward Bohemia, two helpers for one who joined.[14] In 807, between the Seine and the Loire, and in 808, in a larger part of the empire, a varying number, also surely dating from an earlier time, was applicable. Free men whose lands totaled three or four manses all owed service and had to equip themselves. Below this minimum, men who joined were helped to equip themselves by the number of men necessary for attaining this minimum, or nearly so. In 808, for example, a man of three manses who joined the army was helped by a man of one manse, a man of two manses who joined was helped by another man of two manses, and a man of one manse who joined was helped by three men of one manse each.[15] The proportions could vary according to the importance of the expedition or to other circumstances.[16] Perhaps there was a rotation among those who actually served and the helpers. This system remained in force under Louis the Pious[17] and was introduced into Italy where it is found during the reign of Lothair I.[18] It should be noted that the helpers as well as those who joined were considered to have fulfilled military service; their task also was an *exercitare*.[19]

Whatever system was adopted, the king, from the moment when the decision to wage war was made, lacked at least one essential element for establishing his plan of campaign—an idea, even approximate, of the effective forces that he would have at his command. Even if it is conceded that under Charlemagne there might have been at the palace a list, imperfectly and badly kept, of royal landed vassals, there was nothing similar for the other men subject to mobilization. Louis the Pious tried to remedy this lacuna in 829 by charging his *missi* with establishing a numerical register by county.[20]

Mobilization and Concentration, Special Units, and Defensive Organization

In the anticipation of a campaign, how was the mobilization and concentration of the army (*exercitus*) carried out? It is believed that in 755 or 756 under Pepin III, the decision was made not to muster the army in March, as had been done until then, but in May.[21] Although the term *magiscampus* ("field of May") was introduced to designate the concentration of the army, which was often preceded by a session of the assembly, the relationship between these events and the month of May soon disappeared, and *magiscampus* came to designate the concentration of the army and the contingent session of the assembly, even when they took place during another month.[22] It should be noted that under Pepin III the concentration and eventually the session of the assembly took place in May only six times in the course of the dozen years between 756 and 768, and under Charlemagne, a maximum of seventeen times during the forty-five years of his reign from 769 to 813.[23] Under Louis the Pious, even the coincidence between the session of the assembly and the concentration of the army generally ceased to occur.

As far as can be ascertained, the mobilization occurred in two stages, at least beginning with the last decade of the eighth century. The mobilizing authorities received an order of alert whereupon they had to name those who had to join and those who had to help, to insure that the men owing active service were ready to leave with their equipment, and to inspect or assign someone else to inspect their armament.[24] When the order to assemble (*iussio, adnuntiatio*) arrived, these authorities had to call up their men and lead them to the place of concentration (generally called *placitum* because, as has been said, it was often preceded by an assembly).[25] The lapse of time between the alert and the concentration depended on the circumstances; it could be several months.[26] The counts were the principal mobilizing authorities for their own vassals, for the free men of the county owing service, and for the vassals of those lords living in the county who were not mustered. In addition to the counts, however, bishops, abbots, abbesses, royal vassals, and other important lords mobilized their own vassals and their other free dependents.[27] The king sent to the mobilizing authorities his orders of alert or of march, often in writing, by the intermediary of *missi ad hoc*, who were frequently royal vassals.[28] There is extant an order of alert addressed to Fulrad, secular or lay abbot of Saint-Quentin, sent a little after 12 April 806 in the expectation of a summer campaign against the Sorbs.[29]

These methods were unwieldy and slow. It would happen in urgent circumstances that the king or a count invested with superior authority in a particular region would gather troops immediately, ignoring the habitual delay or the distinction between those who joined and those who helped and would then enter into a campaign with them, counting upon being joined later by the *exercitus*.[30]

Charlemagne at the end of his reign, or more likely Louis the Pious, tried to accelerate the mobilization and concentration. The *missi dominici*, having become quasi-permanent,[31] received the order of alert and each transmitted it to the bishops of his *missaticum;* the bishops in turn alerted their own men and also transmitted the order to the abbots, abbesses, counts, and royal vassals of their dioceses so that the latter could do likewise. Upon receiving the order of alert, those who served had to keep themselves ready and completely equipped to begin to march within twelve hours. Used in 817 at the time of the revolt of Bernard of Italy, this method produced satisfactory results.[32]

Besides mobilizing military forces, there were operations of another type. Like Pepin III, Charlemagne used light and rapid small units for particular goals, such as interventions on other operational territory than that of the *exercitus*, for difficult maneuvers, for raids in enemy territory, as garrisons in fortified works, and for surveillance of frontiers. Such units were generally called *scarae*, *excarricati* or *scariti homines*. It seems likely that these detachments were often composed of vassals.[33] When the king left on a campaign or stayed in one of his *palatia*, he evidently had at his command an escort composed chiefly of royal vassals,[34] who certainly played a role in eventual military operations.

In the frontier zones (*marcae*) there were under Charlemagne, certainly by 802 but probably earlier, special obligations for the population—guard duty (*wacta*, *warda*) and a state of alert permitting a rapid defense by the population mobilized on the spot.[35] The same dispositions were instituted in Italy.[36] It has already been said that vassals in the frontier zones were landed, a situation that rendered defense more effective.[37]

Beginning in 800 the maritime zone bordered by the Atlantic Ocean, the English Channel, and the North Sea was under surveillance because of the Norman raids. After the attack on Frisia in 810 by a Danish fleet, there was an increase in security measures involving principally guard service and maintaining a state of alert.[38] In addition, ships were assembled or constructed so as to create flotillas on the coasts, in the vicinity of mouths of rivers, and in harbors, notably at Boulogne-sur-Mer and at Ghent; and orders were given to Louis, king of Aquitaine, to do the same in the estuary of the Gironde and in the delta of the Rhone.[39] Troops could be summoned to embark on these flotillas.[40] However, these measures brought only mediocre results.

Command, Armament, Equipment, Logistic Elements, and Effective Forces

Little is known about the command of the armies. Charlemagne was frequently commander in chief, but Charles the Young, his eldest son, often assumed important commands and was even commander in chief, especially after the imperial coronation. Pepin and Louis also commanded some armies in Italy and on its frontiers, in the country of the Avars, or in Spain. Large units, when not organized in Francia, were often composed of men of the same ethnic group, such as, for example, Alamanni, Bavarians, Thuringians, Frisians, and Saxons. But the commanders of these large units, like those formed in Francia, were frequently Franks, either household officers or counts.[41] Undoubtedly other counts or royal vassals held commands under them, but nothing is known about these subordinate commands.

The Carolingians attached great importance to armament. There is precise information on this subject only for the very end of the eighth century and for the ninth century. It is known that every foot soldier had to be equipped with a lance and a shield—the traditional arms—to which was added, perhaps after the wars against the Avars and the Slavs, a bow.[42] The armament of the cavalry was also traditional but could be more complete.[43] From the earliest evidence of 792/93 we know that it consisted of a lance and a shield, a long sword (*spata*, *gladius*), and a short sword (*semispathium*), a type of dirk having only a single edge.[44] Ninth-century sources indicate the addition of a bow such as was used by the infantry.[45] Certain horsemen were equipped by their lord.[46]

Others in the Carolingian cavalry were armed with more complete equipment. These men wore the *brunia*[47] and were most certainly armored knights.[48] It seems that certain ones also wore a metal helmet (*galea*) as well as metal leg guards (*bauga*, *bagnbergae*).[49] This equipment was extremely expensive. The mount and the complete equipment of the armored knight amounted, in fact, at the time of Charlemagne to thirty-six or forty shillings, according to whether the horse was a mare or a war horse.[50] This was equal to the value of eighteen or twenty cows. By way of comparison, the livestock of the reserve of the royal domain of Annappes (Nord, 2,063 hectares) at the end of Charlemagne's reign or at the beginning of the reign of Louis the Pious included forty-five cows.[51] Only very rich men, whether vassals or free landed men, could therefore afford this equipment. At the beginning of 805 and until much later the wearing of the *brunia* was required of vassals holding a benefice of twelve manses.[52] Moreover, a capitulary of 802/3 made it obligatory for counts to have *bruniae* and helmets in reserve in order to equip horsemen destined to be armored knights.[53]

Although few in number, the units of armored cavalry had an extremely important role, tactical and perhaps strategic: they assured the Carolingian armies of superiority over the Saxons, the Slavs, the Avars, and probably the Danes. This explains the numerous attempts by merchants to buy *bruniae* as well as high-quality Frankish swords and leg guards in the *Regnum Francorum* and to sell them at high prices outside the frontiers. Although this commerce, which favored the enemy, was prohibited and resisted,[54] it was certainly not eliminated.

The fact that all the cavalry, armored or not, seems to have required particular attention on the part of the Carolingians is evident in almost all the documents that have been consulted.[55] Moreover, it was essential in case of operations to take measures assuring the transport horses (pack horses and draft horses) and combat horses the water and especially the grass or fodder necessary. This need, as well as others, was covered by a right to requisition wood, water, grass, and undoubtedly fodder.[56] The movements of the army were conditioned by these necessities,[57] and there were some cases where the absence of pasturage and fodder compelled a Frankish army to retreat.[58]

Charlemagne seemed to have been aware of the importance of problems that are today called logistic. Judging by the capitularies and legal records of 803, 806, 807, and 811, it can be seen that during several campaigns he prescribed the establishment of reserves of provisions, clothes, armaments, gear, and convoys charged with assuring transport, as well as a command and an escort for these convoys.[59] The cartage, provisions, gear, and probably the armament and clothes were procured by the counts, the ecclesiastical and lay lords, and the important royal vassals, who had to furnish them from their domains. The royal domains also had to furnish these supplies.[60] It is possible that the combatants themselves also had to procure supplies, but this fact is not clearly established, and in any event it would be a small matter. Although the quantities of provisions, armament, and equipment to be transported could be determined according to the presumed duration of the campaign, tradition nevertheless set the amounts at a three months supply for provisions and a six months supply for armament and clothes.[61] In 811 an article of a capitulary designated, in view of two anticipated expeditions—one in Spain and the other beyond the Elbe—the points of departure where use of these reserves could be made.[62] However, there is doubt concerning the regular functioning of these logistic services.

Efforts to evaluate the effective forces that Charlemagne was able to mobilize have been in vain.[63] No new research has been undertaken here on this subject for this book: all that can be affirmed is that the armies of Charlemagne were small.

Infractions, Abuses, and Sanctions

Not to join the army or not to contribute to the equipment of a combatant if one was a helper, rendered one guilty of a crime of disobedience punishable by a heavy fine of sixty shillings. This fine, an element of the sanction of the *bannum*, was called *heri-bannum*[64] and was payable in money or even in personal objects of recognized value,[65] preferably those of use to the king. The capitularies of the ninth century issued by Charlemagne and those issued by Louis the Pious contained numerous dispositions regarding the collection and the forms of payment of the fine, which was also owed for nonperformance of *scara* and guard service, as well as for nonperformance of service in the *exercitus*.[66] The importance attached to the *heribannum* and the number of dispositions relating to it reveal that the number of free men who escaped their military duty was rather high. It should be noted that the *heribannum* was introduced into Italy.[67]

Desertion (*herisliz*) was repressed in a celebrated case, that of the duke of Bavaria, Tassilo III, in 788; he was condemned to death but was pardoned insofar as his life was concerned.[68] Later the crime of desertion became, in the course of two years, the object of two different kinds of repression. In 810 Charlemagne, probably with the view of applying an arbitrary punishment, prescribed that the guilty person be put at his disposition, but the following year an article of a capitulary commuted for the guilty person the death sentence,[69] which had been the traditional punishment for this crime. Repression of the crime of *herisliz* was also introduced into Italy.[70]

In order to give an exact picture of military institutions and their functioning, it is essential to take account of the numerous abuses of power that occurred in respect to military service. It seems that the mobilizing authorities exempted from service men who enjoyed their protection by having bought it in one way or another and that they sent on campaign men who ought to have been exempted but who had not gained their favor. The capitularies of the last years of Charlemagne's reign denounced and curbed these abuses.[71] They also curbed the fraudulent maneuvers by which many people escaped military service or the objections they made to orders to join,[72] both serious factors in the diminution of Charlemagne's power.[73]

PART III

"Le droit de juger était avec celui de faire les lois,
le principal attribut de cette royauté omnipotente."
—Fustel de Coulanges,
Les transformations de la royauté à l'époque carolingienne
(Paris, 1892), p. 404.

"Il y annonce le règne de la justice."
—Charlemagne,
in the Programmatic Capitulary of 802; A. Kleinclausz,
Charlemagne (Paris, 1934), p. 308.

Charlemagne and the Administration of Justice

In the complex that judicial organization, competence, and procedure formed at the heart of the Frankish monarchy, it was the judicial organization upon which Charlemagne exerted the greatest influence and which is therefore the principal concern here. The principles determining the application and sources of the law[1] must, however, be discussed briefly.

The Personality of the Law and Sources of the Law

It is almost superfluous to recall that under the Merovingians and the first Carolingians the principle of the personality of the law was in force in the *Regnum Francorum*. Every subject of the king lived, at least in principle, under the authority and protection of the law peculiar to the national group of which he was a member.[2] Charlemagne maintained this rule, and when complaints on the subject of its violation reached him, he ordered the *missi* and the counts to uphold it and see that it was observed by others.[3] More than once in his legislative or regulatory activity Charlemagne not only enforced the rule but prescribed measures for its application.[4] Moreover, traces of its effective application are extant.[5] The application of the personality of the law was actually possible only if the national law of the person demanding its application[6] was that of a great enough number of free men living in the region, so that the necessary judges could be found to constitute the bench of the court. If this condition was not fulfilled there were only two other possibilities: to send the case to a court sitting in a neighboring region where the national law in question was that of a sufficient number of the inhabitants,[7] or to use the national law of the majority of the population that was currently applied in that region. In reality one thus passed from the personality to the territoriality of the law.[8] It should be mentioned that even though the members of the clergy lived under their national law, the churches, at least in the west of the kingdom— and yet with many exceptions—had as their law the Roman law.

The national Germanic laws in force in the *Regnum Francorum* remained throughout the entire reign of Charlemagne first and foremost customary laws known by oral tradition.[9] With only one exception,[10] the *leges* formulated in writing contained only a part of the law peculiar to the various national groups to which the subjects of the king belonged. Charlemagne appeared to have been conscious of the necessity for very careful and comprehensive texts of these laws. The *Lex Saxonum* was put into writing in 785 when the king believed Saxony to be subjugated. Probably in 798 a new text of the *Lex Salica* was prepared, though not promulgated. Perhaps the *Lex Alamannorum* and the *Lex Baiuvariorum* were somewhat superficially revised around 788.[11]

It was, nevertheless, some years later in the realization of his program of imperial government that Charlemagne made a considerable effort to prepare revised and, if possible, completed texts of existing *leges* and written texts of the national laws not yet put into writing. The diet that sat in October 802, and certainly commissions continuing the diet's task up to 803, accomplished an important work to which Charlemagne gave a binding character.[12] In the domain of *leges* there came to light a new and revised text of the Salic law, the *Karolina,* and probably a revised text of the

Ripuarian law.[13] Perhaps the *Lex Saxonum* was revised and a revision of the *Lex Alamannorum* was begun but not completed. Probably some national laws were put into writing,[14] such as those of some of the Thuringian people, including the descendants of the Angles who had not gone to Britain and those Warnes who still survived; those of a group of Franks who had established themselves in the neighborhood of the lower Meuse and the Waal; and those of the Frisians, although in this case perhaps remaining unfinished.[15] Furthermore, in 803 certain dispositions destined to be added to all the laws became the subject of a capitulary; another capitulary revised several articles of the *Lex Ribuaria;*[16] and a third completed the *Lex Baiuvariorum.*[17] Other legislative dispositions of general import were collected in a capitulary of a different type.[18]

While it is known that the capitularies of Charlemagne that did not complete the national *leges* principally contained purely administrative dispositions, certain of these dispositions—and, even more, the normative dispositions that the capitularies also included —sometimes created new law and modified existing law.[19] Whether the *capitula* modifying or completing the Ripuarian law or the Bavarian law were of personal application, as were the laws themselves, all the other capitularies were of territorial application. As for the Roman law, the *Lex Romana Visigothorum* unquestionably remained the most widespread collection of a systematic and general nature; it was certainly known and used not only in the regions where Roman law was the national law of a large part of the population but occasionally elsewhere, and sometimes at the palace itself.[20]

Judicial Organization

THE COUNTY COURT

It is not possible to treat the judicial organization in the Frankish monarchy realistically without also discussing the competence and that part of the procedure preceding the appearance of the parties before the court. The measures that Charlemagne took in this domain had the purpose, on the one hand, of assuring each person a better chance of vindicating his subjective rights and, on the other hand, of assuring respect for objective law. This was a dominant preoccupation of Charlemagne.[21] Consequently, he intended that arbitrary acts capable of hurting people with respect to their lives or their possessions should be prohibited. Violence committed against anyone by a count under the pretext of repression of brigandage, but in reality out of envy and enmity, would entail the dismissal of the count and his condemnation to a fine. To hang a man, whether a free man or a serf, even if he seemed to have been caught in the act, was forbidden, and whoever was guilty of such an abuse had to pay the *wergeld* of the hanged person; a regular procedure had to be observed, whether it was the ordinary procedure or the summary procedure applicable to malefactors caught in the act.[22] The Frankish judicial procedure for objects apparently without owners was introduced into the Bavarian law to prevent the appropriation of objects that might have been lost or stolen.[23] Charlemagne's concern for equity even extended to those who, condemned to death, had been pardoned by the emperor: their person and the possessions they had legally acquired after the grant of pardon had the benefit of protection of the courts.[24]

There is no contradiction between Charlemagne's preoccupation with equity, of which some effects have been indicated, and his anxiety over the increasing number of cases, particularly in the last years of his reign.[25] This anxiety corresponded with the aspiration for stability that so characterized several aspects of his policy. This is what doubtless led him to set a time limit beyond which complaints that might have a repercussion on landed property would no longer have any legal force. While one did not have the right to contest a seisin existing at the time of the death of Pepin III in 768, nevertheless, with a view to avoiding injustices, the emperor restricted the absolute character of this rule by reserving for himself the right to judge any exceptions.[26] Effective observance of the time restriction set at the end of Pepin's reign appeared in the legal records.[27] In Bavaria the time limit was fixed at the accession in 749 of Tassilo III, the duke who was removed in 788.[28]

The counts and subordinate officials were often less than zealous in the exercise of their judicial functions,[29] especially when it concerned plaintiffs whose reactions were less to be feared than those of powerful persons. Charlemagne reacted vigorously against this tendency. A count was not allowed to postpone a session of his court in order to devote himself to some pleasure; he had to treat with diligence and, if necessary, with priority the cases of churches and *miserabiles personae*, that is, widows, orphans, and the poor. But the number of times that such instructions were repeated reveal that they were not too well followed.[30]

The plaintiff could experience serious difficulties in obtaining judgment of a case as a consequence of the ill will of the accused, and this situation was abetted by the fact that Frankish law permitted delays in court attendance that were relatively long and easily extended. In cases under the Ripuarian law, which allowed the largest number of delays, the Capitulary of 803 revising this law reduced the number of delays and, by a more effective intervention of public power, compelled the accused to appear in court.[31] This action suited Charlemagne's firm resolve to maintain the public peace and fight against crime,[32] a resolve manifested in the dispositions of the capitularies destined to prevent or repress the development of brigandage.[33] It has been shown that the inviolability of lands of immunity sustained restrictions intended to facilitate this repression,[34] and for the same reason, even the right of asylum of the churches was limited.[35]

Brigandage was not the only offense that occupied, especially after 802, a larger and larger place in the capitularies of Charlemagne. Violence against the churches and *miserabiles personae*, perjury, incest, certain cases of *faida*, and still other offenses can be cited. These offenses involved sentences of purely penal fines, such as the *bannum*, arbitrary chastisements, corporal punishments, and death. While judgment before the royal court or before the *missi* posed no problem, at the *mallus* the complaint of the damaged party or his representative was usually necessary to set the judicial mechanism in motion, but in many cases there was no complaint, and sometimes it was impossible to get one. Perhaps the count had already proceeded to the *Rügeverfahren*, that is, to an inquest of those whom the *fama publica* placed under suspicion of serious offenses; the result of the inquest substituted for a complaint by a party. It would be rash to state with certainty that Charlemagne had created this institution in Francia, even though it seems probable.[36] But whether according to such a measure or independent of it, it seems certain that in the cases that concern us here the count himself was able to act as the plaintiff.[37] It is not known when Charlemagne authorized this procedure; if there was a written disposition, it has been lost.

The principal reform introduced by Charlemagne in the judicial institutions was aimed at the composition of the county court, the *mallus*.[38] At the beginning of Charlemagne's reign this court, which sat successively in the *pagus* at various places determined by custom, was usually presided over by the count, but a subordinate official (the *vicarius* or *centenarius*) could also preside. There was no change in this respect except that later the assistant of the count, the *missus comitis* or *vicecomes*, was also occasionally president.[39] The president was aided by judgment-finders, men who by practice knew, or were reputed to know, the law and who had the extremely important task of finding the judgment. As in earlier periods they were generally called *rachinburgii* (German, *Urteilfinders*).[40] In Anglo-Saxon England they were known as doomsmen. They were not permanent, and probably the count appointed them for each session. Also sitting on the court, it seems, were other persons, probably notable men and practitioners of the law whom in all likelihood the count admitted. They are believed to be the persons designated by the very vague names *pagenses, francae personae,* and *boni homines,* terms which often also encompassed the judgment-finders.[41] Finally, the free men of that part of the *pagus* where the *mallus* sat had to be present at the sessions, a burden that was very heavy.[42]

From the very first, Charlemagne appears to have substituted for occasional judgment-finders permanent and qualified ones who had acquired from long experience a more thorough knowledge of customary law. This was surely real progress toward the effective administration of justice. These permanent judgment-finders were the *scabini*, who sometimes were still designated by the older name *rachinburgii*[43] and also, we believe, in some regions by the word *iudices*.[44] In a few cases they have been grouped with the other persons who often sat, as formerly, in the company of the qualified judgment-finders under the traditional name of *boni homines* or the more pompous appellation of *magnifici viri;* these expressions, however, were most often reserved for judgment-finders who were not *scabini*.[45]

Perhaps the *scabini* were first created in the north of Francia where they may have existed around 774 and where we later meet them.[46] They then spread into various parts of the realm. In the oldest dated texts we find *scabini* in a normally constituted judicial body exercising their functions in Provence in 780, on the lower Seine in 781, in Franconia in 782, and in the *pagus* of the Moselle probably also in 782.[47] In the first and third texts we find *scabini* at a session of a court of the *missi*; in the second and fourth texts, they are found at a session of the *mallus*; but the *scabini* are always those of the county, the *pagus*. In some capitularies there is mention of the *scabini* and of their *ministerium*, that is, their public function. At least seven *scabini* had to be present at all the sessions.[48] They were closely tied to the count; they were his *scabini*.[49] Also, it appears that they were normally appointed by the count in the presence of the important men of the *pagus*, although the *missi* could likewise appoint them. They had to be chosen from the *pagenses*, that is, the free men of the *pagus*, who were qualified by their virtues; a condemnation to death, even though pardoned, barred a man from becoming a *scabinus*.[50] The *scabini* were under the control of the *missi dominici*, and those who were negligent or guilty of serious faults were brought to the attention of the *missi*, evidently in order to be reproved and, if the case warranted it, removed from office.[51]

In a second move, faithful to his preoccupation so often manifested of protecting free men of modest circumstances,[52] Charlemagne at first limited to two or three, then to three a year, the number of *placita* of the *mallus* in which all free men had to participate. The sessions were probably held on fixed dates without a summons (German, *Ungebotenes Ding*). There has been preserved, it seems, an article of the capitulary by which this measure was proclaimed, but the date of its publication is not known. A *capitulare missorum* of 803, however, applies this rule, and the Capitulary of Thionville of 805 refers to it.[53] Apparently, there were difficulties in putting the rule into practice. Indeed, at first Charlemagne and then Louis the Pious often had to repeat in their capitularies the prohibition against summoning *pagenses* who were not *scabini* and were neither parties nor witnesses to sessions of the *mallus* other than the *tria placita generalia*.[54] In addition to the *scabini*, however, men of superior status and vassals of the count could be required to sit as judgment-finders at all sessions, whether they were general or not.[55]

Under Charlemagne the double reform of creating *scabini* and three *placita generalia* yearly appears to have penetrated into certain parts of the *Regnum* where non-Frankish, Germanic populations lived. This was at least partially the case in Saxony and quite probably in Alamannia.[56] It was certainly so in Italy.[57] In the lands properly called Frankish, particularly between the Loire and the Rhine, this reform had consequences that outlived the *Regnum Francorum*.

The introduction to the courts of a body of judgment-finders, permanent and henceforth better informed, shows the importance that Charlemagne attached to an exact application of the law, even though it was an inadequate reform. The count and those who could replace him as president of the *mallus* had their part in the application of the law. It would seem, therefore, that it was to both the president and the judgment-finders that the article of the Pro-grammatic Capitulary of 802 was addressed, prescribing that the judges (*iudices*) judge according to the written law and not according to their own pleasure. This was an attempt to bind the president and the judgment-finders to written elements of the national laws, elements that the emperor seriously intended to expand at this time. Charlemagne thought that this was the way to eliminate the arbitrary exercise of jurisdiction.[58] To the same end, in the execution of the rule of the personality of the law, the parties were expected to make known their national law and the president to know what national law was applicable.[59] Counts and subordinate officials were urged, in capitularies appearing after 802, to acquire a serious knowledge of the law that would normally be used in the cases submitted to the court over which they presided.[60] Although far from resolving all the difficulties that the application of the various national laws presented, these measures rendered easier the search for methods of resolving difficulties when they did occur.

Another disposition that appeared late in 810 was destined to procure, at least in the most serious cases, a less contingent exercise of jurisdiction by the county courts. Suits dealing with personal liberty or landed property were to be judged at the *mallus* only if it was presided over by the count himself,[61] to the exclusion of the *vicarius* or the *centenarius*, who merited less confidence intellectually, and especially morally.[62] A similar disposition had probably been decreed a little earlier regarding suits that could result in a condemnation to death.[63] Also in 810 Pepin introduced this reform into Italy in his last capitulary.[64] If in a given case the application of the rule proved impossible, the case had to be postponed so that it could be judged at the next assizes of the *missi dominici* unless, to be sure, it was admitted to the palace court. As early as 811 it was necessary to renew the dispositions prohibiting subordinate officials from presiding over the *mallus* in the three kinds of cases that have just been mentioned, probably because those whom it concerned took little care to obey the first dispositions.[65] This reform was, it seems, one of the least effective of those that Charlemagne tried to carry out.[66] Throughout his reign he was concerned not only with the zeal and dignity that the counts, the *vicarii*, and the *centenarii* displayed in the exercise of their judicial functions, but even more, with their honesty and independence. The *missi* had to be on the watch for this.[67] The counts were responsible for the honesty and impartiality of their subordinates.[68] The *missi* themselves were urged to resist all attempts at corruption.[69] Orders and prohibitions applied also to the judgment-finders, that is, to the *scabini* as well as to the presidents of the courts.[70]

There are also in the capitularies dispositions concerning the dignity that parties and witnesses ought to manifest, as well as a disposition prohibiting anyone from going with arms to the *mallus* or to the assizes of the *missi*.[71] Understood less easily at first glance is another disposition, appearing for the first time in the Programmatic Capitulary of 802, stating that it was forbidden to defend before a court a party whose cause was unjust and that to flout this prohibition was an act of infidelity to the emperor.[72] Undoubtedly, it was less a question of a true defender than that of an influential man using his authority or other means to keep an accused person from condemnation. That this disposition was repeated under various forms shows the difficulties encountered in its application.[73]

It should be pointed out that Charlemagne ordered that a place where the *mallus* could sit at all times should be maintained and that a prison as well as forked gallows should be at the disposal of the count.[74] What is more important is that Charlemagne—in whom, it has been said, the aspiration for stability manifested itself in all his actions involving institutions—attached great importance to the authority of judgments at law. To create more respect for the *res iudicata* was the goal of two dispositions dating from the imperial period.

The first disposition repressed the attempt to re-submit to a *mallus* a case that had already received a definitive judgment. Such an attempt was held to be a misdemeanor liable to a fine of reduced *bannum*, that is, fifteen shillings, which could be replaced by fifteen blows with a stick administered by the *scabini* who had rendered the judgment. Since this disposition was even considered important enough to be added to all the national laws, it thus had a widespread and indisputable effect.[75] It corresponded to the traditional clause in the diplomas delivered after a trial at the palace court ordering that the case should be considered settled and terminated.[76] It also corresponded to the custom existing at the *mallus* of handing over to the condemned party (who had yielded) a charter by which the plaintiff (who had obtained satisfaction) guaranteed the condemned person from any new action in the case. This charter, called *securitas*, could be issued following an accord between the parties or in execution of a judgment.[77]

The second disposition was aimed at the person who refused to accept a judgment, but did not dare to initiate the procedure of false judgment against the *scabini*. He was to be put under strong guard until he decided which of the two procedures to follow. Nevertheless, with certain precautions he was to be permitted to take the case before the king. If the king allowed it, a course of new appeal was opened—the action of false judgment before the palace court.[78]

ASSIZES OF THE *Missi Dominici* AND THE PALACE COURT

During the reign of Charlemagne the institution of the *missi dominici* attained considerable importance. The work of the *missi* had, as we have seen, a judicial as well as an administrative aspect.[79] When rendering justice the *missi* acted with extremely broad powers: in this domain as in others it was the king or the emperor who acted through them. The judicial assizes of the *missi* were a sort of detached part of the palace court.[80] This was true especially for the ordinary *missi*, who acted by virtue of a general mandate from the monarch.[81] With this authority they could judge any case that it was convenient for them to receive, to summon, or to evoke to their assizes, but only after having conducted an inquest of the suspected persons, that is, a *Rügeverfahren*.[82] Certain cases could be delegated to them by the king after a complaint that he chose to allow.[83] It appears that procedure had been organized so that in certain circumstances a party could obtain from the monarch at the palace a written order (*breve*) vesting certain *missi* with a particular case.[84]

The composition of the bench in the assizes of the *missi* could vary. It could include bishops, abbots and counts,[85] royal vassals,[86] subordinate officials, *scabini* (or other judges in the regions where the *scabinatus* was not yet introduced),[87] and certainly, as at the *mallus*, important men and local practitioners of the law.[88] But whether a judgment was always influenced by the opinions and the deliberations of the judgment-finders or whether it was often the result of these deliberations,[89] it was through the *missi*—the personal delegates of the king—that the judgment became law.[90] Although the competence of the *missi* was general, because of the nature of the sources, certain types of cases submitted to them are more familiar, for instance, those concerning landed property, the personal status of a free man, and brigandage.[91] Perhaps also in certain cases an appeal to the assizes of the *missi* was possible after a judgment of the *mallus*.[92]

As a consequence of the reorganization of 802, the competence of the assizes of the *missi* was the same as that of the county court in cases where the county court was competent. In 810 this concurrent competence was legally recognized for cases concerning the personal status of a free man, those affecting landed property, and those that could involve condemnation to death.[93] When in 811 it was decided that the *missi* should perform their mission for four months a year and that during each of those months they should hold four assizes in four different places in the presence of the counts,[94] these assizes actually supplanted for a part of the year the *mallus* presided over by the count. One wonders, however, in what measure these regulatory dispositions were observed.

Assizes where numerous judgment-finders were present inspired

Charlemagne and perhaps the parties involved with more confidence than the simple county court. Therefore in 811 the counts of several *pagi* were enjoined to form groups and to hold judicial assizes during the months when the *missi* would not be holding their assizes. This was probably legal confirmation of a custom already existing, at least in certain parts of the *Regnum*.[95]

If the judicial assizes of the *missi dominici* were in large part a new creation, the palace court hardly differed under Charlemagne from what it had been at the time of Pepin III, at least in regard to its composition. Presided over by the monarch himself, it included *proceres* or *fideles* as judgment-finders, among whom were always counts, more rarely a household dignitary, bishops, and abbots. A single *placitum* also mentions royal vassals, but it is believed that they were normally among those judgment-finders not given any other designation, whose names appear after those of the counts in the diplomas of judgment. In one case even some *scabini* are encountered, but this is explained by circumstances peculiar to the case judged.[96] Besides some judgment-finders designated by the king to sit on a case, it seems that other *fideles* or *proceres* were empowered to act as a floating element of the bench, as was the case in the other courts.[97] A count palatine was always present, and it sometimes happened that there might be more than one or that other judgment-finders fulfilled their functions. The *comes palatii* was the expert who knew the law from experience and whose opinion had particular weight.[98] The word "opinion" is used because, although the count palatine assisted the king as did the other judgment-finders, it was the king who handed down the judgment with the help of his judgment-finders. Such, at least, was the law.[99] The count palatine had an office at his command in which scribes drew up diplomas through which the parties who had won their suits could obtain release (*placitum*).

Under Charlemagne there was an important reform. Sometimes the count palatine himself presided over the palace court in the absence of the monarch, and it is believed that these instances were numerous. The increase of cases undoubtedly made necessary in 811 a definition of the competence of the palace court. The emperor reserved for himself cases in which bishops, abbots, counts, and men of high rank were parties, while other cases were to be judged under the presidency of one of the counts palatine, unless for some reason the emperor decided to hear them himself.[100] In particularly serious criminal trials some judgments were rendered by the diet or by an extraordinary assembly under the presidency of Charlemagne. This occurred in the trial at Worms in 786 that concerned those involved in the conspiracy led in 785 by Hardrad; in the trial of Tassilo, duke of Bavaria, at Ingelheim in 788; in the trial of the Gascon rebel Adalaric at Worms in 790; and in the trial of Pepin the Hunchback and his accomplices at Regensburg in 792.[101] In these cases the diet rendering the justice can probably be considered as an enlarged palace court.

The competence of the palace court was evidently general since it was the court of the king. What matters most, however, from a historical point of view, is its real competence, the *id quod plerumque fit*. In the first years of Charlemagne's reign, the cases attributed to the royal jurisdiction by the national laws, particularly the Salic law and the Ripuarian law, constituted the competence of the jurisdiction of the palace court. In addition, individuals or ecclesiastical establishments benefiting from the special protection of the king had the right to take their cases before the palace court,[102] and it seems that most ecclesiastical or lay persons of high rank could also have their important cases judged there.

The fact that this competence, which was first extended to some types of cases during the last decade of the eighth century,[103] was considerably developed after Charlemagne's accession to the empire is an important event in the history of judicial institutions under the Carolingians. The Programmatic Capitulary of 802 assigned to the competence of the palace court cases involving: offenses of the *bannum;* monks whom bishops and abbots could not force to observe the Benedictine Rule; monks who practiced or tolerated sodomy; ecclesiastics who were not holders of an *honor* but who kept dogs or birds of the chase; priests and deacons who maintained concubines; those who harmed a person who had given information in support of the rights of the emperor, if the case was serious enough to warrant a fine in excess of sixty shillings; those who, after committing homicide, refused to pay a composition; those who, after incest or illicit union, refused to submit to the decision of the bishop or to a judgment; those who did not obey the order to join the army; perjurors; and, last, those who were guilty of homicide committed against relatives and did not submit to the judgment of the bishop and a secular court.[104] In 802/3 an article of a capitulary contained the reminder that men of high social rank who caused trouble in a county should be sent to the palace for judgment.[105] An article of the capitulary of 803, intended to complete all the laws, assigned to the same jurisdiction those who in a band resisted a count when he entered lands of immunity in conformance with the law.[106] The *missi* in 803 were instructed both to see that the men whom the counts could not force to observe the laws were sent to the palace for chastisement and also to send to the palace those whose dogs' right shoulders were clipped.[107] The principal reason for these measures, it appears, was Charlemagne's acute sense of responsibility before God, which at this time tortured his conscience.[108] Badly served by chaotic institutions and by incompetent and selfish men, he had the dangerous illusion of thinking that it would be better if he himself could chastise the guilty and bring about in the empire a peace conforming to Divine Will. After the years 802 and 803, dispositions of such a nature were rare.[109]

The enlargement of the competence of the palace court[110] created around the emperor an intolerable atmosphere of which he complained.[111] The crowded docket—to use a modern expression —indefinitely postponed the judgment of cases, especially those in which the parties were of modest circumstances. We know it was the attempt to remedy this situation that led Charlemagne to a division of competence between himself and the counts palatine.[112] But this was a poor remedy. Actually, the increased competence of the palace court was doubtless less catastrophic than it appears to those who read the capitularies of 802/3. It must, indeed, be admitted that many of the dispositions were not obeyed. Bishops, abbots, counts, and subordinate officials were probably unenthusiastic about them; moreover, it was difficult to force individuals involved to present themselves at the imperial residence, sometimes very distant,[113] and then, too, certain dispositions were unrealistic.[114] But in spite of these considerations, the measures taken in 802/3 contributed to producing at the palace a disordered state of affairs, which Louis the Pious attempted to wrestle with after his accession.[115]

Procedure[116]

MODES OF PROOF

The modes of proof of ordinary procedure at the *mallus* and those used most frequently at the royal court under Charlemagne continued to be the ordeals or judgments of God (*iudicia Dei*) and the oath. It is useful to recall that the ordeals were material acts performed by one or several parties at the trial by which it was believed that God would make known which party had right on his side. Most of the judgments of God were originally acts of pagan magic, Christianized in form.[117] As for the oath sworn by one of the parties, generally with some oath-helpers (*coiuratores;* German, *Eideshelfers*), God's intervention was also invoked. It was expected that God would allow the swearing of the oath to be successful if the party had right on his side, or that He would cause the swearing to fail if what the party swore was false. The oath was thus a judgment of God, but of a particular type.[118]

The administration of the proof usually devolved upon the accused and constituted for him a right. Because the accused was reproached with an offense, the trial was always a criminal trial and remained so throughout the Carolingian period. In an earlier period, when the rule came into existence, the accused could reply to the reproach by an act of violence, but he could also deny the infamous accusation by means of an oath with oath-helpers or by the ordeal, an act in whose effectiveness for indicating the truth there was complete faith. This seems to be the most reasonable explanation of the rule,[119] although there were nevertheless some cases in which national laws, and even the Salic law, conferred upon the plaintiff the right of administering the proof.[120]

The oath by which the accused freed himself from the accusation was in current use under Charlemagne. It was always sworn with oath-helpers who were not witnesses and whose number was fixed by judgment in conformance with the law, written or unwritten.[121] Charlemagne decreed new dispositions, some of which enlarged or facilitated, while others restrained, the use of this mode of proof.[122] By a legislative disposition for subjects living under the Ripuarian law and by an article of a capitulary for those living in Saxony, he confirmed a well-established custom: the obligation of swearing the purgatory oath, as it is called later, in a church or at least on some relics.[123]

Among the judgments of God[124] which were performed by the accused alone, the only one that was traditionally used to a large extent in the Frankish national law was the ordeal of boiling water (*iudicium aquae ferventis;* German, *Kesselfang*), whereby the accused plunged his hand into a cauldron (*aeneum, ineum*) full of boiling water in order to retrieve an object. If the arm and hand healed within a fixed period of time, the accused had proved his innocence. In a case in which the accused had to prove that he had not refused to appear at the *mallus* or to carry out the judgment, Charlemagne appears to have eliminated the *Kesselfang* as a means of clearing oneself.[125] On the other hand, he introduced in the *Regnum Francorum* recourse to the proof of the hot iron (*examen vomerum ignitorum;* German, *Pflugscharenlauf*), which consisted of making the accused run with bare feet over nine white-hot plowshares, placed on the ground at intervals. This ordeal was imposed on a person accused of having killed one of his relatives and whose life or demeanor indicated that he was not free of guilt. This disposition was judged important enough to be entered later in all the laws.[126] The same ordeal was prescribed, at least as a mode of subsidiary proof, for a Christian accused by a Jew.[127]

The judicial duel (*campus, duellum*) was, above all, the proof requiring the participation of the two parties.[128] The accused engaged in it in order to free himself from the accusation, the plaintiff in order to prove the accusation well founded.[129] It was employed in cases in which the law prescribed it, and to these cases Charlemagne added others. Some of the dispositions decreed by him in this respect completed the Ripuarian law. Although the goal pursued by the monarch appears to have been to furnish the two parties with more possibilities for inducing God to designate the innocent and the guilty, perhaps he was also concerned with sparing the parties the danger of perjuring themselves by offering them a mode of proof other than the purgatory oath with oath-helpers.[130] The new dispositions sometimes determined the manner in which the duel would be fought, whether with arms or with cudgels and shields.[131] In all these cases, nevertheless, the duel was a mode of subsidiary or alternative proof and sometimes both.[132]

Another judgment of God requiring the participation of the two parties—one that had been created by the first Carolingians under clerical and perhaps monastic influence—was the proof of the cross (*iudicium crucis*), whose origins, of course, were not related to any pagan practice; it is never mentioned in the *leges*. The parties or their representatives each stood before a cross and held their arms outstretched in the form of a cross (*ad Dei iudicium ad crucem exire et adstare*). The first party to tremble, to let his arms fall, or to collapse revealed himself guilty.[133] Some legal records and other texts show that under Charlemagne this proof was used in trials relating to landed property and probably in cases before ecclesiastical jurisdictions involving the marriage law.[134] In three new cases Charlemagne introduced it as a mode of proof that in each case was to be an alternative to the judicial duel and sometimes also to the oath with oath-helpers. The intention was, it seems, to furnish the parties with the option of a reciprocal judicial proof less brutal than the duel. The proof of the cross was later suppressed by Louis the Pious.[135]

All the judgments of God, as well as the oath, required the observance of very strict rules; not to observe them meant to fail in the proof itself or in the swearing of the oath.[136] Perhaps there were some doubts from the time of Charlemagne about the efficacy —indeed, even the religious and moral legitimacy—of the judicial proofs. While this is probable, these doubts were only to be expressed clearly by St. Agobard, metropolitan bishop of Lyons under Louis the Pious. Charlemagne obviously knew that some abuses were possible, and he fought against them;[137] but except for this, his faith in the judgments of God was complete, and he intended that this faith should be shared by his subjects.[138]

The judgments of God and the oath were not the only modes of proof recognized by the law in the Frankish kingdom at the time of the Carolingians. The testimonial proof also existed and had its place in the Salic law and its complements, the Ripuarian law, the Roman law, and even in other Germanic laws. The testimonial proof, as revealed by the sources, was always proposed by one of the parties, who declared that he had witnesses and offered to have them give evidence. The court had to authorize this either in conformity with written or unwritten law—if it contained a disposition on this subject—or according to the facts of the case. The witnesses gave evidence under oath in a church and on relics. In trials concerning landed property the court would order witnesses to go to the designated places and indicate the borders of the lands that were the subject of litigation. The opposing party was not able to pit his witnesses against those who had been permitted to give evidence except, to be sure, if the Roman or the Visigothic law was applicable. Such was the testimonial proof in the relatively numerous legal records from the reign of Charlemagne and, except in what concerned the unilateral character of this mode of proof, in the texts from the first years of the reign of Louis the Pious. After 816, however, Louis decided that the two parties should have the right to produce witnesses and to have them give evidence.[139]

Unlike the oath-helpers, the witnesses had to have a personal knowledge of what they declared in their deposition. Consequently, Charlemagne decided that, unless justified by circumstances, witnesses had to be chosen from the *pagus*.[140] The structure of the state and society, unfavorable to the independence of the individual, sometimes made it very difficult to render an honest deposition. Because this state of affairs greatly concerned Charlemagne, on various occasions he prescribed measures destined to disbar witnesses presumed to be suspect and, if possible, to ascertain their sincerity before hearing their deposition under oath.[141]

Charlemagne may have extended, by means of a normative disposition, the use of the testimonial proof to trials concerning questions of personal status or of real property—trials still enveloped in their penal garb. Although an examination of the legal records seems to suggest this,[142] if it was really so, it is not known how the eventual reform was brought into being.

Under Charlemagne the written proof had a considerably less important role than that of the oath, the judgments of God, and the testimonial proof. It was used only in some trials concerning real property, rights of use, or personal status—trials that, as just noted, had not yet shed their criminal character. Except for a royal act, nothing written had full credence. No doubt it happened that if in a trial one of the parties produced a written document, the opposing party might acknowledge it or even abandon his action;[143] but in other cases written evidence was judged insufficient, and the party who produced it had to bring in another mode of proof, normally the testimonial proof.[144] This was the situation as seen in the legal records at the time of Charlemagne and especially at the beginning of the reign of Louis the Pious.

Even the charters established by the *cancellarius* of the county, which appeared in the Ripuarian law, never completely escaped the pattern.[145] Although Charlemagne had favored the institution of the *cancellarius*,[146] he still had not accorded to its officials the power to establish charters having full credence.[147] Only the royal diploma bore full credence. Therefore, a party who had prevailed at the *mallus* or at an assize of the *missi* sometimes presented to the king during a fictitious trial his notice of judgment, supported by the deposition of witnesses; and in this way the party obtained a judgment from the palace court. On the basis of this, a royal diploma of a special type called *placitum* could be drawn up and delivered to the petitioner.[148]

The last mode of proof that must be considered is the inquest (*inquisitio*). What is meant here is not what has been called the inquest of suspects (German, *Rügeverfahren*),[149] which was employed especially in cases of homicide and was a measure of preparatory inquiry that had as its aim, not to prove an offense, but to determine if there were sufficient charges against one or several persons, so that the result of the inquest could serve as an accusation against them. The inquest that concerns us was a new mode of proof that appeared only during the reign of Charlemagne. What distinguishes the inquest from the ordinary testimonial proof is that it did not arise, like the latter, from an action of a party producing his own witnesses, but rather from an action of authority. The king, the *missi*, and the count presiding over the court convoked witnesses whom they themselves named and ordered them to give evidence under oath.[150] Such were the characteristic traits of the inquest as revealed by the legal records.[151]

This mode of proof appears to have been used first at the palace court and at the assizes of the *missi*, and only later at the *mallus*.[152] At the beginning it was reserved for the king and was aimed at establishing his rights.[153] The king and the *missi* also used it in trials involving real property where a church or even an individual was a party,[154] but this, it seems, was for a long time a favor and had not yet become a right. In 802 the ecclesiastical section of the diet of October beseeched for the churches the right to the procedure of inquest in cases of this type, and it is believed that it largely obtained satisfaction.[155] It seems that resort to the inquest could be admitted, even in trials that in our time would be viewed as having a strictly penal character; however, this was exceptional.[156] Under Louis the Pious the inquest underwent further developments.

EXECUTION OF THE JUDGMENT

It is generally acknowledged that the final judgment in a trial ending in a decision consonant with the complaint condemned the accused to pledge himself to the plaintiff to execute the judgment. This was still the situation during the reign of Charlemagne, at least at the *mallus*. There are in existence some legal records in which the judgment ordered the condemned to undertake to pledge (*per wadium suum* or *rewadiare*) his obligation.[157] This necessitated the delivery of a symbolic token, generally a *festuca* (a "wand" or "rod"), an essential element of the Frankish procedure of the *fides facta* by which one pledged oneself, most often with guarantors. There were analogous procedures in the other Germanic laws in force in the *Regnum Francorum*.

In addition to the *notitiae* (memoranda of legal transactions) just mentioned, there were others in which the judgment of the county court expressly ordered the condemned to pay a certain sum, to invest the plaintiff with a certain piece of land or, if it was a matter of a trial concerning personal status, with his own person. Sometimes the judgment ordered the count himself to invest the plaintiff with certain possessions or with the person of a certain serf or *colonus*. Such *notitiae*, dating from the reign of Charlemagne and from the beginning of the reign of Louis the Pious, were drawn up after judgments rendered at the assizes of the *missi* and also after judgments rendered at the *mallus*.[158] There is nothing extraordinary about this in regard to the assizes of the *missi*, which are an emanation of royal jurisdiction; but in regard to the *mallus* this is, apparently, a new development explained by a reinforcement of authority peculiar to this court, which could henceforth dispense with a pledge made by the condemned party.[159]

A subordinate officer of justice was sometimes charged with proceeding with the formalities of execution.[160] In regions where the personal law of most of the inhabitants was a Germanic law other than the Frankish, this task was accomplished by an officer of execution, the *scultetus* or *sculdahis*; in Septimania it was fulfilled by an officer of execution of Visigothic law, the *sayo*.[161] In a case in which the condemned refused either to execute the judgment or to promise to execute it, it is believed that the *bannum* was used to force the recalcitrant person to obey. Putting a person under the *bannum* (*missio in bannum* or *forbannum*) deprived him to whom it applied of the use of his home and his goods, and placed him temporarily outside the law; it was forbidden to anyone under pain of a fine of fifteen shillings to furnish him shelter or food.[162] Little is actually known about this measure, and its effectiveness remains problematical.[163]

COMPLAINTS OF FALSE JUDGMENT

It is almost unnecessary to recall here that the appeal proper, as it had been known in Roman law and as it is known in modern law, was unknown in the Frankish monarchy. What was known to various Germanic laws in force in the *Regnum*, and especially the Frankish law, was the complaint of false judgment (German, *Urteilschelte*). This was a procedure, introduced by one of the parties, accusing a person or persons who had rendered a judgment contrary to the law of having voluntarily violated the written or unwritten *lex*. What was questioned by the party making a complaint of false judgment was not the knowledge that the accused had of the law, but his moral integrity. It is generally conceded that in the Frankish law this action had to be brought against a single or several *rachinburgii* or *scabini* prior to the pronouncement of the judgment by the count or by another presiding officer. If the plaintiff succeeded in the action of false judgment—no doubt using the oath, an ordeal, or the judicial duel—the new judgment proposed by the plaintiff had to be substituted for the false judgment and had to be declared.[164] This procedure of false judgment existed at the time of Charlemagne, and in one of his capitularies he cited it to the effect that if a party did not wish to falsify (*blasfemare*) the judgment, he had to accept it.[165]

Pepin III had created another means of bringing complaint of false judgment[166] that Charlemagne made more general. It was directed against the whole court, both the presiding officer and the judgment-finders, but instead of being introduced in the same court at the *mallus*, it was taken before the king at the palace court. It was always a false judgment in which the judges were accused of deliberately not judging according to the law in force. It fell to the palace court to judge this case submitted to it, and when its judgment upheld the complaint, it substituted a new judgment for the first and sentenced the first judges to a fine.[167] The palace court could delegate the trial to the *missi dominici*.[168] For Saxony and Bavaria, Charlemagne regulated certain aspects of these complaints of false judgment heard at the palace court.[169] He also made a disposition concerning these complaints in the particular case of those who decided belatedly to use this procedure after having been placed under guard for not having wished at first either to approve a judgment or to falsify it. This disposition of general scope prescribed that the interested party had to obtain a written authorization from the emperor, probably in the form of a writ.[170]

PROCEDURE IN CASES OF APPREHENDED INFRACTIONS

The Frankish law and the other Germanic laws recognized a summary procedure in cases of apprehended infractions that applied not only to a person caught in the act but to a person who, pursued by the victim or his relatives and by neighbors aroused by the cries of the victim (German, *Schreimannen*), had been seized by them with the stolen object or the weapon of the crime in his possession, had blood on his hands, or showed other evidence of guilt. He could be bound by the victim and his pursuers in order to be presented to the judge, who was generally the count but was sometimes a *missus* or a viscount. The regular procedure was not used in such a case. The judge alone, without judgment-finders, had to verify if it was indeed a matter of apprehension in the act itself. The victim or his kindred who had taken the initiative of the pursuit could be introduced in this case to swear with oath-helpers that the apprehension had arisen in circumstances constituting incontestable crime. If the facts were indeed thus, the arrested individual had no plea of defense, and the judge ordered him to be hanged.[171]

Charlemagne does not appear to have changed anything in this summary procedure. It had a special importance in the repression of brigandage. He thus protected officials and all other persons who in this repression used this procedure or participated in its use, and yet he also took measures against abuses that such a procedure could easily produce.[172] In a capitulary devoted entirely to the fight against brigands, Charlemagne clearly made a distinction between the arrest of a brigand caught in the act itself and the accusation of brigandage; in the first case he formally confirmed the validity of the *antiqua consuetudo*, that is, the summary procedure.[173]

Faida

Although a discussion of some developments involving *faida* ("vengeance") may appear surprising in an account of the administration of justice, it seems necessary: first, because a number of conflicts did not end in a judicial suit, but in *faida*, and second, because the measures taken by Charlemagne in regard to *faida* had the same goal as those taken in regard to the administration of justice—the maintenance of public peace.

Because *faida* was a permanent and most pressing danger to the public peace, to which Charlemagne was so dedicated, he had to fight against it.[174] Yet the legitimacy of vengeance was so firmly established in the juridical and moral conscience of the populations living according to the Frankish law or most of the other Germanic laws[175] that Charlemagne could not prohibit *faida*. Instead, he decided in 779 to use administrative measures designed to eliminate it as much as possible by promoting a settlement in money or by substituting a judicial settlement. If the author of the act requiring vengeance proposed to the victim or his relatives a settlement in money that was refused, the victim or the person who represented his relatives would be placed at the disposition of the king, who would assign to him a place of residence where he could not do any harm. If the victim or his relatives invited the author of the act prompting recourse to *faida* to pay a composition or summoned him to appear in court and he refused to do either, it was he whom the king sent to reside elsewhere.[176] The immediate effect sought by these measures was to render recourse to *faida* possible only if both parties rejected a settlement in money or a judicial procedure. When Charlemagne declared in 789 in the *Admonitio generalis* that his *iudices* had to prosecute homicide committed out of vengeance, he referred to similar methods of suppressing *faida*.[177] In Saxony, a land incompletely subjugated, where vengeance was a particularly dangerous cause of trouble, it was by using the *bannum*, a heavy fine of sixty shillings or even a multiple of sixty shillings, that Charlemagne strove to prevent, or at least to limit, recourse to *faida*.[178]

Sometime after the coronation of 800 when the emperor, haunted by his increased responsibilities before God,[179] became engrossed in combatting homicides, whose growing number distressed him, he was faced once more with the problem of *faida*. This time he went beyond the dispositions in force. The author of the guilty act had to offer an adequate compensation, that is at least the *wergeld*, to the relatives of the victim. If he did not do so, he would be sent to the palace for judgment and his possessions would be seized. From that moment the emperor could impose upon him an arbitrary punishment and could declare the confiscation of his possessions. The relatives of the victim were obliged to accept a settlement in money, but no sanction other than that of 779 was provided in case the relatives would not accept it.[180] This naturally applied only when the relatives of the victim had not summoned the guilty party to appear in court.

Some years later it was evident that the situation remained dangerous. Besides other measures designed to make the public peace respected,[181] in an article of the Capitulary of Thionville in 805 Charlemagne ordered the *missi* and, through them, the counts to examine with care all cases involving *faida*. After determining which party refused to reach an agreement, the *missi* or the counts were to compel him to do so. If this was not successful, it would be necessary to send the recalcitrant parties to the emperor. Though it was more precise and extended the sanction to the two parties, this was a confirmation of the rule of 802.[182] Charlemagne addressed himself also to those who, after a sworn agreement or a judicial decision, nevertheless committed an act of vengeance, and he treated them in a particularly severe manner. He who in violation of such an agreement killed his adversary would be condemned to pay both the *wergeld* and the fine of the *bannum* and would have his right hand cut off, the punishment for perjury.[183] Charlemagne subsequently repeated this order more than once to the *missi dominici*.[184]

There is every reason to believe that these measures and those taken by Charlemagne's successors were often ignored,[185] and that *faida* continued to be freely practiced in the whole of the *Regnum Francorum*.[186]

NOTES

DA   *Deutsches Archiv für Geschichte des Mittelalters:*
                  VIII, *Deutsches Archiv für Erforschung des*
                  Mittelalters (1950)

HZ   *Historische Zeitschrift*

MG.   *Monumenta Germaniae historica*

    Capit.   Capitularia

    Const.   Constitutiones

    D(D)   Diploma(ta)

    D(D)Kar.   Diploma(ta) Karolinorum

    Epp.   Epistolae

    Poet. lat.   Poetae latini

    SS.   Scriptores

    SS. rer. Germ.   Scriptores rerum Germanicarum in usum
                  scholarum separatim editi

NA   *Neues Archiv der Gesellschaft für ältere*
                  deutsche Geschichtskunde

NF.   Neue Folge

NS.   Nova Series

Regesten   J. F. Böhmer, *Regesta imperii:*
                  I, *Die Regesten des Kaiserreichs unter den Karolingern,*
                  751–918. Revised by E. Mühlbacher and
                  completed by J. Lechner (Innsbruck, 1908);
                  reprinted with additions by C. Brühl and
                  H. H. Kaminsky (Hildesheim, 1966).

Notes

In cross references to other notes in this book, part numbers are given only when the note to which attention is being called does not occur in the same part as the note referring to it.

The reader should realize that the dates given to the capitularies and related documents often differ from the dates given in the edition of Boretius-Krause. Most of these changes are justified in the tables of capitularies compiled by my colleague A. E. Verhulst, professor at the University of Ghent, which appear at the end of my study referred to below, n. 3. A few new dates have resulted from some of my research not yet published. The historical-geographical framework of this study is solely the Regnum Francorum. *Italy has been excluded, being a subject in itself. The imperial powers of Charlemagne have been discussed only briefly because they are dealt with elsewhere. See O. Bertolini, "Carlomagno e Benevento," and P. E. Schramm, "Karl der Grosse im Lichte seiner Siegel und Bullen sowie der Bild- und Wortzeugnisse über sein Aussehen," in* Karl der Grosse: I, Persönlichkeit und Geschichte, *ed. H. Beumann (Düsseldorf, 1965), 609–71, 15–23. Because Charlemagne remained king of the Franks and of the Lombards after his accession to the empire, one seems justified in using the noun "king" and the adjective "royal" in connection with events after Christmas 800.*

Part I

1. The following works contain excellent discussions of the institutions of the Frankish monarchy in the Carolingian period: G. Waitz, *Deutsche Verfassungsgeschichte*, III, IV (2nd ed.; Berlin, 1883–85); H. Brunner, *Deutsche Rechtsgeschichte*, I (2nd ed.; Leipzig, 1906), II, rev. by C. von Schwerin (2nd ed.; Berlin and Munich, 1928); R. Schröder, *Lehrbuch der deutschen Rechtsgeschichte*, rev. by E. von Künszberg (7th ed.; Berlin and Leipzig, 1932); H. Conrad, *Deutsche Rechtsgeschichte*, I (2nd ed.; Karlsruhe, 1962); L. Halphen, *Charlemagne et l'empire carolingien* (2nd ed.; Paris, 1949); R. Folz, *Le couronnement impérial de Charlemagne* (Paris, 1964). See also my study, "Les traits généraux du système d'institutions de la monarchie franque," in *Il passagio dall'Antichità al Medioevo in Occidente. Settimane di studio del Centro italiano di studi sull'alto medioevo*, IX (Spoleto, 1962); and "The Impact of Charlemagne on the Institutions of the Frankish Realm," *Speculum*, XL (1965).

2. One distinguishes them notably in the diplomas of immunity granted by Charlemagne to the church of Trier, *ao.* 772; to the abbey of Saint-Germain-des-Prés, *ao.* 772; to the churches of Metz, *ao.* 775; and of Paris, *ao.* 774–800: DDKar., Nos. 66, 71, 91, 193.

3. See my *Recherches sur les capitulaires* (Paris, 1958), pp. 3–7, 18–21 (rev. German edition, *Was waren die Kapitularien?* trans. by W. A. Eckhardt [Darmstadt and Weimar, 1961], pp. 13–18, 35–40).

4. *MG.* Capit. I, No. 20. See my article, "Une crise dans le règne de Charlemagne. Les années 778 et 779," in *Mélanges Charles Gilliard* (Lausanne, 1944). Herstal, Belgium, province of Liège.

5. C. De Clercq, *La législation religieuse franque de Clovis à Charlemagne* (Louvain and Paris, 1936), p. 159.

6. *MG.* Capit. I, No. 22 (Admonitio generalis), No. 23 (Duplex legationis edictum), No. 24 (Breviarium missorum Aquitanicum). On the importance of the Admonitio generalis, see De Clercq, pp. 172–76; Halphen, *Charlemagne et l'empire carolingien*, pp. 209–10; and my article, "L'Eglise et le pouvoir royal sous Pépin III et Charlemagne," in *Le Chiese nei regni dell'Europa Occidentale e i loro rapporti con Roma sino all' 800. Settimane di Studio del Centro italiano di studi sull'alto medioevo*, VII (Spoleto, 1960), 104–5, 121–22.

7. On this celebrated collection: G. Le Bras, in P. Fournier and G. Le Bras, *Histoire des collections canoniques en Occident depuis les Fausses Décrétales jusqu'au Décret de Gratien*, I (Paris, 1931), 95–98; H. E. Feine,

Kirchliche Rechtsgeschichte. Die Katholische Kirche (4th ed.; Cologne and Graz, 1964), pp. 94–95, 151.

8. C. 62: *Omnibus. Ut pax sit et concordia et unianimitas cum omni populo christiano inter episcopos, abbates, comites, iudices et omnes ubique seu maiores seu minores personas, quia nihil Deo sine pace placet* . . . The biblical citations appear in the following order: Matt. 5, 23, and 24; Lev. 19, 18; Matt. 5, 9; John 13, 35; I John 3, 10.

9. Duplex legationis edictum, c. 18; Breviarium missorum Aquitanicum, inscriptio, doubtless contemporary. See also p. 13 and n. 67.

10. *MG.* Capit. I, No. 28; *MG.* Concilia II, No. 19, G, pp. 165–71. See De Clercq, pp. 183–91, and my article, "Observations sur le synode de Francfort de 794," in *Miscellanea historica in honorem A. De Meyer,* I (Louvain and Brussels, 1946).

11. On this crisis see my "Note sur deux capitulaires non datés de Charlemagne," in *Miscellanea historica in honorem L. van der Essen,* I (Brussels and Paris, 1947).

12. A. Hauck, *Kirchengeschichte Deutschlands,* II (8th ed.; Berlin and Leipzig, 1954; reprint), 303–21, 324–43; H. von Schubert, *Geschichte der Christlichen Kirche im Frühmittelalter* (Tübingen, 1921), pp. 378–87; E. Caspar, *Das Papsttum unter fränkischer Herrschaft* (Darmstadt, 1956; reprint), pp. 76–104; E. Amann, "L'époque carolingienne," *Histoire de l'Eglise publiée sous la direction de A. Fliche et V. Martin,* VI (Paris, 1947), 107–45.

13. Jurisdiction over clergy: c. 6, 30, 39; prices, weights, and measures: c. 4; money: c. 5.

14. Boretius, *MG.* Capit. I, No. 33, henceforth referred to as the Programmatic Capitulary. The name Capitulare missorum generale given by the editor does not correspond to the nature of the document; see my *Recherches sur les capitulaires,* p. 52 and n. 207 (=*Was waren die Kapitularien?,* p. 84 and n. 207). For the date: Annales Iuvavenses maiores, *ao.* 802, ed. H. Bresslau, *MG. SS.* XXX, p. 736.

15. See Folz, pp. 178–87.

16. Responsibility: acts and attitudes of the subjects, c. 3, 5, and 40 of the Programmatic Capitulary; acts and attitudes of the officials, c. 13, 14, 15.

17. I have in mind c. 13, 14, 16, 17, 32, 33, 36; toward the end of these articles a change in the wording, often with a shift from the third to the first person and to an emotional and "direct" tone in the text, suggests a personal role of Charlemagne that was probably oral and had the objective of emphasizing the import of the disposition.

18. See my study, "Le programme de gouvernement impérial de Charlemagne," in *Renovatio Imperii. Atti della giornata internazionale*

di studio per il millenario. Ravenna 4–5 November 1961 (Faenza, 1963).

19. C. 2–9 of the capitulary.

20. Annales Laureshamenses, *ao.* 802, ed. G. H. Pertz, *MG.* SS. I, p. 38.

21. Rather than using the edition Boretius, *MG.* Capit. I, No. 34 (Capitularia missorum specialia), it is better to refer to the very superior edition of W. A. Eckhardt, "Die capitularia missorum specialia von 802," *DA*, XII (1956).

22. It was a double capitulary. The first section, very brief, was purely ecclesiastical, while the second, very long, had a general character: *MG.* Capit. I, Nos. 43 and 44. See my commentary in *Recherches sur les capitulaires*, pp. 73–74 (*=Was waren die Kapitularien?*, pp. 114–16). Thionville (German, Diedenhofen), France, Moselle department.

23. On this expression see my *Recherches sur les capitulaires*, p. 44, n. 169 (*=Was waren die Kapitularien?*, p. 73, n. 169).

24. This state of uncertainty and anxiety appears clearly in the prooemium to the Divisio Regnorum of 6 February 806 (see the following note). In two extremely important works, H. Beumann ("Nomen imperatoris. Studien zur Kaiseridee Karls des Grossen," *HZ*, CLXXXV [1958]) and W. Schlesinger ("Kaisertum und Reichsteilung. Zur Divisio Regnorum von 806," in *Forschungen zu Staat und Verfassung. Festgabe für Fritz Hartung* [Berlin, 1958], included in the collection of studies of W. Schlesinger, *Beiträge zur deutschen Verfassungsgeschichte des Mittelalters*, I [Göttingen, 1963]) have also thrown light on the state of uncertainty existing on the eve of the settlement of 806. No position is taken here on the views of these two learned colleagues on the significance of the Divisio.

25. *MG.* Capit. I, No. 45, and Annales Regni Francorum, *ao.* 806, ed. F. Kurze, SS. rer. Germ. (1895), p. 121.

26. Capitulare legibus additum; Capitulare legi Ribuariae additum; Capitulare Aquisgranense; Capitulare missorum; *MG.* Capit. I, Nos. 39, 41, 77, 40. For the date of No. 77 see my article, "Zur Datierung eines Aachener Kapitulars Karls des Grossen," *Annalen des historischen Vereins für den Niederrhein*, CLV–CLVI (1954).

27. Capitula ad legem Baiwariorum addita and Capitulare Baiwaricum, *MG.* Capit. I, Nos. 68, 69. This is a mere probability based on the decision taken in October 802 to proceed with the revision of the national *leges* with the co-operation of the *legislatores,* that is, of men with a practical knowledge of these *leges*: Annales Laureshamenses, *ao.* 802 (see above, n. 20).

28. Capitula post annum 805 addita, particularly c. 3, *MG.* Capit. I, No. 55.

29. *Recherches sur les capitulaires*, pp. 74–85 (*=Was waren die Kapitularien?*, pp. 117–30).

30. My work, cited in the preceding note, pp. 91–93 (=pp. 139–41). My eminent colleague Aug. Dumas formulated this observation in terms so striking ("La parole et l'écriture dans les capitulaires carolingiens," in *Mélanges d'histoire du moyen âge dédiés à la mémoire de Louis Halphen* [Paris, 1951], p. 216) that I quote them here: "Charlemagne a passé son règne à rabâcher les mêmes choses à ses missi, qui avaient de la peine à les faire exécuter."

31. Capitulare missorum, *ao.* 803, c. 3; Capitulare Aquisgranense, *ao.* 809, c. 1 and 11; Capitulare missorum Aquisgranense primum, *ao.* 809, c. 13, 22 (in the important mss. of the group Paris lat. 9654 and Vatic. Palat. 582), c. 28; Capitulare missorum italicum (there is some doubt on the "Italian" character), *ais.* 802–10 (I agree with the date of De Clercq [see n. 5], p. 381), c. 12; Capitulare incerti anni, *ais.* 805–13?, c. 1 and 2; Pippini capitulare italicum, *ais.* 806–10 (dispositions of Frankish law introduced into Italy), c. 4: *MG.* Capit. I, Nos. 40, 61, 62, 99, 86, 102. Obviously all these dispositions only come after the *scabini* appear in the legal records.

32. Capitula de causis diversis, *ao.* 806, c. 2 and 3; for the date see my article, "Observations sur la date de deux documents administratifs émanant de Charlemagne," *Mitteilungen des Instituts für Österreichische Geschichtsforschung,* LXII (1954); Memoratorium de exercitu in Gallia Occidentali praeparando, *ao.* 807, c. 2; Capitulare missorum de exercitu promovendo, *ao.* 808, c. 1: *MG.* Capit. I, Nos. 49, 48, 50.

33. Only the oral juridical act was essential; see Dumas (n. 30), and my *Recherches sur les capitulaires,* pp. 18–21 (=*Was waren die Kapitularien?,* pp. 35–40).

34. On the changes in residence see A. Gauert, "Zum Itinerar Karls des Grossen," in *Karl der Grosse,* I, 307–21 (see especially the map). The talks referred to occurred at the assemblies (see pp. 21–23) or in sessions comparable to assemblies at which the "interventions" mentioned in the *narratio* of many of the diplomas took place.

35. See pp. 23–26.

36. DDKar. I, No. 81.

37. I am not concerned here with the problems raised by the historical event of the accession of Charlemagne to imperial dignity, nor even with the general import of this event, but rather with the principal effects that the coronation of 25 December 800 had on the institutions of the *Regnum Francorum.* For the events and their import, see the abundant literature consecrated to them and especially the following, relatively recent works: L. Halphen, *Charlemagne et l'empire carolingien* (see above, n. 1); H. Fichtenau, "Karl der Grosse und das Kaisertum," *Mitteilungen des Instituts für Österreichische Geschichtsforschung,* LXI (1953); P. Munz, *The Origin of the Carolingian Empire* (Leicester,

1960); R. Folz, *Le couronnement impérial de Charlemagne* (see above, n. 1); P. Classen, "Karl der Grosse, das Papsttum und Byzanz. Die Begründung des karolingischen Kaisertums," in *Karl der Grosse*, I, 537–608.

38. DDKar. I, No. 197. See P. Classen, "Romanum gubernans imperium," *DA*, IX (1952); and P. Bonenfant, "L'influence byzantine sur les diplômes des Carolingiens," *Université libre de Bruxelles; Annuaire de l'Institut de philologie et d'histoire orientales*, XI (1951) (=*Mélanges Henri Grégoire*, III). See also the important commentary of P. E. Schramm, "Karl der Grosse im Lichte der Staatssymbolik," in *Karolingische und Ottonische Kunst* (Wiesbaden, 1957), pp. 35–37.

39. See especially H. Beumann, "Nomen imperatoris. Studien zur Kaiseridee Karls des Grossen," *HZ*, CLXXXV (1958).

40. H. Brunner and C. von Schwerin, *Deutsche Rechtsgeschichte*, II, 123: *Potenzierung des fränkischen Königtums*.

41. See, for example, Letter 257, from Alcuin to Charlemagne, *ao.* 802, *MG. Epp.* IV, p. 415. See also Halphen, pp. 213–22; Folz, pp. 183–86; L. Wallach, *Alcuin and Charlemagne* (Ithaca, 1959), pp. 7, 16–19, 50, 73.

42. See pp. 6–7. The text cited belongs to the Programmatic Capitulary of 802, c. 3. *MG. Capit.* I, No. 33: . . . *ut unusquisque et persona propria se in Sancto Dei servitio . . . pleniter conservare studeat . . .*

43. See pp. 13–14.

44. See pp. 25 and 82.

45. See pp. 7–8 and 72–73.

46. See pp. 78–79.

47. *MG. Capit.* I, No. 33. See pp. 6–7. For all of these measures see also E. Ewig, "Vom Regnum Francorum zum Imperium Christianum" and "Die Entfaltung der karolingischen Theokratie," in *Handbuch der Kirchengeschichte*, ed. H. Jedin, III, Pt. 1 (Freiburg im Breisgau, 1966), 97–118.

48. For further comment on the relation between the imperial and royal power, see P. Classen, "Karl der Grosse, das Papsttum und Byzanz," in *Karl der Grosse*, I, 537–608.

49. The *bannum* is essentially a command or prohibition, but given the general character that it assumes in the texts, one seems warranted in stating that since the Carolingian period the word also designated the power by virtue of which one commanded or prohibited.

50. (*1*) Capitulare Saxonicum, *ao.* 797, c. 1: . . . *ut de illis capitulis pro quibus Franci, si regis bannum transgressi sunt solidos sexaginta conponunt . . . Hec sunt capitula: primum ut ecclesiae, viduae, orfani et minus potentes iustam et quietam pacem habeant; et ut raptum et*

*fortiam nec incendium infra patriam quis facere audeat presumtive; et
de exercitu nullus super bannum domini regis remanere praesumat.*
(*2*) Capitulare missorum of 802, c. 18 of the missatica A and D, 19 of the
missatica B and C: *De banno domno imperatoris et regis, quod* (A and
D, *an* B and C) *per semet ipsum consuetus est bannire* . . . (six cases:
house assault and arson are missing). (*3*) Capitula a misso cognita
facienda, probably *ao.* 802, c. 1: text practically identical to the preceding. (*4*) Capitula ad legem Baiwariorum addita, probably *ao.* 803, surely
an old title:*Capitula quae ad legem Baiwariorum domnus Karolus . . .
addere iussit, ut bannum ipsius quislibet inruperit conponere debeat.*
C. 3, *in fine:* . . . *Haec octo capitula in assiduitate; reliqua autem
reservata sunt regibus, ut ipsi potestatem habeant nominativae demandare
unde exire debent.* The eight cases of no. (*1*). (*5*) Fragment of another
version of the Capitulare missorum of 802 inserted in the collection of
the capitularies of Gerbald, bishop of Liège, probably in 806: see above
(*2*); but the eight cases of no. (*1*). (*6*) Summula de bannis, reign of
Charlemagne or of Louis the Pious, perhaps an annotation of private
origin; old title, *De octo bannus unde domnus noster vult quod exeant
solidi LX. MG.* Capit. I, Nos. 27, 34 (better: W. A. Eckhardt [see above,
n. 21], p. 503), 59, 68, 104 (c. 6) (better: W. A. Eckhardt, *Die Kapitulariensammlung Bischof Ghaerbalds von Lüttich [Germanenrechte* NF.,
Deutschrechtliches Archiv, V; Göttingen, 1955], No. LXII, p. 96), 110.
The *bannum* applied to military service is frequently cited in the texts
of the period.

51. See the texts reproduced in the preceding note, especially nos.
(*1*) and (*4*).

52. Affirmation of the general character of the *bannum*: see n. 50,
no. (*4*). Examples of application: (*1*) Capitulary of Herstal, *ao.* 779, c. 19.
(*2*) Programmatic Capitulary, *ao.* 802, c. 38. *MG.* Capit. I, Nos. 20
and 33.

53. For example: Tractoria of Charlemagne for Saint-Denis, *ais.* 774/
75, DKar., No. 88, p. 128, l. 23; Responsa misso cuidam data, *ais.* 802–13,
c. 5, *MG.* Capit. I, No. 58.

54. See texts (*1*); (*4,* c. 1); (*6*). See also c. 30 of a collection of articles
for the *missi* of 806 appearing in the collection of capitularies of the bishop Gerbald, W. A. Eckhardt, *Kapitulariensammlung,* p. 85 (=*MG.* Capit.
I, No. 35, c. 57). The fine itself is called *bannum*.

55. Capitulare Saxonicum, *ao.* 797, c. 9, *MG.* Capit. I, No. 27.

56. Programmatic Capitulary, *ao.* 802, c. 8, *MG.* Capit. I, No. 33.

57. See my study cited in n. 6, and H. Büttner, "Mission und Kirchen-
organisation des Frankenreiches bis zum Tode Karls des Grossen," in
Karl der Grosse, I, 454–87.

58. Formulae Salicae Merkelianae, No. 63, Zeumer, *MG. Formulae,* p. 262; Capitulare episcoporum, *ais.* 792/93 (on the events and the date, see my article cited above, n. 11); Capitulare missorum of Thionville, *ao.* 805, c. 4; Capitulare missorum Aquisgranense primum, *ao.* 810, c. 5, and Capitulare missorum Aquisgranense alterum, c. 1: *MG.* Capit. I, Nos. 21, 44, 64, and 65.

59. Prooemium of the Admonitio generalis, *ao.* 789, *MG.* Capit. I, No. 22, p. 53, ll. 26–43. I quote the affirmation of royal power: *Quapropter et nostros ad vos direximus missos, qui ex nostri nominis auctoritate una vobiscum corrigerent quae corrigenda essent.*

60. See p. 5 and, in n. 8, the text of c. 62.

61. Capitulary issued at the completion of the council of Frankfurt, *ao.* 794, c. 6 (implicitly); Programmatic Capitulary of 802, c. 14; Capitulare missorum of 802, c. 18a of missaticum A, c. 20 of the missatica B and C; fragment of a capitulary, perhaps of another version of the Capitulare missorum of 802, preserved in the collection of capitularies of Gerbald, bishop of Liège, W. A. Eckhardt, *Kapitulariensammlung,* No. LXII, p. 95 (=Capitula francica, c. 5); Capitulare Baiwaricum, probably 803, c. 4; Capitula a missis dominicis ad comites directa, *ao.* 806, c. 1, preserved in the collection of Gerbald, Eckhardt, *Kapitulariensammlung,* No. LXIV, c. 1, p. 100; Capitula de canonibus excerpta, *ao.* 813, c. 9 (text intended to provide the basis for a capitulary not drawn up); Boretius, *MG.* Capit. I, Nos. 28 and 33; W. A. Eckhardt, "Capitularia" (see n. 21), p. 503 (=Boretius, No. 34); W. A. Eckhardt, *Kapitulariensammlung,* p. 95, *in fine* (=Boretius, No. 104); Boretius, *MG.* Capit. I, No. 69; Eckhardt, *Kapitulariensammlung,* p. 100 (=Boretius, No. 85); Boretius, *MG.* Capit. I, No. 78. One finds the same disposition in a notice addressed to the counts of a certain region, which, however, has not been identified; Boretius, *MG.* Capit. I, No. 97, gives the date as 779/800; De Clercq (see n. 5), pp. 161–62, as 779–81; both believe that it concerned Italy. In any event the rule appears in a capitulary of Pepin, king of Italy, *ao.* 810, c. 5, Boretius, *MG.* Capit. I, No. 102.

62. This results not only from frequent repetitions but from an article appearing in a list of matters to be dealt with at the diet in 811, c. 5: necessity of discovering the reason why clerics and laymen find fault with each other; this is obviously a reference to the authorities, *MG.* Capit. I, No. 71.

63. Programmatic Capitulary, c. 1 and 3, *MG.* Capit. I, No. 33.

64. On this point see my study, "Charlemagne et le serment," in *Mélanges d'histoire du moyen âge dédiés à la mémoire de Louis Halphen* (Paris, 1950).

65. This is not the place to discuss whether this fidelity was of

Germanic origin or not; the problem does not concern our subject. W. Schlesinger has treated this problem with erudition and intelligence: "Randbemerkungen zu drei Aufsätzen über Sippe, Gefolgschaft und Treue," in *Alteuropa und die moderne Gesellschaft. Festschrift für Otto Brunner* (Göttingen, 1963), included in the collection of W. Schlesinger, *Beiträge zur deutschen Verfassungsgeschichte des Mittelalters*, I (Göttingen, 1963).

66. *Lex Ribuaria*, 72 (69), 1, ed. F. Beyerle and R. Buchner (*MG. Leges nationum Germanicarum* III, Pt. II), p. 123. The disposition has also been included in the Capitulatio de partibus Saxoniae of 785, c. 11, *MG. Capit.* I, No. 26. This disposition was in force throughout the *Regnum*.

67. Duplex legationis edictum, *ao.* 789, c. 18 (formula for the oath); Breviarium missorum Aquitanicum, *ao.* 789, an old inscriptio; Capitulare missorum, *ais.* 792/93, c. 1–4: *MG. Capit.* I, Nos. 23, 24, 25.

68. Programmatic Capitulary, c. 2, *MG. Capit.* I, No. 33. For the original negative character see H. Mitteis, *Lehnrecht und Staatsgewalt* (Weimar, 1933), p. 48.

69. See my study cited above, n. 18. The principal texts are the Programmatic Capitulary; the Capitularia missorum specialia (see above, n. 21); and probably some communications made by a *missus* in 802 (Capitula a misso cognita facienda, c. 12, *MG. Capit.* I, No. 59).

70. Programmatic Capitulary, c. 3–9.

71. Two formulas closely related to each other have been preserved, *MG. Capit.* I, appendices to No. 34, pp. 101–2. Comparison with the oath of vassalage given by Tassilo III in 757 (Annales Regni Francorum, *h. ao.*, ed. Kurze, p. 14) removes any doubt. Aug. Dumas, "Le serment de fidélité et la conception du pouvoir du Ier au XIe siècle," *Revue historique de droit français et étranger* (1931), p. 295, has challenged the view that Tassilo became a vassal in 757; H. Krawinkel, *Untersuchungen zum fränkischen Benefizialwesen* (Weimar, 1937), pp. 48–65, is of the same opinion. They have been refuted respectively by F. Lot, "Le serment de fidélité à l'époque franque," *Revue belge de Philologie et d'Histoire*, XII (1933), 575, and by C. Odegaard, *Vassi and fideles in the Carolingian Empire* (Cambridge, Mass.; 1945), pp. 90–96.

72. This did not stop Dumas, p. 293, from believing that Charlemagne appeared to the person swearing the oath as a lord rather than as the king; these views have been refuted by Lot, pp. 751–52.

73. P. E. Schramm, "Die Anerkennung Karls des Grossen als Kaiser," *HZ*, CLXXII (1951), 496, and in brochure (Munich, 1952), p. 52, believes that the goal was to extend the duties of subjects in relation to the head of the state. It is reassuring to state that the opinion of this

excellent connoisseur of Carolingian history is close to mine on this point.

74. Capitulare missorum of Thionville, *ao.* 805, c. 9 (*in fine;* in the critical apparatus see some of the dispositions differing in form but having the same general meaning in other manuscripts); Capitulare missorum of Nijmegen, *ao.* 806, c. 2; Capitulare de iustitiis faciendis, *ao.* 811, c. 13: *MG.* Capit. I, Nos. 44, 46, 80.

75. It is, moreover, striking to state that not only G. Waitz, always prudent and reserved, abstains in the page that he devotes to the *gratia* (*Verfassungsgeschichte,* III [2nd ed.], 326), from giving it a definition, but that Brunner and von Schwerin, with all of their experience and ability in the rigorous definition of concepts, are very vague on this subject ([see above n. 1], pp. 106–7). *Gratia regis* is translated in German by *Königshuld.* This aspect of royal power remained very important in Germany for centuries. See R. Köstler, *Huldentzug als Strafe* (Stuttgart, 1910), and my article, "La 'gratia' des monarques francs," *Anuario de estudios medievales,* III (1966).

76. Formulae marculfinae aevi carolini, No. 18 (beginning of the reign of Charlemagne: the clause appears in the Carolingian revision), and Cartae Senonicae, No. 18 (same epoch), *MG.* Formulae, pp. 121 and 193; writ for the abbey of Honau, *ais.* 772–74, and tractoria for the abbey of Saint-Denis, *ais.* 774/75, DDKar., Nos. 77 and 88; writ to Baugulf, abbot of Fulda, end of eighth century (de litteris colendis), L. Wallach, "Charlemagne's De litteris colendis and Alcuin," *Speculum,* XXVI (1951), 289–92 (a better edition than that of Boretius, *MG.* Capit. I, No. 29; Wallach has used the oldest text discovered and edited by P. Lehmann, *Fuldaër Studien,* NF., *Sitzungsberichte der Bayerischen Akademie der Wissenschaften, Philologisch-Historische Klasse* [1927], Abh. 2); tractoria for Hilderic, judicial representative of the abbey of Farfa, *ao.* 791, DKar., No. 172; writ of mobilization for Fulrad, abbot of Saint-Quentin, *ao.* 806, and writ in favor of Spanish refugees established in Septimania and in the future Spanish march, *ao.* 812: *MG.* Capit. I, Nos. 75 and 76 (=DKar., No. 217, and R. d'Abadal i de Vinyals, *Catalunya Carolingia,* II, pt. 2 [Barcelona, 1952], Preceptes per a particulars, No. 2).

77. Diplomas of immunity for Trier and Metz, *ais.* 772–75, DDKar., Nos. 66 and 91.

78. The formula is: *Taliter exinde agite, qualiter gratia nostra vultis habere* (DKar., No. 88), . . . *si gratiam Dei et nostram habere vultis* (*ibid.,* No. 172), or it is comparable to one of those cited here.

79. Programmatic Capitulary of 802, c. 21 and 28, *MG.* Capit. I, No. 33.

80. Capitula tractanda cum comitibus, episcopis et abbatibus, *ao.* 811, c. 2 and 5, *MG.* Capit. I, No. 71.

81. See chiefly the Programmatic Capitulary of 802, c. 21.

82. By an act of grace: the former duke of Bavaria, Tassilo, at the synod of Frankfurt in 794, c. 3, *MG.* Capit. I, No. 28; perhaps the Lombard Aio, in 799, DKar., No. 187. After a judgment: Peter, bishop of Verdun, at the synod of Frankfurt, c. 9; Count Theodold, in 797, DKar., No. 181.

83. Religious institutions: diploma for the abbey of Gorze, *ais.* 772–74, and diploma for Saint-Martin of Tours, *ao.* 782, DDKar., Nos. 76 and 141. Individuals: Cartae Senonicae, No. 19, and Formulae Salicae Bignonianae, No. 1, both at the beginning of the reign of Charlemagne, *MG.* Formulae, pp. 193 and 228; diplomas for Theodold and for Aio, see n. 82.

84. At the time of the Italian expedition in 774; *Liber Pontificalis. Vita Hadriani,* c. 31 (310), ed. L. Duchesne, I (2nd ed.; Paris, 1955), 495.

85. Capitulary of Herstal, *ao.* 779, prooemium *(consenserunt decretum);* Capitulatio de partibus Saxoniae, *ao.* 785, c. 1 *(placuit omnibus),* c. 15 *(consenserunt omnes);* synod of Frankfurt, *ao.* 794, c. 4 *(consentienti sancta synodo),* c. 6, 7, 9, 10 *(statutum* or *definitum est a domno rege et sancta synodo),* c. 55, 56 *(omnis synodus consensit);* Capitulare saxonicum, *ao.* 797, c. 1 *(omnes unianimiter consenserunt et aptificaverunt),* c. 3, 9 *(item placuit),* c. 6, 7 *(statuerunt),* c. 8 *(convenit);* second letter of Charlemagne to Gerbald, bishop of Liège, *ao.* 805 *(cum consensu et pari consilio):* MG. Capit. I, Nos. 20, 26, 28, 27, 124 (and W. A. Eckhardt, *Kapitulariensammlung* [see n. 50], No. LXIX, p. 116).

86. I agree with the view of Fustel de Coulanges, *Les transformations de la royauté pendant l'époque carolingienne* (Paris, 1892), pp. 465–76; and especially with that of G. Seeliger, *Die Kapitularien der Karolinger* (Munich, 1893), pp. 41–51; and Seeliger, "Volksrecht und Königsrecht," *Historische Vierteljahrschrift,* I (1898), 320–30. My opinion is expressed in *Recherches sur les capitulaires,* pp. 30–34 (=*Was waren die Kapitularien?,* pp. 53–59). In his recent and remarkable work *Aequitatis iudicium* (Frankfort on the Main, 1959), pp. 70 ff., E. Kaufmann, whose thinking follows lines quite different from mine, doubts that *consensus* was an essential element in giving an obligatory force to the capitularies. Recently, however, he appears to have deviated from this position.

87. This is established principally by two texts. (*1*) The letter of Charlemagne to Pepin in 806-10, *MG.* Capit. I, No. 103. It concerns those who *nolunt ea oboedire nec consentire neque pro lege tenere; ea* are the Capitula legibus addenda of 803. Charlemagne ordered his son: . . . *oboedire atque inplere praecipias; consentire,* therefore, accompanies *oboedire* and is understood in *inplere,* that is, to conform to the new dispositions: it is something that one is obliged to do. (*2*) Capitu-

lare missorum of Nijmegen, *ao.* 806, c. 2, *MG.* Capit. I, No. 46. Charlemagne ordered *Ut hi qui antea fidelitatem partibus nostris non promiserunt promittere faciant et insuper omnes denuo repromittant, ut ea quae inter filios nostros propter pacis concordiam statuimus pleniter omnes consentire debeant.* In the second part of the article, aiming at the settlement of the succession of 806, the king's subjects are enjoined to make a promise, and this consisted of consenting to the settlement: it is a thing to which the subjects are bound. Just as the duty of fidelity existed before the swearing of the oath, so the duty of conforming to new dispositions existed before the *consensus* was given.

88. The Capitulare missorum of 803, c. 19 (*MG.* Capit. I, No. 40), prescribed the invitation to the *populus*—that is, the great ecclesiastics and laymen—to *consentire* to the Capitula legibus addenda of this year. A *notitia (ibid.,* No. 39, p. 112, ll. 14-21) describes the execution of this instruction as it was carried out at Paris; at the request of the count of Paris, acting as an imperial *missus,* the *scabini* of the various counties of the region, *in uno consenserunt quod ipsi voluissent omni tempore observare usque in posterum.* This is a *consensus* completely analogous to that which Charlemagne demanded for the same *capitula* in Italy; it was not given freely.

89. For these, see pp. 30–31 and nn. 216 and 218.

90. Divisio imperii, *MG.* Capit. I, No. 45.

91. The term *imperium* is interpreted only in its geographical sense; when there is a question of imperial power (c. 33: *potestas imperialis*), it is concerned exclusively with that of Charlemagne.

92. C. 15.

93. See n. 41.

94. My views on this point agree with those of D. Bullough, *The Age of Charlemagne* (London, 1965), p. 197. With great erudition and remarkable ingenuity (see n. 24), H. Beumann and W. Schlesinger have defended the opinion that the regulation of 806 marked a shifting of the imperial idea and imperial power toward a conception more hegemonial and Frankish and less Roman than that of 800–802. They consider that this conception was reconcilable with the division and that the future cosharers became collectively coholders of the imperial power. I do not believe that this interpretation agrees with the texts. A critical examination of the conceptions of my learned colleagues cannot be undertaken here. H. Beumann has greatly influenced the views of R. Folz, *Le couronnement impérial de Charlemagne* (see above, n. 1), pp. 197–201.

95. If Bernard had been regarded as being entitled to the rights of his father, Charles's share would have been divided between Louis and Bernard in conformance with Article 4 of the *Divisio.*

96. This coronation represents the manner in which Charlemagne himself had very likely wished to be crowned on 25 December 800, that is, without any intervention by the pope. The ceremony of 813 could have been inspired by that of the coronation of an associate emperor in Byzantium; W. Ohnsorge, "Das Mitkaisertum in der abendländischen Geschichte des frühen Mittelalters," *Zeitschrift der Savigny Stiftung für Rechtsgeschichte*, Germanistische Abt. (1950), pp. 310–11 (=*Abendland und Byzanz* [Darmstadt, 1958], p. 262).

97. DDKar., Nos. 62, 78, 118, 128, 161, *ais.* 771, 772–74, 777, 779, 788. Capitulary issued at the conclusion of the synod of Frankfurt, *ao.* 794, c. 55; Capitulare de villis, *ais.* 771–800, c. 9, 15, 16, 47: *MG.* Capit. I, Nos. 28 and 32. Annales Regni Francorum, rev. text, *ao.* 796, ed. Kurze, p. 99; Annales Laureshamenses, *ao.* 802, *MG.* SS. I, p. 38. It is in this sense that Adalard, cousin and adviser of Charlemagne, used the word *palatium* in the title of his short treatise on the De ordine palatii, which Hincmar used in composing his treatise on the same subject, see c. 12, ed. V. Krause, in *MG.* Capit. II, p. 522, and ed. M. Prou (with French translation) (Paris, 1884), p. 32. Along with C. Brühl, "Hinkmariana," I, *DA*, XX (1964), I agree that such a treatise by Adalard existed and that it was used by Hincmar, but as he saw fit.

98. See E. Ewig, "Descriptio Franciae," in *Karl der Grosse*, I, 166 ff., and Ewig, "Résidence et capitale pendant le haut moyen âge," *Revue historique*, CCXXX (1963), 53–65; C. Brühl, "Königspfalz und Bischofsstadt in fränkischer Zeit," *Rheinische Vierteljahrsblätter*, XXIII (1958), W. Metz, "Die Agrarwirtschaft im karolingischen Reiche," in *Karl der Grosse*, I, 489–500.

99. See the chapter of H. Gauert (cited in n. 34), and J. Fleckenstein, "Karl der Grosse und sein Hof," in *Karl der Grosse*, I, 24–50.

100. See W. Kaemmerer, "Die Aachener Pfalz Karls des Grossen," in *Karl der Grosse*, I, 322–48; L. Falkenstein, *Der "Lateran" der karolingischen Pfalz zu Aachen* (Cologne, 1966).

101. Programmatic Capitulary, c. 15, 17, 19, 24, 31–34, 36–39, *MG.* Capit. I, No. 33. See my study, "Le programme de gouvernement impérial de Charlemagne" (n. 18, above), pp. 83–85. On the obstruction and disorder see particularly: Capitulare missorum Aquisgranense primum, *ao.* 809, c. 2; Capitulare missorum Aquisgranense primum, *ao.* 810, c. 1: *MG.* Capit. I, Nos. 62 and 64.

102. See my article, "La fin du règne de Charlemagne. Une décomposition," *Zeitschrift für Schweizerische Geschichte*, XXVIII (1948), 447–50.

103. Seneschal: Annales Regni Francorum, *ao.* 786, the two texts, ed. Kurze, pp. 72–73; epitaph of the seneschal Eggihard, ed. E. Dümmler, *MG.* Poet. lat. I, p. 109: ... *regi summus in aula fuit;* Hincmar, *De ordine*

palatii, c. 23 (see above, n. 97), supposedly following Adalard, ed. Krause, p. 525, ed. Prou, pp. 58 ff. Butler: Annales Regni Francorum, *ao*. 781, 2 texts, pp. 58–59; Hincmar, *De ordine palatii*, c. 23. Chamberlain: Annales Regni Francorum, *ais*. 782 and 791, rev. text, pp. 61 and 89; DKar., No. 204, *ao*. 806; Hincmar, *De ordine palatii*, c. 22, supposedly following Adalard, ed. Krause, p. 525, ed. Prou, pp. 56 and 58. Constable: Annales Regni Francorum, *ao*. 782, rev. text, *ao*. 807, pp. 61 and 124; DKar., No. 138, *ao*. 781; Hincmar, *De ordine palatii*, c. 23.

104. Marshals: Capitulare Aquisgranense, *ais*. 802/3, c. 10, *MG.* Capit. I, No. 77. Sacellarius: Hincmar, c. 17 (see n. 97), supposedly following Adalard, ed. Krause, p. 523, ed. Prou, p. 46. Ostiarius: *Codex Carolinus*, No. 82, *ao*. 788, ed. W. J. Gundlach, *MG.* Epp. III, p. 615; Hincmar, *De ordine palatii*, c. 17.

105. In the address of the following diplomas: DDKar., Nos. 66, 91, 98, 99, 123 (in the sanctio), 125, 141 (in the address and in the sanctio), 142, 175, *ais*. 772–92, are cited some *domestici*, some of whom had functions at the court; it is, however, necessary to ask whether this is not explained by the use of a formula that inadequately expresses the real situation. The mention of *domestici* along with counts, bishops, and abbots in the Capitulare missorum of Nijmegen in 808, c. 18 (*MG.* Capit. I, No. 46), has more weight; but probably these were regional *domestici* still existing in certain parts of the territory.

106. Capitulare de villis, *ais*. 771–800, c. 16 and 47, *MG.* Capit. I, No. 32.

107. Hincmar, *De ordine palatii* (see nn. 97 and 103), c. 22.

108. In 794 a Count Richard was *villarum suarum provisor*, Astronome, *Vita Hludowici*, c. 6, *MG.* SS. II, p. 610.

109. See pp. 83–84.

110. Military commands: 778, Spanish campaign, seneschal and count palatine; 782, campaign in Saxony, chamberlain, constable, count palatine; 786, campaign against the Bretons, seneschal; 791, campaign against the Avars, chamberlain; 807, campaign on the sea against the Saracens in the waters around Corsica, constable. See Einhard, *Vita Karoli*, c. 9, ed. O. Holder-Egger, *MG.* SS. rer. Germ. (1911), p. 12, and the references in the passages of the Annales (above, n. 103). Diplomatic missions: 788, at Rome, usher (see n. 104); 802, at Constantinople; and 808, at Rome, Count Helmgaud, who had been count palatine, Annales Regni Francorum, *ao*. 802, p. 117, and Leonis Papae epistolae X, ed. K. Hampe, *MG.* Epp. V, pp. 87 ff., No. 1; 811, negotiations with the Danes, Burchard, who had been constable, Annales Regni Francorum, *ao*. 811, p. 134.

111. J. Fleckenstein, "Die Hofkapelle der deutschen Könige. I, Grun-

dlegung. Die Karolingische Hofkapelle," *Schriften der Monumenta Germaniae historica*, XVI (Stuttgart, 1959). It suffices to refer to this very well documented and intelligent work, particularly to pp. 5–67. On Fulrad and his successors, pp. 27 and 45–47. For Angilram and Hildebold, see especially DKar., No. 161, *ao.* 788, and the capitulary issued after the synod of Frankfurt, *ao.* 794, c. 55, *MG.* Capit. I, No. 28.

112. *Gesta Sanctorum Patrum Fontanellensis Coenobii*, c. XIII, *Gesta Ansegisi*, ed. F. Lohier and L. Laporte (Rouen and Paris, 1936), p. 93. The assimilation to the *vassi dominici* appears in some texts a bit later, such as Walafrid Strabo, *De exordiis et incrementis rerum ecclesiasticarum*, c. 32, *MG.* Capit. II, p. 515; one seems justified in using this source. Cf. Fleckenstein, pp. 30–31, 92–93.

113. Fleckenstein, pp. 57–61. If the sources did not generally omit adding a title to a name when it did not concern a superior authority, one could undoubtedly multiply the examples.

114. Capitulare missorum de exercitu promovendo, c. 8, *MG.* Capit. I, No. 50.

115. On the relations between the office that drew up diplomas and the chapel, H. W. Klewitz, "Cancellaria," *DA*, I (1937), and Fleckenstein, pp. 75–81. On the personnel, H. Bresslau, *Handbuch der Urkundenlehre für Deutschland und Italien*, I (3rd ed.; Berlin, 1960, reprint of the 2nd ed.; 1912), 378–85.

116. I avoid using the term "chancery," which is anachronistic and gives rise to confusion; see the preceding note.

117. Bresslau, pp. 380–82. For the capitularies see also my *Recherches sur les capitulaires*, pp. 39–52 (=*Was waren die Kapitularien?*, pp. 65–83).

118. Annales Laureshamenses, *ao.* 802, ed. G. H. Pertz, *MG.* SS. I, p. 38, apropos sending *missi* in the spring of this year (see pp. 6–7): Charlemagne ... *noluit de infra palatio pauperiores vassos suos transmittere ad iustitias faciendum propter munera* ...

119. Capitulary of Boulogne, *ao.* 811, c. 7, *MG.* Capit. I, No. 74: disposition concerning the ... *vassis dominicis qui adhuc intra casam serviunt et tamen beneficia habere noscuntur*. The royal vassals without benefices, of which there is question in c. 9 of the Capitulary of Herstal of 779 (*ibid.*, No. 20), have, in the context, their own landed estates and do not appear to have been ranked among the *pauperiores vassi* whose service in the palace was permanent.

120. Hincmar, *De ordine palatii*, c. 31 and 32, ed. Krause, pp. 527–28, ed. Prou, pp. 78 ff., supposedly after Adalard; but except for some facts, pure verbiage.

121. Contemporary title in a manuscript (Paris lat. 4613), of the Capitulare legibus additum of 803, *MG.* Capit. I, No. 39: *Haec sunt*

capitula quae domnus Karolus magnus imperator iussit scribere in consilio suo et iussit eas ponere inter alias leges. Beginning of the prooemium of the Admonitio generalis, *ao.* 789, *ibid.,* No. 22: . . . *una cum sacerdotibus et consiliariis nostris.* Letter of Alcuin to Arn, *ao.* 799 ex., ed. E. Dümmler, *MG.* Epp. IV, No. 186, p. 313; he replied to the archbishop of Salzburg, who had begged him to intervene with the king on the selection of *missi:* . . . *Scias certissime et hoc me saepius fecisse et suis quoque suadere consiliariis.*

122. One thinks of a person such as the cousin of the emperor, Count Wala, brother of Adalard, who had great influence over Charlemagne to the end of his reign: for Wala, see S. Abel and B. Simson, *Jahrbücher des fränkischen Reiches unter Karl dem Grossen,* II (Leipzig, 1883), 466, n. 1, and L. Weinrich, *Wala* (Hamburg, 1963).

123. See pp. 3–8.

124. The term *populus* inserted in the expression *generalis populi sui conventus* and in similar expressions should not be deceiving: it concerns elements of the population who counted, that is, members of the ecclesiastical and lay aristocracy; likewise, mention of *Franci* present at the assembly, which appears in several texts, does not exclude subjects of the king belonging to other ethnic groups.

125. Assembly of Herstal, Capitulary of Herstal, prooemium, *ao.* 779, *MG.* Capit. I, No. 20; assembly of Worms, Annales Regni Francorum, 1st text, *ao.* 787, ed. Kurze, p. 76; assembly of Aachen, Capitulare Saxonicum, *ao.* 797, c. 1, *MG.* Capit. I, No. 27; assembly of Aachen, *ao.* 802, October, Annales Laureshamenses, *h. ao.,* *MG.* SS. I, p. 39, and Capitulare missorum of 803, c. 14, *MG.* Capit. I, No. 40; assembly of Thionville, 806, February, Annales Regni Francorum, *h. ao.,* p. 121; assembly of Ingelheim, *ao.* 807, probably August, Chronicon Moissiacense, *MG.* SS. II, p. 258; assembly of Aachen, *ao.* 808, Capitula cum primis conferenda, inscriptio, *MG.* Capit. I, No. 51; 1st assembly of Aachen, *ao.* 811 (for the dispositions to be enforced after the death of Charlemagne), Einhard, *Vita Karoli,* c. 33, ed. Holder-Egger, pp. 37–41; 2nd assembly of Aachen, *ao.* 811, Capitula tractanda cum comitibus, episcopis et abbatibus, c. 1, *MG.* Capit. I, No. 71.

126. I have not noted any mention of assemblies for the years 774 (the Italian campaign of Charlemagne), 778 (the Spanish campaign), 796 (the king at Aachen and in Saxony), 799 (the king at Aachen and in Saxony), 801 (the emperor returns from Italy, then at Aachen).

127. What is said here (without noting variant readings) rests on a reconstruction that I am unable to quote due to lack of space. I have made this reconstruction with the assistance of two texts from the Annales Regni Francorum, from the Annales Laureshamenses, Sancti

Amandi, Mosellani, Petaviani, and Mettenses priores, from the Chronicon Moissiacense, and from diplomas and capitularies of Charlemagne. This reconstruction forms the basis of my exposition on the assemblies. *Synodus* has been particularly used in the sense of an ordinary diet by the first original text of the Annales Regni Francorum, especially up to 788; the revised text and the sole text (from 801 onward) utilize by preference *conventus generalis*; after Charlemagne became emperor the legal records frequently cite the imperial *placitum:* the same word designated the concentration of the army and the diet.

128. For the evidence on the assemblies see the preceding note.

129. Beginning at the time when military movements began to bother Charlemagne—for the evidence: in 808, Capitula cum primis conferenda, inscriptio, *MG.* Capit. I, No. 51; in 811, second assembly, Annales Regni Francorum, *h. ao.*, p. 134 *(et placito generali secundum consuetudinem Aquis habito);* in 812, *ibid.*, pp. 136–37; in 813, *ibid.*, p. 138. In 806 the holding of the ordinary *placitum*, which was held at the place where the army was concentrated, was put under the authority of the commander of the army, Charles the Young; Charlemagne was sojourning elsewhere, Karoli ad Fulradum abbatem epistola, *in fine, MG.* Capit. I, No. 75, and Chronicon Moissiacense, *h. ao., MG.* SS. II, p. 258.

130. Annales Mosellani, *ao.* 781, ed. I. M. Lappenberg, *MG.* SS. XVI, p. 497: Worms, not before July . . . *magnum conventum Francorum id est magiscampum;* the army was ready to march against Tassilo. Annales Laureshamenses, *ao.* 790, *MG.* SS. I, p. 34: Worms, after 9 April and before 9 June, Charlemagne, having no military expedition to make, sent the troops back to their homes: . . . *Conventum habuit in Wormatia, non tamen magiscampum.* We know that Pepin III had fixed the session of the diet for May.

131. Perhaps in 770, 771, 773, 777, 789, 790, 811, 812. The month of May is excluded for all the other sessions, known and datable, of ordinary and extraordinary diets.

132. In 773, extraordinary diet (=d.e.) at Thionville and ordinary diet (=d.o.) at Geneva, Annales Regni Francorum, 2 texts, pp. 34–39. In 775, d.e. at Quierzy and d.o. at Düren, *ibid.*, *ais.* 774 and 775, 2 texts, pp. 40–41. In 779, d.e. at Herstal and d.o. at Düren, Capitulary of Herstal, prooemium, *MG.* Capit. I, No. 20, and Annales Regni Francorum, 2 texts, pp. 54–55. In 789, perhaps d.e. at Aachen and d.o., probably also at Aachen, Admonitio generalis, prooemium, *MG.* Capit. I, No. 22, and Annales Regni Francorum, 1st text, p. 84. In 802, only two d.e. at Aachen; the 1st: Annales Iuvavenses maiores, ed. H. Bresslau, *MG.* SS. XXX, p. 736; Annales Sancti Amandi, ed. G. H. Pertz, *MG.* SS. I, p. 14; Annales Guelferbytani, *ao.* 801 (misdated a year early), ed. G. H. Pertz,

MG. SS. I, p. 45; the 2nd: Annales Laureshamenses, p. 39. In 805, no trace of d.o.; the capitularies of Thionville, *MG.* Capit. I, Nos. 43 and 44, scarcely conceivable without a d.e. In 806, d.e. at Thionville, d.o. at Waldau, Annales Regni Francorum, p. 121; Karoli ad Fulradum epistola, *MG.* Capit. I, No. 75, and Chronicon Moissiacense, p. 258. Perhaps two diets in 808, at Aachen, Capitula cum primis conferenda, inscriptio, and c. 12, *MG.* Capit. I, No. 51. In 811 d.e. and d.o. at Aachen, Einhard, *Vita Karoli,* c. 33, ed. Holder-Egger, pp. 37-41; Annales Regni Francorum, p. 134, and Capitula tractanda, c. 1, *MG.* Capit. I, No. 71. In 813, d.e. and d.o. at Aachen, Annales Regni Francorum, p. 138, and Chronicon Moissiacense, p. 259.

133. That of Herstal in 779, those of Aachen certainly in 802 and 813.

134. Herstal and Aachen, 802, see pp. 4-5 and 6-7. Aachen, 813, where Louis, king of Aquitaine, was crowned associate emperor by his father, Annales Regni Francorum, p. 138.

135. This results from annalistic texts in which it is frequently said that Charles *synodum* or *conventum habuit, tenuit, congregavit* or even that he *plaidavit.* Some more explicit texts show the king presiding over sessions of the council of Frankfurt in 794 (see above, n. 10) and the emperor presiding over the secular section of the diet of October 802 at Aachen. See, for 794, the Libellus sacrosyllabus episcoporum Italiae in *MG.* Concilia II, No. 19, D, p. 131; for 802, Annales Laureshamenses, p. 39.

136. Some of these preparatory documents have been preserved. Among these is one used at the 1st diet of 808 and three others used at the ordinary diet of Aachen in 811, *MG.* Capit. I, Nos. 51, 71, 72, 73.

137. 786, Worms, Annales Laureshamenses, *MG. SS.* I, p. 32; 792, Regensburg, Annales Regni Francorum, rev. text, p. 91, and Annales Petaviani, ed. G. H. Pertz, *MG. SS.* I, p. 18; 794, Frankfurt, see above, n. 10, and Annales Regni Francorum, rev. text, p. 95; 797, Aachen, Capitulare Saxonicum, c. 1, *MG.* Capit. I, No. 27, and Annales Sancti Amandi, *ao.* 797, p. 14; 802, October, Annales Laureshamenses, p. 39. Probably 809, at Aachen; ecclesiastical synod, Annales Regni Francorum, p. 129; the capitularies of Aachen of 809 (*MG.* Capit. I, Nos. 61, 62, 63) seem to us to imply an assembly. 811, Aachen, the three preparatory documents (*ibid.,* Nos. 71, 72, 73) and in particular c. 1 of the Capitula tractanda (No. 71): *In primis separare volumus episcopos et comites nostros et singulariter illos alloqui.* See my article, "Note sur les 'Capitula de causis cum episcopis et abbatibus tractandis' de 811," *Studia Gratiana,* XIII (1967).

138. This was not always the case; Capitulare missorum of 803, c. 14, *MG.* Capit. I, No. 40: *De episcopis, abbatibus, comitibus qui ad placitum*

nostrum non venerunt. This concerns the great extraordinary diet of October 802.

139. *Legislatores,* as they are described by the Annales Laureshamenses (see above, n. 132), that is, men well acquainted by practice with the national laws in use in the *Regnum Francorum.*

140. See pp. 14–16.

141. This is affirmed *expressis verbis* in several texts relating to ordinary and extraordinary diets: 773, Thionville, d.e., Annales Regni Francorum, 1st text, p. 34; 776, Worms, d.o., *ibid.,* p. 46; 784, Worms, d.o., *ibid.,* p. 68; 786, Worms, d.o., *ibid.,* p. 72; 789, Aachen, d.o., *ibid.,* p. 84; 791, Regensburg, d.o., *ibid.,* p. 88; 802, October, Aachen, d.e., Annales Laureshamenses, p. 39; 806, Thionville, d.e., Annales Regni Francorum, p. 121; 811, Aachen, the three preparatory documents for the d.o., *MG.* Capit. I, Nos. 71, 72, 73; 813, Aachen, perhaps d.o. and certainly d.e., Einhard, *Vita Karoli,* c. 30, ed. Holder-Egger, p. 34.

142. Hincmar has given, in his *De ordine palatii,* c. 29, 30, 34–36 (ed. Krause, pp. 527, 528–29; ed. Prou, pp. 70–79, 84–95), a description of the organization and functioning of the assemblies, which certainly contains some exact information taken from Adalard (e.g., c. 34, on the preparatory documents; see above, n. 136). But on the whole this treatise presents a systematic character, which does not agree with the evidence of contemporary sources; moreover, it contains some details which one should view with great reserve. Nevertheless, as has been seen, in regard to this work I do not agree with the absolute skepticism of L. Halphen, "Le 'De ordine palatii' d'Hincmar," *Revue Historique,* CLXXXII (1938), and in the collection of articles of Halphen, *A travers l'histoire du moyen âge* (Paris, 1950). See n. 97.

143. The voluminous article of V. Krause, "Geschichte des Institutes der missi dominici," *Mitteilungen des Instituts für Österreichische Geschichtsforschung,* XI (1890), is very valuable despite certain parts less satisfactory than others. The tables that accompany it contain some errors but are useful to consult.

144. In the order of citations: Duplex legationis edictum, *ao.* 789, c. 37; Admonitio generalis, *ao.* 789, prooemium; Capitula a missis dominicis ad comites directa, *ao.* 806, prooemium; Capitulare missorum Aquisgranense alterum, *ao.* 809, c. 11: *MG.* Capit. I, Nos. 23, 22, 85 (p. 184, l. 1 =W. A. Eckhardt, *Kapitulariensammlung* [see n. 50], No. LXIV, p. 99), 63. On the instructions to the *missi,* see pp. 53–54 and n. 403.

145. The name *missus* is also given by the sources to persons to whom the king had confided a diplomatic mission or an important military command; this is justified by the fact that these persons also received from the king a large delegation of his powers.

146. Some *missi ad hoc* are cited in the following legal records: (*1*) 777, private charter, E. E. Stengel, *Urkundenbuch des Klosters Fulda*, I (Marburg, 1958), No. 83 (perhaps). (*2*) 780, *notitia* of a judgment, I. H. Albanès and U. Chevalier, *Gallia Christiana Novissima*, III (Marseilles, Valence, 1899), No. 42 (=B. Guérard, *Cartulaire de l'abbaye de Saint-Victor de Marseille*, I [Paris, 1857], No. 31) (perhaps). (*3*) 781, DKar., No. 140. (*4*) 782, *ibid.*, No. 148. (*5*) 782, *notitia* of a judgment, K. Glöckner, *Codex Laureshamensis*, II (Darmstadt, 1933), No. 228. (*6*) 787, *Gesta Sanctorum Patrum Fontanellensis Coenobii*, XI, *Gesta Vuitlaici* (see n. 112), c. 3, p. 82. (*7*) 790, DKar., No. 165. (*8*) 794, Astronome, *Vita Hludowici*, c. 6 (see n. 108). (*9*) 806, DKar., No. 203. (*10*) 812, Praeceptum pro Hispanis, *MG. Capit.* I, No. 76. (*11*) 813, DKar., No. 218. (*12*) 801-13, Formulae Bituricenses, No. 14, *MG. Formulae*, p. 174.

147. In addition to the cases cited in the texts, which appear below in nn. 165 and 170, one meets ordinary *missi* in the following legal records, all being *notitiae* of judgments: (*1*) 782, C. Devic and J. Vaissete, *Histoire générale de Languedoc*, II, ed. Privat (Toulouse, 1875), Preuves, No. 6 (V). (*2*) and (*3*) Toward the end of the eighth century, Formulae Augienses, B., Nos. 22 and 23, *MG. Formulae*, p. 357. (*4*) 791, R. Poupardin, *Recueil des chartes de l'abbaye de Saint-Germain-des-Prés*, I (Paris, 1909), No. 22. (*5*), (*6*), and (*7*) 791-93, 793, T. Bitterauf, *Die Traditionen des Hochstifts Freising*, I (Munich, 1905), Nos. 142, 143, 166. (*8*) 795, P. de Monsabert, *Chartes de l'abbaye de Nouaillé* (Poitiers, 1936), No. 7 (*missi* of Louis the Pious, king of Aquitaine, who followed the rules prescribed by his father). (*9*) 796, M. Prou and A. Vidier, *Recueil des chartes de l'abbaye de Saint-Benoît-sur-Loire*, I (Paris and Orléans, 1900), No. 9 (=E. Pérard, *Recueil de plusieurs pièces curieuses servant à l'histoire de Bourgogne* [Paris, 1664], p. 34). (*10*) 804, 806, 806/7, Bitterauf, Nos. 193, 227, 232. One will recall that the text (*1*) and (*2*) of 777 and 780, cited above in n. 146 might not involve *missi ad hoc* but ordinary *missi*.

148. The expression is employed in this sense in regard to functions of *missi* in the following texts: Capitulare legi Ribuariae additum, *ao.* 803, c. 8; Capitulare Karoli Magni de latronibus, *ao.* 804, c. 8; Capitula a missis dominicis ad comites directa, *ao.* 806, c. 6; Capitula de missorum officiis, *ao.* 810 (*iustitiam;* the same sense), c. 3 and 5; Capitulare de iustitiis faciendis, *ao.* 811, c. 12: *MG. Capit.* I, Nos. 41, 82, 85 (=W. A. Eckhardt, *Kapitulariensammlung*, No. LXIV, p. 102), 66, 80.

149. The definition of the authority that the *missi* ought to exercise, given by c. 1 of the Programmatic Capitulary of March 802, corresponds to all that we know about this authority before and after this date. See

also the Capitula de missorum officiis of 810, c. 1 and 2. *MG.* Capit. I, Nos. 33 and 66.

150. Capitulare Haristallense, *ao.* 779, c. 21; Capitulare missorum, *ais.* 792/3, c. 5; Programmatic Capitulary of March 802, c. 1; Capitula a missis dominicis ad comites directa, *ao.* 806, prooemium and c. 4–7; Capitula de iustitiis faciendis, *ao.* 811, c. 8: *MG.* Capit. I, Nos. 20, 25, 33, 85 (=W. A. Eckhardt, *Kapitulariensammlung*, No. LXIV, pp. 99–102), 80.

151. Dispositions of the Programmatic Capitulary of 802 and of three other capitularies communicated by one of the *missi* in the spring of 802; *notitia* of the publication of the Capitulare legibus additum of 803 by the count of Paris in his capacity as *missus*; Capitula de missorum officiis, *ao.* 810, c. 2; Capitula per missos cognita facienda, *ais.* 805–13, particularly c. 6: *MG.* Capit. I, Nos. 59, 39 (p. 112, ll. 14–20), 66, 67.

152. Duplex legationis edictum, *ao.* 789, c. 27 and 37; Capitulare missorum of Thionville, *ao.* 805, c. 12 and 15 (and c. 12 in the text of the mss. of the group Paris lat. 9654 and Vatic. Palat. 582); Capitula de rebus exercitalibus in placito tractandis, *ao.* 811 (the collection results from an inquest of *missi*); Capitulare de iustitiis faciendis, *ao.* 811, c. 9: *MG.* Capit. I, Nos. 23, 44, 73, 80.

153. Duplex legationis edictum, *ao.* 789, c. 35; Breviarium missorum Aquitanicum, *ao.* 789, c. 6; Capitulare missorum, *ao.* 802, c. 10; Capitula a misso cognita facta (1st text cited in n. 151), *ao.* 802, c. 3; Capitulary of Aachen, *ais.* 802/3, c. 4; Capitulare missorum of Nijmegen, *ao.* 806, c. 6 and 7, and Capitula de causis diversis (fragment of a capitulary of Nijmegen), *ao.* 806, c. 4; Capitulare missorum primum and Capitulare missorum alterum of Aachen, *ais.* 809 and 810, c. 9, c. 9, c. 14, c. 9; Capitulare de iustitiis faciendis, c. 5, 6, and 7: *MG.* Capit. I, Nos. 23, 24, 34 (better: W. A. Eckhardt, "Capitularia" [see n. 21], c. 10 and 9, p. 501), 59, 77, 46, 49, 62–65, 80.

154. Breviarium missorum Aquitanicum, *ao.* 789, c. 1; Programmatic Capitulary of 802, c. 1; Capitulare missorum of Nijmegen, *ao.* 806, c. 2, 3, 5, 8, 10; Capitulare missorum, *ais.* 807–13, c. 1–4; Capitula a missis dominicis ad comites directa, *ao.* 806, prooemium, *in fine*: *MG.* Capit. I, Nos. 24, 33, 46, 60, 85 (=W. A. Eckhardt, *Kapitulariensammlung*, No. LXIV, p. 100).

155. Capitulare missorum of 803, c. 27; Capitulare missorum Aquisgranense primum, *ao.* 809, c. 15; Capitula de missorum officiis, *ao.* 810, complete; Capitulare missorum, *ais.* 806–13, c. 4: *MG.* Capit. I, Nos. 40, 62, 66, 60.

156. Inquests on the subject of personal or real rents owed to the emperor and the control over their collection: Capitulare missorum of Thionville, *ao.* 805, c. 20; Capitulare de iustitiis faciendis, *ao.* 811, c. 10

and 11: *MG.* Capit. I, Nos. 40 and 80. Inquests on the subject of *heribannum*, control, and on occasion, collection: Capitulare missorum generale of Thionville, c. 19; Capitulare missorum of Nijmegen, *ao.* 806, c. 5; Capitulare missorum de exercitu promovendo, *ao.* 808, c. 2; Capitulare missorum Aquisgranense primum et alterum, *ao.* 810, c. 12 and 11; Capitula de missorum officiis, *ao.* 810, c. 4; Capitula de rebus exercitalibus in placito tractanda, *ao.* 811, c. 6; Capitulary of Boulogne, *ao.* 811, c. 2 and 9: *MG.* Capit. I, Nos. 44, 46, 50, 64, 65, 66, 73, 74. Measures preparatory to a campaign: Memoratorium de exercitu, *ao.* 807, c. 3; Capitulare missorum de exercitu promovendo, all of the capitulary: *MG.* Capit. I, Nos. 48, 50. Power of nomination of subordinate officers, correlative to the power of dismissal (see above, n. 152): Capitulare missorum of 803, c. 3; Capitulare missorum generale of Thionville, c. 12: *MG.* Capit. I, Nos. 40, 44.

157. See Part III.

158. See p. 14.

159. Protection. For Saxony: Capitulare Saxonicum, *ao.* 797, c. 7: triple *wergeld.* Fragment of a capitulary preserved in the collection of Ansegise, c. 1: armed resistance to a *missus* whose position is known, penalty of death; if his position is unknown, fine of the *bannum* (sixty shillings): *MG.* Capit. I, Nos. 27 and 70. Maintenance: Capitulary of Herstal, *ao.* 779, c. 17; Capitulare de villis, *ais.* 771–800, c. 27; Programmatic Capitulary of 802, c. 28; Capitulare missorum of 802, c. 14; Capitulare missorum of 803, c. 17 and 5 (for the *heribannitores*, "collectors of the *heribannum*"); collection of articles of capitularies for the use of *missi* in 806, c. 53; Capitulare missorum Aquisgranense alterum, *ao.* 809, c. 10; Capitula omnibus cognita facienda, *ais.* 802–13, c. 2 (for the *heribannitores*): *MG.* Capit. I, Nos. 20, 32, 33, 34 (=W. A. Eckhardt, "Capitularia," c. 14 or 15, p. 502), 40, 35 (W. A. Eckhardt, *Kapitulariensammlung*, No. LIX, c. 26, p. 85), 63, 57.

160. Capitulare missorum, *ais.* 792/93, c. 4; Programmatic Capitulary, *ao.* 802, c. 1; Capitulare missorum, *ao.* 803, c. 3 and 25; Capitula a missis dominicis ad comites directa, *ao.* 806, prooemium; Capitulare missorum Aquisgranense primum, *ao.* 810, c. 12; Capitula per missos cognita facienda, *ais.* 805–13: *MG.* Capit. I, Nos. 25, 33, 40, 85 (=W. A. Eckhardt, *Kapitulariensammlung*, No. LXIV, p. 100), 64, 67. There is preserved a report of one of the *missi* (*ad hoc* or ordinary) working in Provence in 780 (see above, n. 146 (2), and n. 147, *in fine*), Albanès and Chevalier, *Gallia Christiana Novissima*, III, No. 41, cols. 33–34.

161. The existence of these secretaries of the *missi* is implied by the texts cited in the preceding note; they are, moreover, cited under the name of *brebitarii* ("compilers of *brevia*") in c. 1 of the Programmatic Capitulary of 802.

162. Capitulare missorum generale of Thionville, *ao.* 805, c. 13, and Responsa cuidam misso data, *ais.* 806-13, *MG.* Capit. I, Nos. 44 and 58.

163. See above, n. 147 and below, n. 170.

164. I agree with Krause (see n. 143), pp. 205-6, that this resulted from c. 21 of the Capitulary of Herstal, *MG.* Capit. I, No. 20.

165. Krause, pp. 214-17, notes the reasons why ordinary *missi* would before 802 have been named and sent out on missions each year; but I believe that the sources he cites do not permit such a conclusion. The character of the mission confided to the *missi* in 779, 789, and 793 implies that they were sent throughout the *Regnum;* see pp. 5-7 and 13-14. The mission of Leidrade, bishop designate of Lyons, and of Theodulphe, bishop of Orléans, in a large part of the south of Gaul in 798, can be explained by reasons peculiar to these regions; but it seems more likely that their mission was but part of one that applied to all of the realm; Versus Teudulfi episcopi contra iudices, ed. E. Dümmler, *MG.* Poet. lat. I, pp. 493-520.

166. See pp. 6-7.

167. See the text in the Annales Laureshamenses, *ao.* 802, *MG.* SS. I, p. 38, in which the principal passage is reproduced above, n. 118. The picturesque account that Theodulphe has left of the mission accomplished by Leidrade and himself in the south of Gaul shows that the men of the region were very surprised not to see them succumb to the attraction of presents offered to them; these had normally been accepted by their predecessors; see the work cited in n. 165, vv. 167-68, 171-254, 259-60.

168. Annales Laureshamenses, the passage (pp. 38-39) following that referred to in the preceding note: . . . *sed elegit in regno suo archiepiscopos et reliquos episcopos et abbates cum ducibus et comitibus, qui iam opus non abebant super innocentes munera accipere.* It is possible to believe that Leidrade and Theodulphe (see nn. 165 and 167) informed Charlemagne of the attempts at corruption that were common in their *missaticum* (vv. 167-68, 171-254, 259-60). At the request of Arn, Alcuin intervened in 799 with some councilors of Charlemagne to obtain the designation of incorruptible *missi* (see above, n. 121, *in fine*).

169. *Missaticum:* Capitulare missorum of Nijmegen, *ao.* 808, c. 1; Capitula per missos cognita facienda, *ais.* 805-13, c. 4; Capitulare de iustitiis faciendis, *ao.* 811, c. 5, 9, and 12: *MG.* Capit. I, Nos. 46, 67, 80. *Legatio:* last capitulary cited, c. 7. *Missaticum* can have the sense of "mission confided to a *missus*," as in a fragment of a capitulary preserved by Ansegise, c. 1; *legatio,* also, Capitulare de iustitiis faciendis, c. 8: *MG.* Capit. I, Nos. 70 and 80.

170. W. A. Eckhardt, "Capitularia," has well shown that such was the rule in 802. He has, thanks principally to the study of the Capitulare missorum of this year, identified six *missatica* and the *missi* of four,

perhaps of five of them; these *missi* agree with all the characteristics indicated in the text. They are the abbot of Saint-Denis, the archbishop of Rouen, the archbishop of Sens, the archbishop designate of Reims, and three counts, one of whom was the count of Paris. One is able to make a similar observation for Bavaria: Arn, archbishop of Salzburg, is *missus* in 802; M. Heuwieser, *Die Traditionen des Hochstifts Passau* (Munich, 1930), Nos. 50 and 54; Bitterauf, *Die Traditionen des Hochstifts Freising*, I, Nos. 183–86.

171. To me this appears to result from the large number of *capitularia missorum* for this period.

172. It would seem that one could state this in 806: Capitula a missis dominicis ad comites directa, prooemium, *MG.* Capit. I, No. 85 (=W. A. Eckhardt, *Kapitulariensammnlung*, No. LXIV, p. 99). These *missi* are all very important persons.

173. Capitulare de iustitiis faciendis, *ao.* 811, c. 8, *MG.* Capit. I, No. 80.

174. W. A. Eckhardt, "Capitularia," pp. 515–16, has produced some serious arguments for this conclusion. See also E. Ewig, "Descriptio Franciae," in *Karl der Grosse*, I, 170–71.

175. One may see an echo of the anxiety that this state of affairs caused Charlemagne in at least two capitularies: Capitulare missorum, *ao.* 802–13, c. 4; Capitula per missos cognita facienda, *ais.* 805–13, c. 6: *MG.* Capit. I, Nos. 60 and 67.

176. For example: Formulae Salicae Bignonianae, Nos. 7 and 9; Formulae Salicae Merkelianae, Nos. 28 and 38; Formulae Senonenses recentiores, Nos. 2–6: *MG.* Formulae, pp. 230, 231, 252, 256, 211–14. Diplomas of Charlemagne, DDKar., Nos. 63 and 194, *ais.* 771, 785–800. Poupardin, *Recueil des chartes de . . . Saint-Germain-des-Prés*, I, No. XXII, *ao.* 791. H. Wartmann, *Urkundenbuch der Abtei Sankt Gallen*, I (Zurich, 1863), No. 187, *ais.* 806/7.

177. Capitulary of Herstal, *ao.* 779, c. 11; Capitulatio de partibus Saxoniae, *ao.* 785, c. 24 and 28; Capitulary of Boulogne, *ao.* 811, c. 5: *MG.* Capit. I, Nos. 20, 26, 74. Survey of the comital institution, studied in the framework of what will become Catalonia: R. d'Abadal i de Vinyals, "La institució comtal carolingia en la Pre-Catalunya del segle IX," *Anuario de estudios medievales*, I (1964).

178. Adrevald, *Miracula Sancti Benedicti*, c. 18, ed. O. Holder-Egger, *MG.* SS. XV, I, p. 486 (=ed. E. de Certain, *Les miracles de Saint Benoît* [Paris, 1858], l. 1, c. 18, p. 43).

179. The best-known members of these families are ranked in the *Reichsaristokratie* by G. Tellenbach, *Königtum und Stämme in der Werdezeit des Deutschen Reiches* (Weimar, 1939), pp. 41 ff. Some examples are: the dynasty of the Thierry related to the king; one Thierry is

count in Ripuaria, Annales Regni Francorum, rev. text, *ais.* 782, 793, pp. 61, 63, 93; his brother, William, is count of Toulouse and duke in 790 ("Saint Guilhem"), Astronome, *Vita Hludowici,* c. 5, *MG.* SS. II, p. 609; see L. Auzias, *L'Aquitaine carolingienne* (Toulouse, 1937), p. 37. The dynasty of the Nibelungen, perhaps originally from Hesbaie, is also related to the royal family; several members of this family were counts: among them Childebrand II, count and *missus* in the Autunois, Prou and Vidier, *Recueil des chartes de . . . Saint-Benoît-sur-Loire,* I, No. 9, *ao.* 796; see L. Levillain, "Les Nibelungen historiques," *Annales du Midi,* XLIX–L (1937 and 1938). The Lambert family, originally from the Moselle region, DKar., No. 148, *ais.* 782/83; Guy, count in the march of Brittany and *praefectus,* Annales Regni Francorum, two texts, *ao.* 799, p. 108; head of the dynasty of Spoleto. The Unroch family, probably from the region of the Scheldt and the Meuse; the first by this name is noted as count and *missus* in 806 and as count in 811, *MG.* Capit. I, No. 85, Einhard, *Vita Karoli,* c. 33, ed. Holder-Egger, p. 41, and Annales Regni Francorum, *ao.* 811, p. 134; head of the dynasty of the Frioli. The family of Audulf, count in the Taubergau, in Franconia, DKar., No. 206, *ao.* 786, seneschal, Annales Regni Francorum, *ao.* 786, pp. 72–73, then successor of Gerold, as holder of a superior power in Bavaria, in 799; see Tellenbach, p. 44.

180. For example, Alamanni: Gerold, brother of Queen Hildegard, count, then *praefectus* of Bavaria, killed in 799; he was considered an Alamannian because his mother was one, but his father seems to have been a Frank, according to K. F. Werner, "Bedeutende Adelsfamilien im Reich Karls des Grossen," in *Karl der Grosse,* I, 111. Eric, count, duke in Friuli, killed in 799; Annales Regni Francorum, 1st text, *ao.* 799, p. 108; see Tellenbach, pp. 51–52. Both are ranked in the *Reichsaristokratie* by this scholar. Saxony: Count Bennit, DKar., No. 213, *ao.* 811. Bavaria: the *iudex* Orendil (802), count in 807; Bitterauf, *Traditionen des Hochstifts Freising,* I, Nos. 184, 186, 258. Goth: Bera, count of Barcelona in 803; Astronome, *Vita Hludowici, MG.* SS. II, p. 613.

181. Gunthramnus: royal vassal in 777, Stengel, *Urkundenbuch des Klosters Fulda,* I, No. 83; count in 782, Glöckner, *Codex Laureshamensis,* II, No. 228, *ao.* 782.

182. The two types of counts: Capitulare episcoporum, *ais.* 792/93, *MG.* Capit. I, No. 21. The *comites mediocres* were assimilated to royal vassals who possessed domains comprising two hundred or more manses; it is true that a part of these estates may have been benefices. One finds very important donations of landed estates made by counts. I cite, for example, those made by Count Gerold to Saint-Gall (Wartmann, *Urkundenbuch der Abtei Sankt Gallen,* I, No. 108, *ao.* 786); by Count

Theudald to Saint-Denis (J. Tardif, *Monuments historiques, Cartons des Rois* [Paris, 1866], No. 97, *ao*. 797; see also DKar., No. 181, *ao*. 797). One could multiply these examples without difficulty.

183. *Honor:* see the texts cited in n. 177. *Ministerium:* Capitula a missis dominicis ad comites directa, *ao*. 806, *MG*. Capit. I, No. 85 (=W. A. Eckhardt, *Kapitulariensammlung*, No. LXIV, pp. 99-102).

184. *Ministerium:* Capitulary of Herstal, *ao*. 779, c. 21, and the Programmatic Capitulary of 802, c. 21, 28, *MG*. Capit. I, Nos. 20 and 33; Cartae Senonicae, No. 18, *MG*. Formulae, p. 193. *Comitatus:* Capitulatio de partibus Saxoniae, *ao*. 785, c. 24; Capitulare missorum, *ais*. 792/93, c. 4; Capitulare Aquisgranense, *ais*. 802/3, c. 9, 11, 12, 14; Capitulare missorum of Thionville, *ao*. 805, c. 11; Divisio Regnorum, *ao*. 806, c. 1; Capitula de causis diversis, *ao*. 806, c. 4: *MG*. Capit. I, Nos. 26, 25, 77, 44, 45, 49. Glöckner, *Codex Laureshamensis*, III (1936), Nos. 3139 and 3637, *ais*. 772/73 and 777-83; DKar., No. 206, *ao*. 807. *Grafia:* Cartae Senonicae, No. 31, *MG*. Formulae, p. 199.

185. This results from numerous texts establishing a relation between the exercise of comital authority and the *pagus* or its inhabitants, the men of the *pagus (pagenses):* Capitulare missorum, *ais*. 792/93, c. 5; Capitulare missorum of Thionville, *ao*. 805, c. 11; Capitula de rebus exercitalibus, *ao*. 811, c. 1; Capitulare Bononiense, *ao*. 811, c. 7; Capitulare de iustitiis faciendis, *ao*. 811, c. 3: *MG*. Capit. I, Nos. 25, 44, 73, 74, 80. DKar., No. 138, *ao*. 781; Formulae Senonenses recentiores, No. 4, *MG*. Formulae, p. 213. With the reservation indicated in the text I agree with the interpretation of J. Prinz, "Pagus und Comitatus in den Urkunden der Karolinger," *Archiv für Urkundenforschung*, XVII (1941).

186. S. Krüger, *Studien zur sächsischen Grafschaftsverfassung im 9. Jahrhundert* (Göttingen, 1950); and the review of H.-J. Freytag in *Niedersächsisches Jahrbuch für Landesgeschichte*, XXIII (1951).

187. DKar., No. 129, *ao*. 780 (=H. Weirich, *Urkundenbuch der Reichsabtei Hersfeld*, I, Pt. I [Marburg, 1936], No. 14): . . . *decima de Hassega* (=Hochseegau), *de comitatos, quos Albericos et Marcoardus . . . tenere visi sunt . . .* and further on . . . *decima de Hassega, que de illos duorum comitatos comites nostri exactaverunt . . .*

188. The case is anticipated in 808 in the Capitulare missorum de exercitu promovendo, *MG*. Capit. I, No. 50, c. 4: . . . *ut quanta ministeria unusquisque comes habuerit . . . ,* c. 8: . . . *comes in cuius ministeriis haec facienda sunt.* The county is indicated by the words in c. 4: *ministerium eius,* which excludes any other interpretation. The statement that beyond frontier zones Charlemagne never entrusted to any of his counts more than a county, has for its author the monk of Saint-

Gall (Notkerus Balbulus, *Gesta Karoli Magni Imperatoris*, c. 13, ed. H. F. Haefele, *MG*. SS. rer. Germ., NS. I [1959], p. 17); the statement is without any authority.

189. This number is merely an approximation.

190. Capitula a missis dominicis ad comites directa, *ao*. 806, c. 1, *MG*. Capit. I, No. 85 (=W. A. Eckhardt, *Kapitulariensammlung*, No. LXIV, p. 100). It is by virtue of this that the counts received under penalty of destitution the order to pursue and to condemn to a fine of sixty shillings those who refused to accept payment in the new pennies coined as royal "money" (Capitulare missorum Aquisgranense alterum, *ao*. 809, c. 7, *MG*. Capit. I, No. 63).

191. See, for example, DDKar., Nos. 180 and 205, *ais*. 797 and 807.

192. Capitulatio de partibus Saxoniae, *ao*. 785, c. 31; Capitulare missorum Aquisgranense primum, *ao*. 809, c. 11: *MG*. Capit. I, Nos. 26 and 62.

193. Capitulary of Herstal, *ao*. 779, c. 9 and 11; Programmatic Capitulary of 802, c. 25; Capitulare legibus additum, *ao*. 803, c. 2; Capitulare missorum, *ao*. 803, c. 24; Capitulare missorum Aquisgranense primum, *ao*. 810, c. 2; Capitulare de iustitiis faciendis, *ao*. 811, c. 12: *MG*. Capit. I, Nos. 20, 33, 39, 40, 64, 80.

194. See Part III.

195. See pp. 42–44.

196. Capitulare Aquisgranense, *ais*. 802/3, c. 9, 10, 17; Capitula de causis diversis, *ao*. 806, c. 3; Capitulare missorum de exercitu promovendo, *ao*. 808, all of the capitulary and particularly c. 1; Capitulare Bononiense, *ao*. 811, all of the capitulary and particularly c. 7; Capitula per episcopos et comites nota facienda, *ais*. 802–13, c. 2: *MG*. Capit. I, Nos. 77, 49, 50, 74, 54. See J. F. Verbruggen, "L'armée et la stratégie de Charlemagne," in *Karl der Grosse*, I, 420–36, and Part II of the present volume.

197. Among these ordinary administrative tasks was that of the investiture of estates given by the king to individuals and ecclesiastical establishments if it had not been done by *missi ad hoc;* Mühlbacher, DKar., No. 116, note (or better: Stengel, *Urkundenbuch des Klosters Fulda*, I, No. 83, *ao*. 777). Swearing of the oath of 792/93: activity of the counts and establishment of writings, Capitulare missorum, c. 4, *MG*. Capit. I, No. 25; probably there was an analogous procedure in 802 and later.

198. See p. 25 and n. 156, and p. 32, as well as Part III.

199. Capitulatio de partibus Saxoniae, *ao*. 785, c. 29 (in a regional framework). Principle enunciated in the Admonitio generalis of 789 (see p. 5 and n. 8). Programmatic Capitulary of 802, c. 14; Capitulare missorum, *ao*. 802, c. 18a (=W. A. Eckhardt, "Capitularia" [see n. 21], c. 18a and 20, p. 509); Capitulare Baiwaricum, probably *ao*. 803, c. 4;

Capitula a missis dominicis ad comites directa, *ao.* 806, c. 1 (obedience to the bishop in affairs related to his functions is recommended to the counts); Capitulare Aquisgranense, *ao.* 809, c. 4; Capitulare missorum Aquisgranense primum, *ao.* 809, c. 4 and 11; Capitulare missorum italicum (?), *ais.* 802–10 (see above, n. 31), c. 2: *MG.* Capit. I, Nos. 26, 22, 33, 34, 69, 85 (=W. A. Eckhardt, *Kapitulariensammlung* [see n. 50], No. LXIV, p. 100), 61, 62, 99.

200. Capitula tractanda, *ao.* 811, c. 2–5; Capitulare de iustitiis faciendis, *ao.* 811, c. 2; Capitula e canonibus excerpta, *ao.* 813, c. 9 and 10 (elements selected from among the canons of the five councils of this year in order to serve as a basis for the preparation of a capitulary; c. 10 includes the recommendation of 806, see n. 199): *MG.* Capit. I, Nos. 71, 80, 78 (=ed. Werminghoff, *Appendices ad Concilia anni 813*, A, *MG.* Concilia II, I, pp. 294–97).

201. *Iuniores*: Programmatic Capitulary of 802, c. 25; Praeceptum pro Hispanis, *ao.* 812; Capitula a missis dominicis ad comites directa, *ao.* 806, c. 1 and 2: *MG.* Capit. I, Nos. 33, 76, 85 (=W. A. Eckhardt, *Kapitulariensammlung*, No. LXIV, pp. 100–101). *Vassi comitum*: Capitulare missorum de exercitu promovendo, *ao.* 808, c. 4 (utilized in view of the maintenance of the public peace); Capitulare Aquisgranense, *ao.* 809, c. 5, and Capitulare missorum Aquisgranense primum, c. 13, following ms. Paris lat. 9654 (used as judgment-finders at the *mallus*): *MG.* Capit. I, Nos. 50, 61, 62.

202. *Tertia*: in the older texts of the *leges*, which had kept their authority, one can also cite for the reign of Charlemagne an Italian capitulary introducing Frankish law into Italy, *ao.* 787, c. 5, and the Capitulary of Boulogne, *ao.* 811, c. 2, *MG.* Capit. I, Nos. 95 and 74. For the toll, see my study, "A propos du tonlieu à l'époque carolingienne," in *La città nell'alto Medioevo, Settimane di studio del Centro italiano di studi sull'alto medioevo*, VI (Spoleto, 1959), 507–8 and see also p. 44 and n. 326.

203. *Ministerium*: Capitulare de villis, *ais.* 771–800, c. 27, *MG.* Capit. I, No. 32. The meaning of the word is justified by comparison with its use in a diploma of Louis the Pious for the church of Tournai, *ao.* 817, *Recueil des historiens des Gaules et de la France*, VI, 509. *Beneficium*: it is probably an element of the endowment that is designated thus in DKar., No. 206, *ao.* 807; it is less certain that it is this way in DKar., No. 154, *ao.* 786, and in Prou and Vidier, *Recueil des chartes de . . . Saint-Benoît-sur-Loire*, I, No. IX, *ao.* 796. C. 6 of the Capitulare missorum of Nijmegen, *ao.* 806 (*MG.* Capit. I, No. 46), envisages every benefice held from the king by a count.

204. E. Lesne, *Histoire de la propriété ecclésiastique en France*, II,

Pt. 1 (Lille and Paris, 1922), 126, for the reign of Charlemagne, cites only one incontestable example from a diploma of Louis the Pious, *Recueil des historiens des Gaules et de la France*, VI, 553, *ao*. 827.

205. See pp. 21–22.

206. One takes this into account by stating that there were always several counts among the judgment-finders on the palace court, DDKar., Nos. 65, 110, 138, 148, 204, 216, *ais*. 772, 775, 781, 782/83, 806, 812.

207. See the texts indicated above, in nn. 146, 147, 170.

208. See the chapter of J. F. Verbruggen cited in n. 196 and Part II of this volume.

209. See my study, "Les relations extérieures de la monarchie franque sous les premiers souverains carolingiens," *Annali di Storia del diritto*, V–VI (1961/62; appeared in 1964), 14–17.

210. Capitulare de iustitiis faciendis, *ao*. 811, c. 8, *MG*. Capit. I, No. 80.

211. Allusion to this activity by a neighboring count: Capitula per episcopos et comites nota facienda, *ais*. 802–13, prooemium, *MG*. Capit. I, No. 54.

212. Capitulary of Herstal, *ao*. 779, c. 21; Duplex legationis edictum, *ao*. 789, c. 17; Capitula de causis diversis, *ao*. 806, c. 1; Capitula a missis dominicis ad comites directa, *ao*. 806, c. 2: *MG*. Capit. I, Nos. 20, 23, 49, 85 (=W. A. Eckhardt, *Kapitulariensammlung*, No. LXIV, pp. 100–101): dispositions taken against negligent behavior.

213. These are the dispositions issued against these abuses that made them better known. Annales Laureshamenses, *ao*. 802, *MG*. SS. I, p. 38, and Programmatic Capitulary of 802, c. 1; Capitulare missorum of Thionville, *ao*. 805, c. 15; Capitulare missorum de exercitu promovendo, *ao*. 808, c. 3, 6, 7; Capitulare Aquisgranense, *ao*. 809, c. 7; Capitula de rebus exercitalibus in placito tractanda, *ao*. 811, c. 2, 3, 4, 5; Capitulare Bononiense, *ao*. 811, c. 9; Praeceptum pro Hispanis, *ao*. 812; Capitula omnibus cognita facienda, *ais*. 802–13, c. 2: *MG*. Capit. I, Nos. 33, 44, 50, 61, 73, 74, 76 (=d'Abadal [see above, n. 76], II, Pt. 2, Preceptes per a particulars, No. 2, pp. 312–14), 57. Also the last text cited in n. 212.

214. This has been vigorously emphasized by H. Fichtenau, *Das Karolingische Imperium* (Zurich, 1949), p. 116.

215. Einhard, *Vita Karoli*, c. 11, ed. Holder-Egger, p. 14; *neque provincia . . . ulterius duci, sed comitibus ad regendum commissa est.*

216. For Aquitaine, G. Eiten, *Das Unterkönigtum im Reiche der Merowinger und Karolinger* (Heidelberg, 1907), pp. 40–46; Auzias, *L'Aquitaine carolingienne*, pp. 68–70; and P. Wolff, "L'Aquitaine et ses marges," in *Karl der Grosse*, I, 293–95.

217. See above, nn. 180 and 179.

218. *Annales Mettenses priores, ao*. 790, ed. B. von Simson, *MG*. SS.

rer. Germ. (1905), p. 78. One does not find Charles the Young subsequently in this region: in general he exercises military commands in the east of the *Regnum Francorum*. He becomes king only in 800. Liber Pontificalis, *Vita Leonis III*, c. XXIII/376, ed. Duchesne, II, 7; Maine was not organized into a kingdom.

219. As strongly underlined by Fichtenau, p. 118.

220. There at least remains reference to *duces* among personnages designated as *missi* in March 802 and among the members of the diet of Aachen in October 802, Annales Laureshamenses, *ao*. 802, *MG*. SS. I, p. 39. There is also reference to *duces* in the address of the Capitulary of Aachen, which is related to the work of the diet of 802, *MG*. Capit. I, No. 77. Tellenbach (see n. 179), pp. 58–59, thinks that *dux* was a title peculiar to members of the *Reichsaristokratie*.

221. Astronome, *Vita Hludowici*, c. 5, p. 609. See above, n. 179.

222. *Marca* does not seem to me to have any other meaning than frontier zone in Annales Regni Francorum, 1st text, *ao*. 773, p. 36; Capitulary of Herstal, *ao*. 779, c. 19; Capitulare missorum, *ao*. 803, c. 7 (in the ms. Vatic. Palat. 773); letter of Charlemagne to Gerbald, bishop of Liège, *ao*. 805; Capitulary of Boulogne, *ao*. 811, c. 8 (fiction of a frontier): *MG*. Capit. I, Nos. 20, 40, 124 (p. 245, l. 38 =W. A. Eckhardt, *Kapitulariensammlung*, No. LXIX, p. 118), 74. The term appears to imply a defensive organization in the following texts: Annales Regni Francorum, 1st text, *ao*. 788, p. 84; Capitulare Baiwaricum, probably *ao*. 803, c. 9; Capitula cum primis conferenda, *ao*. 808, c. 9, and Capitula cum primis constituta, *ao*. 808, c. 1; Karoli Magni Capitulare missorum italicum (?), *ais*. 802–10, c. 3 and 4; Capitula tractanda, *ao*. 811, c. 2: *MG*. Capit. I, Nos. 69, 51, 52, 99 (see above, n. 31), 71.

223. Annales Regni Francorum, 1st text, *ao*. 799, p. 108: *Wido comes, qui in marcam Brittaniae praesidebat, una cum sociis comitibus Brittaniam ingressus* . . .

224. *Praefectus* and especially *praefectus limitis*, expressions of the classical world, are used to the end of the reign of Charlemagne and into the time of Louis the Pious: Annales Regni Francorum, 1st text, *ao*. 799, p. 108: *Geroldus comes Baioariae praefectus;* Annales Regni Francorum, rev. text, *ao*. 799, p. 109: *Wido comes ac praefectus Brittanici limitis;* Einhard, *Vita Karoli*, c. 9, ed. Holder-Egger, p. 12: *Hruodlandus Brittannici limitis praefectus. Marchio*, or the plural *marchiones*, is rare in the time of Charlemagne; in the texts which follow, the word seems to designate counts of a frontier region: Karoli Magni Capitulare missorum italicum (?), *ais*. 802–10, c. 5, *MG*. Capit. I, No. 99 (see above, n. 31); Astronome, *Vita Hludowici*, c. 4, p. 609, *ao*. 785 (the text was drawn up at the time of Louis the Pious, employing for this part of the work a

source which was much older). On the complexity of the terminology, see J. Dhondt, "Le titre du marquis à l'époque carolingienne," *Archivum latinitatis medii aevi. Bulletin du Cange,* XIX (1946).

225. R. d'Abadal, "Nota sobre la locución 'marca hispanica,'" *Boletin de la Real Academia de Buenas Letras de Barcelona,* XXVII (1957/58), seems to have demonstrated that the existence of a Spanish march cannot be proved for the time of Charlemagne. Likewise on the future eastern march of Bavaria (*Ostmark*), there is no definite information for the epoch of Charlemagne; if it already existed as such it must have been under the superior authority of the *praefectus* of Bavaria. Perhaps Count Werner, one of the *missi* exercising authority in the eastern and south-eastern frontier zones of the empire in 805 (Capitulare missorum of Thionville, c. 7, *MG.* Capit. I, No. 44) and residing at Lorsch in the Traungau, may have been recognized as the chief of the *Ostmark*; see E. Klebel, "Herzogtümer und Marken bis 900," *DA,* II (1938), 17 and 38.

226. Cartae Senonicae, Nos. 28, 35, 36; Formulae Senonenses recentiores, No. 11; Formulae Salicae Lindenbrogianae, No. 17: *MG.* Formulae, pp. 197, 200, 201, 217, 278. DKar., No. 87, *ao.* 774. See also, below, n. 229.

227. The inferior rank of the *centenarii* and *vicarii* appears, among other places, in the Capitulare missorum of 792/93, c. 4; while the counts took the oath of fidelity between the hands of the *missi,* the *centenarii* and *vicarii* took it between the hands of the counts. Their dependence upon the counts is indicated by the fact that they are called *vicarius* or *centenarius* of such a count: Formulae Salicae Bignonianae, Nos. 7 and 13, *MG.* Formulae, pp. 230, 232; Capitula de rebus exercitalibus in placito tractanda, *ao.* 811, c. 2; Capitula omnibus cognita facienda, *ais.* 802–13, c. 4: *MG.* Capit. I, Nos. 73 and 57. Written instructions given by a count to a *vicarius:* Formulae Salicae Merkelianae, No. 51, p. 259. Obligation of the inferior officers to execute orders of the count and control of their activities by the count, Programmatic Capitulary of 802, c. 25, No. 33.

228. This results from the identity of functions (see below, n. 234). Particularly decisive is the disposition imposing upon the counts and their subordinate officers the knowledge of their national law: the Capitula omnibus cognita facienda, *ais.* 802–13, c. 4, use the words *comites et vicarii eorum;* a fragment of a *capitulare missorum* from the same years, c. 3, uses the expression *comites quoque et centenarii, MG.* Capit. I, Nos. 57 and 60.

229. One will easily find these passages thanks to the excellent index of the Mühlbacher edition, *MG.* DDKar., pp. 546 and 559, *vis. centenarius* and *vicarius,* subrubrics Adresse and Publikation.

230. The part of the territory administered by one of these officers is

called a *ministerium*, like that of the county in which it is a division: Formulae Salicae Merkelianae, No. 51, *MG*. Formulae, p. 259; Capitulare Aquisgranense, *ais*. 802/3, c. 8; Capitula de causis diversis, *ao*. 806, c. 4: *MG*. Capit. I, Nos. 77, 49. *Centena*: Formulae Salicae Bignonianae, No. 18; Formulae Salicae Merkelianae, Nos. 3, 5, 7–8, 10–11, 16–17, 19–20, 25, 27, 29, 33, 35–36, pp. 235, 241–55; Capitulare missorum, *ais*. 792/93, c. 4, No. 25. *Vicaria* is attested to on the eve of the reign of Charlemagne and immediately after: Formulae Bituricenses, No. 15, p. 175, and Formulae Imperiales, Nos. 3 ff., pp. 289 ff.

231. An intriguing hypothesis suggested for Aquitaine by M. Garaud, "L'organisation administrative du comté de Poitou au Xe siècle et l'avènement des châtelains et des châtellenies," *Bulletin de la Société des Antiquaires de l'Ouest* (1953), p. 413.

232. *Ministerium* in this sense: Formulae Salicae Merkelianae, No. 51 (in addition to a territorial sense), *MG*. Formulae, p. 259; and Capitulare Aquisgranense, *ao*. 809, c. 11, *MG*. Capit. I, No. 61.

233. See, for example, Capitulare Aquisgranense, *ais*. 802/3, c. 5, 6, 8; Capitulare de causis diversis, *ao*. 806, c. 4; Capitulare missorum de exercitu promovendo, *ao*. 808, c. 3: *MG*. Capit. I, Nos. 77, 49, 50. For the judicial functions see Part III.

234. Formulae Salicae Merkelianae, No. 51, *MG*. Formulae, p. 259; Capitulare Aquisgranense, *ao*. 809, c. 11 (text of the ms. Paris lat. 4628A); Capitulare missorum Aquisgranense primum, *ao*. 809, c. 22 (text of the mss. of the group Paris lat. 9654, Vatic. Palat. 582); Capitula omnibus cognita facienda, *ais*. 802–13, c. 3: *MG*. Capit. I, Nos. 61, 62, 57.

235. Capitulare missorum, *ao*. 803, c. 3; Capitulare missorum of Thionville, *ao*. 805, c. 12; Capitula francica (fragments), c. 5, *ais*. 802–6; Karoli Magni Capitulare missorum italicum (?), c. 6: *MG*. Capit. I, Nos. 40, 44, 104 (=W. A. Eckhardt, *Kapitulariensammlung*, No. LXII, p. 97), 99 (see above, n. 31).

236. Capitulare Aquisgranense, *ais*. 802/3, c. 13 and 15; Capitulare missorum de exercitu promovendo, *ao*. 808, c. 3 and 7; Capitula de rebus exercitalibus in placito tractanda, *ao*. 811, c. 2 and 3; Capitula omnibus cognita facienda, *ais*. 802–13, c. 2; Capitula e canonibus excerpta, *ao*. 813, c. 22; Capitula incerti anni, *ais*. 806–13, c. 2: *MG*. Capit. I, Nos. 77, 50, 73, 57, 78, 86. Compare with p. 30 and nn. 212 and 213.

237. See p. 30 and nn. 210–11.

238. Alamannia: Wartmann, *Urkundenbuch der Abtei Sankt Gallen*, I, Nos. 195, 196 (*vicarius*), 214 (*centenarius*), *ais*. 807, probably 807, 814; in addition the *centenarius* is known in the *Lex Alamannorum*, XXXVI, 1 and 3, ed. K. A. Eckhardt, *Leges Alamannorum*, II (Witzenhausen, 1962), 37–38. Bavaria: *Centenarius*: Statuta Rhispacensia, *ao*. 799, c. 15,

MG. Capit. I, No. 112 (=Werminghoff, *MG.* Concilia II, No. 24, Decretum synodale, XV, p. 209); Bitterauf, *Die Traditionen des Hochstifts
Freising*, No. 299, *ao.* 811. *Vicarius: ibid.*, No. 268a, *ao.* 807.

239. Bavaria: *ibid.*, Nos. 176, 288, 244, *ais.* 798, 809, 806–11. Alamannia:
Wartmann, I, No. 21, *ao.* 789.

240. Two *missi Frodaldi comitis*, exercising judicial functions, A. de
Courson, *Cartulaire de l'abbaye de Redon* (Paris, 1863), No. 191, pp.
147–48, *ao.* 797. Capitula per episcopos et comites nota facienda, *ais.*
802–13, c. 5: *una cum missis illorum* [sc. *comitum*] *qui in exercitu sunt,*
MG. Capit. I, No. 54.

241. As in the Capitulare missorum Aquisgranense primum, *ao.* 809,
c.2; in the Capitula a missis dominicis ad comites directa, *ao.* 806, c. 4:
MG. Capit. I, Nos. 64 and 85 (=W. A. Eckhardt, *Kapitulariensammlung,*
No. LXIV, p. 101). See also a *notitia* of judgment, *ao.* 780, in De Monsabert, *Chartes de l'abbaye de Nouaillé*, No. 5.

242. Devic and Vaissete, *Histoire générale de Languedoc*, ed. Privat,
II, Preuves, Nos. 10 (VII) and 15 (XI), cols. 57–58 and 64–65, *ais.* 791
and 802.

243. See p. 48.

244. In a diploma of Charlemagne for Saint-Denis, *ao.* 774, DKar.,
No. 87, one finds the enumeration *nullus comes nec vicecomis nec vicarius
nec centenarius* . . . , but the original is not extant, and it is quite possible
that *vicecomis* was interpolated in a copy.

245. Capitula incerti anni, *ais.* 806–13, c. 3: *De pravis advocatis et
vicedominis et vicecomitis* . . . Legal records can be cited from the first
years of the reign of Louis the Pious; they indicate that the use of the
term was current and that the institution functioned to the end of the
reign of Charlemagne. Diploma of Louis the Pious for Saint-Denis, *ao.*
814, J. Tardif, *Monuments historiques. Cartons des Rois*, No. 107 (date
rectified according to *Regesten*, No. 554): *nullus comes vel vicecomes
aut vicarius vel centenarius* . . . *Notitiae* of judgment: Prou and Vidier,
Recueil des chartes de Saint-Benoît-sur-Loire, I, No. XI, *ao.* 817, *Blitgarius, vicecomes* at Autun; F. Bougaud and J. Garnier, *Chronique de
l'abbaye de Saint-Bénigne de Dijon, suivie de la chronique de Saint-
Pierre de Bèze* (Dijon, 1875), p. 252, *ais.* 817/18, *Balactarium vicecomitem
ad vicem Hildegarni comitis.* Between 818/19 and 840 one meets a *Gen-
esius vicecomes*, as a judgment-finder at an assize of the *missi* at Orléans;
Miracula Sancti Benedicti, I, c. 25, *MG.* SS. XV, I, p. 490.

246. Three *notitiae* of judgment: *ao.* 815, Balactarius (see n. 245),
sent by the count in order to examine on the spot the lands that were
the subject of the action, . . . *misso secum Balactario illustri viro*, Bougaud and Garnier, pp. 250–51 (=M. Thévenin, *Textes relatifs aux institu-*

tions privées et publiques aux époques mérovingienne et carolingienne [Paris, 1887], No. 115, pp. 169-70); *ao.* 819, Autun, Blitgarius (see n. 245), presides over the *mallus* as *misso vir inluster Theoderico comite,* Prou and Vidier, I, No. XVI, 36-37; *ao.* 815, Poitiers, *Godilus, missus illustri viro Bernardo comiti,* De Monsabert, No. 10.

247. W. Sickel, *Der fränkische Vicecomitat* (n.p., 1907), gives, on pp. 8-21, a list of texts that permit one to follow the spread of the institution; the list is useful but not totally trustworthy.

248. Even when the sources mention numerous prisoners of war taken by the Frankish armies, they furnish no evidence on their lot. C. Verlinden, *L'esclavage dans le monde médiéval,* I (Brugge, 1955), 706, argues with wisdom for prudence in this respect.

249. Some references to booty in the Saxon wars: Annales Regni Francorum, 1st text, *ais.* 772, 774, 775, 785, rev. text, *ao.* 783, pp. 34, 40, 42, 68, 65; in a campaign against Benevento, *ao.* 800, p. 110. On the treasures of the Avars and their transfer to Aachen, Annales Regni Francorum, the two texts, *ao.* 796, *initio* and *in fine,* pp. 98-100.

250. From the following texts put together: Annales Regni Francorum, *ais.* 786 and 799, the two texts, and 818, pp. 72-73, 108-9, 148.

251. From the following texts: Annales Regni Francorum, *ais.* 787 and 800, the two texts; 801; 812 (tribute worth 25,000 gold shillings); 814 (tribute established on the basis of the tax of 787, that is, 7,000 gold shillings); pp. 74-75, 110-11, 114, 137.

252. The most important work is that of W. Metz, *Das karolingische Reichsgut* (Berlin, 1960). See also his short survey, very much to the point, "Die Agrarwirtschaft im karolingischen Reiche," in *Karl der Grosse,* I, 489-500. See also E. Ewig, "Descriptio Franciae," *ibid.,* pp. 168-69.

253. Some examples in the diplomas of Charlemagne, DDKar. I, Nos. 83, 84, 103, 104, 121, 144, 188. See also: Capitulare de villis, *ais.* 771-800, c. 4, 6, 52, 62; Capitulare de iustitiis faciendis, *ao.* 811, c. 7; Brevium exempla, Nos. 25, 30, 32, 34, 36: *MG.* Capit. I, Nos. 32, 80, 128.

254. Metz, *Reichsgut,* pp. 232-33.

255. For example, the lands ravaged by the wars against the Saracens in Septimania, DDKar. I, No. 179, *ao.* 795, and Praeceptum pro Hispanis, *ao.* 812, *MG.* Capit. I, No. 76 (=d'Abadal, *Catalunya Carolingia,* II, Pt. 2, Preceptes per a particulars, Nos. 1 and 2). These lands were ceded in large part to refugees from Spain authorized to practice the *aprisio;* they did not help to furnish revenues to the king since they were freed from rents or other payments. See A. Dupont, "L'aprision et le régime aprisionnaire dans le Midi de la France," *Le Moyen Age* (1965).

256. *MG.* Capit. I, No. 32. The most recent important studies on the

Capitulare de villis are those of K. Verhein, "Studien zu den Quellen zum Reichsgut der Karolingerzeit: Pt. 1, Das Capitulare de villis," *DA*, X (1954); and of Metz, *Reichsgut*, pp. 77–87, and "Agrarwirtschaft," pp. 497–99 (with references to the abundant literature).

257. Verhein, Pt. 1, pp. 385–87; Metz, *Reichsgut*, pp. 84–85. A. Dopsch, *Die Wirtschaftsentwicklung der Karolingerzeit*, I (3rd ed.; Darmstadt, 1962), 32–39, thoroughly defined the objectives and the goal of the Capitulare de villis and showed that it was not an ordinance that created a new, grandiose, and complete organization of the royal domains, as had been thought.

258. Capitulary of Aachen of 802/3, *MG*. Capit. I, No. 77, c. 3, 8, 10, 18, 19. See Metz, *Reichsgut*, pp. 82–83.

259. All the erudite efforts to contest the unity of the Capitulare de villis and to see in it or in its principal part an ordinance of Louis the Pious applicable only in his kingdom of Aquitaine have been in vain.

260. C. 1: . . . *villae nostrae, quas ad opus nostrum serviendi institutas habemus.*

261. See p. 25 and n. 153. C. 4 of the Capitulare de causis diversis, *ao.* 806, and c. 5–7 of the Capitulare de iustitiis faciendis, *ao.* 811, *MG*. Capit. I, Nos. 49 and 80, are particularly explicit. I quote c. 7 of the second of these capitularies: *Ut non solum beneficia episcoporum, abbatum, abbatissarum atque comitum sive vassallorum nostrorum sed etiam nostri fisci describantur, ut scire possimus quantum etiam de nostro in uniuscuiusque legatione habeamus.*

262. These were the *episcopatus* or the *abbatia*, which included lands, tithes, and churches granted by the king. They were frequently held in benefice; E. Lesne, *Histoire de la propriété ecclésiastique en France*, II, Pt. 1, 121–32.

263. Lands that constituted the benefices serving as the endowment for the comital office (see p. 29 and n. 203), and lands that constituted the benefices of royal landed vassals (see p. 51 and nn. 383–87). On this subject see Metz, *Reichsgut*, pp. 201–7.

264. *Dominici*, because they remained in the possession of the *dominus* or, in other words, because they were a part of the royal *indominicatum*.

265. *MG*. Capit. I, No. 128, c. 25 ff. On the Brevia, see Verhein, Pt. 2, "Die Brevium Exempla," *DA*, XI (1955), and Metz, *Reichsgut*, pp. 24, 26–46, 52, 78–80. On the connection between the Capitulare de villis and the Brevium exempla, Verhein, Pt. 1, pp. 378–79, Metz, pp. 78–80.

266. I have not concerned myself here with two important *polyptyques (Urbar)* describing the imperial landed estates, one for the region of the middle Rhine called the Lorsch *polyptyque (Lorscher Reichsurbar)* drawn up between 830 and 850, and the other for the Grisons

(German, *Graubünden*) and adjoining regions called the *polyptyque* of Raetia *(Churrätische Reichsurbar)* drawn up between 840 and 843, both of which are considerably later than the reign of Charlemagne. They have been edited, respectively, by K. Glöckner, *Codex Lauresh-amensis*, III (Darmstadt, 1936–63), No. 367; and E. Meyer-Marthaler and F. Perret, *Bündner Urkundenbuch*, I (Chur, 1955), Appendix, 373–96. See Metz, *Reichsgut*, pp. 53–65.

267. Metz, *Reichsgut*, pp. 11, 122–40, with a cartographic outline, p. 135. See also his "Agrarwirtschaft," pp. 497–98 (with the same outline). Aquitaine: Astronome, *Vita Hludowici*, c. 6–7, ed. G. H. Pertz, *MG. SS*. II, pp. 610–11 (=ed. R. Rau, *Quellen zur karolingischen Reichsge-schichte*, I [Berlin,1956], 268).

268. See p. 36 and n. 265.

269. P. Grierson, "The Identity of the Unnamed Fiscs in the 'Brevium exempla ad describendas res ecclesiasticas et fiscales,' " *Revue belge de Philologie et d'Histoire*, XVIII (1939), 437–61.

270. C. 19.

271. Annappes (1,156 hectares) plus Flers, which formerly had been made a part of it (907 hectares); *mansioniles*—Gruson appears only under its own name; the two others are identified (Wattiesart is a hamlet of Seclin). Cysoing (1,351 hectares) plus Bouvines and Louvil, which were a part of it (268 and 248 hectares, respectively). Somain-en-Ostrevant (987 hectares) plus Rieulay and Villers Campeau, which were a part of it (174 and 245 hectares, respectively); the total, 1,406 hectares, is quite close to the 1,368 hectares that are obtained from information in a charter of 868/69 (I. de Coussemaker, *Cartulaire de l'abbaye de Cysoing* [Lille, 1886], I, No. 3). Vitry-en-Artois, see the text. The numbers are those of the actual communes that reproduce those of the ancient parishes, which, it is generally agreed, correspond roughly to the extent of the ancient large domains of the kings or the church. This is, nevertheless, only a simple probability, and I use these figures only to give an idea of the size. There could indeed be on the land some landed estates belonging to other proprietors (see Metz, *Reichsgut*, pp. 189–93); this was probably the case at Somain-en-Ostrevant.

272. Brevium exempla, before c. 25 ff.: *De ministerio illius maioris vel ceterorum*. On all of this, Verhein, Pt. 2, pp. 359–66; Metz, *Reichsgut*, pp. 95–96, 111–19, 155–62, "Agrarwirtschaft," pp. 490, 495–96.

273. C. 36. *Treola* is also called *fiscus dominicus*. Identification: J. Vannérus, "Une énigme toponymique: 'Treola,' " *Bulletin de la Commis-sion Royale de Toponymie et de Dialectologie*, XXII (1948). Just as many ecclesiastical establishments had acquired vineyards in wine-producing regions, the administrators of *fisci* attached to them domains

in the same regions in order to have at their disposal more and especially better wine than that produced in the north and northwest of Gaul. See H. van Werveke, "Comment les établissements religieux se procuraient-ils du vin au moyen âge," *Revue belge de Philologie et d'Histoire*, II (1923). See also Verhein, Pt. 2, pp. 361–63; Metz, *Reichsgut*, pp. 156–57.

274. Diploma of Louis the Pious, *ao.* 817, *Recueil des historiens des Gaules et de la France*, VI, 509; explained by a charter of Count Hilduin, *ais.* 879–98, C. Duvivier, *Actes et documents anciens intéressant la Belgique*, I (Brussels, 1898), No. 1, and by a diploma of Charles the Simple, *ao.* 898, P. Lauer, *Actes de Charles III le Simple* (Paris, 1940), No. 2. See H. Pirenne, "Le fisc royal de Tournai," in *Mélanges d'histoire du moyen âge offerts à M. Ferdinand Lot* (Paris, 1925).

275. The *fiscus* very likely included the town of Tournai (left bank) and the adjacent commune of Orcq as well as the dependent domain of Marquain, a true *mansionilis* (Belgium, Hainaut, arrondissement of Tournai). But two parts of the *fiscus* had been granted in benefice to a royal vassal and to the count, respectively; later, these two parts, along with another part, were given to the church of Tournai. Although very close to each other the *ministerium* of Annappes and the *fiscus* of Tournai do not appear to have been under a common authority.

276. For example, from the charter of 868/69 briefly describing the landed elements of the *fiscus* of Somain; see n. 271.

277. On the *fiscus* of Theux and its woods, see the diploma of Louis the Pious and Lothair of 25 May 827, J. Halkin and C. G. Roland, *Recueil des chartes de l'abbaye de Stavelot-Malmedy*, I (Brussels, 1909), No. 29; it is valid for the reign of Charlemagne. It is evident from later diplomas that at least an important part of the *silvae* was a *forestis*, notably from a diploma of Charles the Simple, *ao.* 915, ed. Lauer (see n. 274), No. 81. The meaning of *forestis* appears clearly in the Capitulare de villis, c. 36. See the important works of C. Petit-Dutaillis, "De la signification du mot 'forêt' à l'époque franque," *Bibliothèque de l'Ecole des Chartes*, LXXVI (1915); and E. Fairon, "Les donations de forêts aux Xe et XIe siècles en Lotharingie et en Allemagne," *Revue belge de Philologie et d'Histoire*, IV (1925) (=*Miscellanées historiques* by the same author [Liège, 1945], pp. 123 ff.). For the *forestarii*, Capitulare Aquisgranense of 802/3, c. 18 (see n. 258).

278. Capitulare de villis; the *iudex* has been cited so frequently that it is not necessary to note the articles where he appears. *Actor:* Capitulare de disciplina palatii Aquisgranensis, dating, I believe, from the beginning of the reign of Louis the Pious, c. 2, *MG. Capit.* I, No. 146; Diplomas of Louis the Pious and Lothair, *ao.* 827, see n. 277 (the *actor* Alberic evidently had, under Charlemagne, a predecessor with the same

title), and of Louis the Pious of 8 January 823, Migne, *Patrologia Latina*, CIV, col. 1107 (report of facts dating from the reign of Charlemagne). For the titles of the stewards see also Metz, *Reichsgut*, pp. 144–55 (in a broader chronological framework).

279. See n. 272. Probably each of the *fisci* described in the Brevium exempla was administered by a *maior*, but that of Annappes had some authority over the other *maiores*.

280. Capitulare de villis, c. 10, 26, 36, 60.

281. Capitulare Aquisgranense, *ao.* 802/3, c. 19 (see n. 258). In this source are attributed to the *villicus* tasks and powers that in the Capitulare de villis are attributed to the *iudex*.

282. In addition to the two capitularies cited in n. 261, see the capitulary cited in n. 281, the same article, and what is said on p. 36 concerning the origin of the Brevium exempla, c. 25 ff. See also Metz, *Reichsgut*, pp. 17–18.

283. See p. 19 and nn. 105 (Capitulare de villis, c. 16 and 47), 106, and 107. Add the *De ordine palatii* (see n. 97), c. 23 (ed. Krause, p. 525, ed. Prou, pp. 58–61), where there is a discussion of the role of the seneschal, the butler, and the constable. See also Metz, *Reichsgut*, p. 12.

284. See p. 19 and n. 108. Count Richard demonstrated what he was capable of by the establishment in 787 of an inventory of the possessions of the abbey of Saint-Wandrille, and in 794 by the restoration of the royal landed patrimony in Aquitaine, which had suffered numerous usurpations; *Gesta sanctorum patrum Fontanellensis coenobii*, ed. F. Lohier and J. Laporte (Rouen, 1936), XI, Pt. 3, 82–83; and Astronome, *Vita Hludowici*, c. 7 (see n. 267).

285. Verhein, Pt. 1, pp. 386–87.

286. Capitulare de villis, c. 30, c. 32, c. 31, c. 33. See (also for n. 287) Metz, *Reichsgut*, pp. 79–80, and especially (also for nn. 287 and 289) M. Bloch, "La Organización de los dominios reales carolingios y las teorias de Dopsch," *Anuario de historia del derecho español* (1926).

287. Capitulare de villis, c. 55.

288. *Ibid.*, c. 28.

289. *Ibid.*, c. 44 and 62.

290. Brevium exempla, c. 25, 30–35. See Metz, *Reichsgut*, pp. 53, 79–80.

291. See n. 284.

292. Astronome, *Vita Hludowici* (see n. 267), c. 6 and 7.

293. For what precedes, notably for the notion of *Winterpfalz* and for some examples, P. Classen, "Bemerkungen zur Pfalzenforschung am Mittelrhein," in *Deutsche Königspfalzen*, I (Göttingen, 1965), 75–78.

294. Metz, *Reichsgut*, pp. 12, 127–28; especially Classen, pp. 77–79, and particularly p. 78. In the sense of what is said in the text, an important passage of Hincmar, *De ordine palatii*, quoting very probably a writing

of Adalard (see above, n. 97), c. 23, ed. Krause, p. 525, ed. Prou, pp. 58–61.

295. This possibility, and no more, is suggested by the articles of the Capitulare de villis that prescribe to the *iudex* certain tasks and certain deliveries *quando servierit* (c. 23, 24, 39, 59, 61).

296. Classen, p. 77.

297. This is only a hypothesis; it does not exclude the support of the king by the ecclesiastical establishment itself for a brief time. For these sojourns: C. Brühl, "Königspfalz und Bischofsstadt in fränkischer Zeit," *Rheinische Vierteljahrsblätter*, XXIII (1958).

298. See the chapter of W. Metz cited in n. 98.

299. The study of money departs from the framework of this work; one should refer to the remarkable chapter of P. Grierson, "Money and Coinage under Charlemagne," in *Karl der Grosse*, I, 501–36. I limit myself to some very general information on coinage as an institution.

300. It is necessary to add the *obolus*, or the half-penny, and the quarter-penny. Let us recall the existence of two moneys in name only: the shilling, worth 12 pennies; and the pound, worth 20 shillings, or 240 pennies.

301. The excellent account of Grierson, pp. 511–27.

302. Capitulare missorum of Thionville, *ao.* 805, c. 18, and Capitula cum primis constituta, *ao.* 808, c. 7, *MG.* Capit. I, Nos. 44 and 53. This disposition, it seems to me, ought to be interpreted as "in one of our *palatia*."

303. Capitulary published at the end of the synod of Frankfurt, *ao.* 794, c. 5; Capitulare missorum Aquisgranense alterum, *ao.* 809, c. 7: *MG.* Capit. I, Nos. 28 and 63. In addition, Capitulare missorum of Thionville and Capitula cum primis constituta, cited in n. 302, c. 18, *in fine*, and c. 7, *in fine*, respectively.

304. See the words *fredus* or *Friedensgeld* in the index of the *Lex Salica (Pactus Legis Salicae*, ed. K. A. Eckhardt, II, Pt. 1 and 2 [Göttingen, 1955/56] =edition done by the same scholar in the *MG.* Leges nationum Germanicarum IV, Pt. I; the references permit one easily to find in such a case the corresponding passages from the Karolina), of the *Lex Ribuaria* (ed. F. Beyerle and R. Buchner, *MG.* Leges nationum Germanicarum III, Pt. 2), of the *Lex Alamannorum* (ed. K. A. Eckhardt; see above, n. 238), of the *Lex Baiuuariorum* (ed. E. von Schwind and E. Heymann, *MG.* Leges nationum Germanicarum V, Pt. 2), etc.

305. Capitulare de villis, *ais.* 771–800, c. 4; Capitulare missorum Aquisgranense primum, *ao.* 810, c. 15; Capitula de missorum officiis, *ao.* 810; Capitulare de iustitiis faciendis, *ao.* 811, c. 10: *MG.* Capit. I, Nos. 32, 64, 66, 80.

306. See the *leges* cited in n. 304 and the texts cited above, n. 202.

307. Capitulare legibus additum, *ao.* 803, c. 7, *MG.* Capit. I, No. 39.

308. See pp. 11–12 and nn. 54, 55, 56.

309. Capitulare Aquisgranense, *ais.* 802/3, c. 6; Capitulare missorum of Thionville, *ao.* 805, c. 19; Capitulare missorum de exercitu promovendo, *ao.* 808, c. 1 and 2; Capitulare missorum Aquisgranense primum, *ao.* 810, c. 12; Capitulare de missorum officiis, *ao.* 810, c. 4; Capitulare Bononiense, *ao.* 811, c. 1: *MG.* Capit. I, Nos. 77, 44, 50, 64, 66, 74.

310. Capitulare Bononiense, *ao.* 811, c. 2, *MG.* Capit. I, No. 74.

311. Insolvent debtors: they will pledge themselves as serfs until payment; Capitulary of Herstal, *ao.* 779, c. 19; Capitulare missorum Aquisgranense primum, *ao.* 810, c. 12; Capitulare Bononiense, *ao.* 811, c. 1; Capitula Karoli apud Ansegisum servata, c. 3: *MG.* Capit. I, Nos. 20, 64, 74, 70. Remission of the *bannum*: Programmatic Capitulary of 802, c. 29, No. 33.

312. Capitulare missorum of Thionville, *ao.* 805, c. 19, No. 44: the fine of £3 (=sixty shillings) was able to be reduced to thirty shillings, ten shillings, and five shillings in proportion to the personal wealth of the individual.

313. Text cited in the preceding note and c. 2 of the Capitulary of Boulogne (see n. 310).

314. This was notably the case with the estates of those who had taken part in the conspiracies against Charlemagne, those of Hardrad and Thuringian aristocrats in 785 and that of Pepin the Hunchback in 792: Annales Nazariani, *ao.* 786, ed. G. H. Pertz, *MG.* SS. I, p. 43; Annales Laureshamenses, *ao.* 792, *ibid.*, p. 35. See also DKar., No. 181, *ao.* 797 (restitution of the estates after confiscation, when the person involved had proved his innocence).

315. Annales Regni Francorum, *ais.* 779 (the two texts), 787, 793 (1st text), 797, 798, 799 (the two texts), 801, 802, 807, pp. 52–54, 74, 94, 102–3, 102–5, 108–9, 115–16, 117, 123–24. See my study, "Les relations extérieures de la monarchie franque" (see n. 209), pp. 37–39.

316. See p. 14. Programmatic Capitulary of 802, c. 8, *MG.* Capit. I, No. 33.

317. Capitulary of Aachen, *ais.* 802/3, c. 6; Capitulare missorum of Thionville, *ao.* 805, c. 20; Capitulare de iustitiis faciendis, *ao.* 811, c. 10 and 11: *MG.* Capit. I, Nos. 77, 44, 80.

318. As F. Lot maintained in his *L'impôt foncier et la capitation personnelle sous le Bas-Empire et à l'époque franque* (Paris, 1928), pp. 107, 114–15.

319. A very simplified résumé of the views of Th. Mayer, "Königtum und Gemeinfreiheit im frühen Mittelalter," *DA,* VI (1943); in the collection of Mayer's works, *Mittelalterliche Studien* (Lindau and Constance,

1959); "Die Königsfreien und der Staat des frühen Mittelalters," in *Das Problem der Freiheit. Vorträge und Forschungen*, ed. Th. Mayer, II (Lindau and Constance, 1955); H. Dannenbauer, "Hundertschaft, Centena und Huntari," *Historisches Jahrbuch*, LXIII/LXIX (1949); in the collection of Dannenbauer's articles, *Grundlagen der mittelalterlichen Welt* (Stuttgart, 1958); and "Freigrafschaften und Freigerichte," in *Das Problem der Freiheit*.

320. See F. Lot, "Un grand domaine à l'époque franque, Ardin en Poitou," in *Cinquantenaire de l'Ecole Pratique des Hautes Etudes. Mélanges* (Paris, 1921).

321. Karoli ad Fulradum abbatem epistola, *ao*. 806; Memoratorium de exercitu in Gallia Occidentali praeparando, *ao*. 807, c. 3; Capitula omnibus cognita facienda, *ais*. 802-13, c. 5: *MG*. Capit. I, Nos. 75, 48, 57. Hincmar, *De ordine palatii*, c. 29, ed. Krause, p. 527 (=ed. Prou, p. 74); probably according to Adalard.

322. Capitulary of Aachen, *ais*. 802/3, c. 5 and 6, *MG*. Capit. I, No. 77.

323. As all the contemporary texts related to the toll, such as the capitularies, diplomas, and narratives, indicate. One will find a good number of these texts in my study, "A propos du tonlieu à l'époque carolingienne" (see n. 202). I cite here as particularly clear c. 13 of the Capitulare missorum of Thionville, *ao*. 805, Capit. I, No. 44: *De teloneis placet nobis ut antiqua et iusta telonea a negotiatoribus exigantur, tam de pontibus quam et de navigiis seu mercatis . . .* The texts from the time of Louis the Pious are even more explicit.

324. Capitulare missorum of Thionville, c. 13 (see the preceding note), the rest of the article; also exempted are the commodities transported by those who go to the palace or to the army and who return from those places.

325. This appears notably in diplomas granting or confirming privileges (see nn. 346-47) and in the dispositions of capitularies containing the conditions for the legitimate collection of the toll (see below, nn. 327-28).

326. The competence of the count results chiefly from his presence in the address of the diplomas concerned with privileges related to the toll. Examples for the reign of Charlemagne: Cartae Senonicae, No. 36, *ais*. 768-75, *MG*. Formulae, pp. 201-2; *MG*. DDKar., No. 122, *ao*. 779 (=Poupardin, *Recueil des Chartes de . . . Saint-Germain-des-Prés*, I, No. XIX), No. 192, *ao*. 800. The *telonearii* appear as the collectors of the toll in an account of the *Miracula Sancti Benedicti;* they will be discussed later, n. 331. The right of the count and, if it was the case, of subordinate officers to receive for themselves a certain portion of the toll results, I believe, from the terms of a diploma for Saint-Denis granted by Pepin

III, *ao.* 753; there, it is said that normally the proceeds from the toll *ad parte nostra seu et ad omnes agentes nostros potuerat sperare,* DKar., No. 6, p. 10, ll. 37–38. It is hardly possible that the rule had changed.

327. Capitulary of Herstal, *ao.* 779, c. 18; Capitulare missorum of Thionville, *ao.* 805, c. 13; Capitulare missorum of Nijmegen, *ao.* 806, c. 10; Capitula omnibus cognita facienda, *ais.* 802-13, c. 7 (texts from various mss.); Responsa cuidam misso data, *ais.* 802-13, c. 6: *MG.* Capit. I, Nos. 20, 44, 46, 57, 58.

328. Capitulare missorum of Thionville (see the preceding note), c. 13: *. . . nova vero seu iniusta . . . in quibus nullum adiutorium iterantibus praestatur . . . ut non exigantur.* Such also appears to be the sense of c. 7 of the Capitula omnibus cognita facienda (see preceding note), where the existence of a bridge and of a passage of water are sufficient conditions for legitimate collection of the toll.

329. Dispositions of a lost diploma of Charlemagne for the church of Strasbourg, which are contained in a diploma of confirmation coming from Louis the Pious, *ao.* 831, W. Wiegand, *Urkundenbuch der Stadt Strassburg,* I (Strasbourg, 1879), No. 23. Gervold, abbot of Saint-Wandrille, *procurator,* in *Gesta Sanctorum Patrum Fontanellensis Coenobii,* XII, *Gesta Gervoldi,* c. 2, ed. F. Lohier and J. Laporte, pp. 86–87.

330. See pp. 46–47.

331. In Adrevald, *Miracula Sancti Benedicti,* c. 19, ed. O. Holder-Egger, *MG.* SS. XV, Pt. 1, p. 487 (=E. de Certain, *Les miracles de Saint-Benoît,* I, c. 19, pp. 46–47), there is a lively and picturesque account of the violation of privileges to the detriment of the abbey of Fleury (Saint-Benoît-sur-Loire) by the toll collectors of the count of Orléans at the time of Charlemagne.

332. This is proved by the capitularies and the diplomas related to the toll.

333. Notice of 811 relating to the division of the chattels in the fortune of Charlemagne, in Einhard, *Vita Karoli,* c. 33, ed. Holder-Egger, pp. 37–41. With this, one is able to compare the similar division of Louis the Pious, in Astronome, *Vita Hludowici,* c. 63, *MG.* SS. II, p. 647. See my "Note sur le 'Praeceptum Negotiatorum' de Louis le Pieux," in *Studi in onore di Armando Sapori,* I (Milan, 1957).

334. See p. 19.

335. For the presents that the ambassadors offered to the chiefs of state to whom they presented themselves, see my study cited above, n. 209, p. 39.

336. See, for example, how the major part of the treasures of the Avars, which came into the royal treasury in 796, was distributed, Annales Regni Francorum, *ao.* 796, pp. 98–99.

337. Formulae Bituricenses, No. 14, *MG*. Formulae, p. 174: a woman who was under the royal protection begged Charlemagne to protect her from the results of an arbitrary action that had deprived her of her estates. Concession of the privilege of protection to physical persons: Cartae Senonicae, No. 28, *MG*. Formulae, p. 197; DKar., No. 69, *ao*. 772.

338. DDKar., Nos. 72, 89, 173, *ais*. 772, 775, 792.

339. *Ibid.*, Nos. 62, 70 (=C. Wampach, *Geschichte der Grundherrschaft Echternach*, I, Pt. 2 [Luxembourg, 1930], No. 68, pp. 132–33), 128, 178, *ais*. 771, 771/72, 779, 794. The first three are actually confirmations for Saint-Calais and Echternach; the last is a concession to Caunes. Recommendation of the protected: Cartae Senonicae, No. 28; of the abbot: DDKar., Nos. 72, 178. In some of the cases noted here and in n. 338, the concession or the confirmation of the *mundeburdis* accompanied that of other privileges (privileges of ecclesiastical order or immunity) or even a landed donation.

340. The clause of prohibition appears in Cartae Senonicae, No. 28, DDKar., Nos. 69, 72, 178; it is implied by Formulae Bituricenses, No. 14. See pp. 11–12 and nn. 50–51.

341. Cartae Senonicae, No. 28, DDKar., Nos. 62, 69, 128, 178.

342. See pp. 11–12; see also the Programmatic Capitulary of 802, c. 30, as well as the Capitulare missorum of 802, c. 15 (=W. A. Eckhardt, "Capitularia" [see n. 21], c. 15–16, p. 502), and the collection of *capitula* for the *missi* of 806, c. 54 (=W. A. Eckhardt, *Kapitulariensammlung* [see n. 50], No. LIX, c. 27, p. 85): *MG*. Capit. I, Nos. 33, 34, 35.

343. Capitulare Aquisgranense, *ais*. 802/3, c. 2, *MG*. Capit. I, No. 77. In lieu of the palace court the competence of the *missi* was recognized.

344. See the discussion on pp. 43–45, as well as my study cited in n. 202 and R. Doehaerd, "Exemption d'impôts indirects et circulation privilégiée en Europe Occidentale pendant le haut moyen âge," in *Hommage à Lucien Febvre*, II (Paris, 1953).

345. Confirmation of the cession to Saint-Denis of the toll in the *pagus* of Paris during the fair of October, *ais*. 774/75, DKar., No. 88. Cession to Saint-Germain-des-Prés of the bureau of the toll at Villeneuve-Saint-Georges, *ao*. 779, DKar., No. 122 (=Poupardin [see above, n. 326], No. XIX). Cession to the church of Orléans of half of the toll in the *pagus* of Orléans, from a diploma of Louis the Pious, *ao*. 814, Formulae Imperiales, No. 19, *MG*. Formulae, p. 300. Confirmation to the church of Utrecht of the tithe of the toll at Utrecht and perhaps at Duurstede, from a diploma of Louis the Pious, *ao*. 815, M. Gijsseling and A. C. F. Koch, *Diplomata Belgica ante annum millesimum centesimum scripta* (Brussels, 1950), No. 179. Cession to Flavigny of the toll in its domains, *ao*. 775, DKar., No. 96.

346. Saint-Denis, *ao.* 775, confirmation, DKar., No. 93. Flavigny, *ao.* 775, DKar., No. 96. Saint-Germain-des-Prés, *ao.* 779, confirmation, DKar., No. 122 (=Poupardin, No. XIX). Honau, *ao.* 781, DKar., No. 137. The following concessions and confirmations are only known by some diplomas of confirmation of Louis the Pious: Echternach, *ao.* 819, Wampach (see n. 339), No. 138, pp. 204–6. Jumièges, *ais.* 814/15, confirmation, Formulae Imperiales, No. 24, *MG.* Formulae, pp. 303–4 (=J. J. Vernier, *Chartes de l'abbaye de Jumièges,* I [Rouen, 1916], No. 1). Murbach, *ao.* 816, *Recueil des historiens des Gaules et de la France,* VI, 494, No. 55, Paris, *ao.* 814, R. de Lasteyrie, *Cartulaire général de Paris,* I (Paris, 1887), No. 30. Saint-Martin de Tours (on land), *ao.* 816, *Recueil des historiens des Gaules,* VI, 508, No. 55. General exemption except for the bureaus of Duurstede, Quentowic, and the *clusae:* church of Strasbourg, see above, n. 329.

347. Exemption limited to a certain number of boats: Saint-Paul-de-Cormery, *ao.* 800, 2b, DKar., No. 192. All the other concessions and confirmations are known by some diplomas of later confirmation: Church of Angers, 3b, Louis the Pious, *ao.* 816, *Recueil des historiens des Gaules,* VI, 496, No. 59. Fleury (Saint-Benoît-sur-Loire), 4b, and total exemption on land, confirmation, Louis the Pious, *ao.* 818, Prou and Vidier, *Recueil des Chartes de . . . Saint-Benoît-sur-Loire,* I, No. 15, and the account of the *Miracula Sancti Benedicti* (see above, n. 331). Saint-Germain d'Auxerre, 4b, confirmation of Louis the Pious, *ao.* 816, *Recueil des historiens des Gaules,* VI, 488, No. 45. Saint-Martin of Tours, 12b, Louis the Pious, *ao.* 816, E. Mühlbacher, "Unedierte Diplome, III, No. 2," *Mitteilungen des Instituts für Österreichische Geschichtsforschung,* VII (1886), 438–39. Saint-Philibert of Noirmoutier, 6b, Pepin I of Aquitaine, *ao.* 826, L. Levillain, *Actes de Pépin I et de Pépin II, rois d'Aquitaine* (Paris, 1926), No. 6. On the diplomas of exemption, see G. Tessier, *Diplomatique royale française* (Paris, 1962), p. 66, and my study, cited in n. 202, pp. 501–2.

348. Cartae Senonicae, No. 36, *MG.* Formulae, pp. 201–2.

349. Privilege for pilgrims: Charlemagne confirmed the validity as well as the limitations in a letter to Offa, king of Mercia, *ao.* 796, *MG.* Epp. IV, No. 10, p. 145.

350. Judicious observations of L. Levillain, *Etudes sur l'abbaye de Saint-Denis à l'époque mérovingienne,* IV, *Les documents d'histoire économique. Bibliothèque de l'Ecole des Chartes,* XCI (1930). They are also valid for the Carolingian epoch.

351. See in particular the discussions of M. Kroell, *L'immunité franque* (Paris, 1910); Brunner and von Schwerin (see n. 1), pp. 382–415, and my study, "L'immunité dans la monarchie franque," in *Les liens de vas-*

salité et les immunités, Recueils de la Société Jean Bodin, I (2nd ed.; Brussels, 1958). The remarkable work of E. E. Stengel, *Die Immunität in Deutschland bis zum Ende des 11. Jahrhunderts,* I (Innsbruck, 1910), is especially important for the period after Charlemagne.

352. All the diplomas of Charlemagne preserved in the original give *emunitas;* the classical form *immunitas* only appears in copies.

353. DDKar., No. 73, Lorsch, *ao.* 773; No. 82, *id., ao.* 774; No. 87, Saint-Denis, *ao.* 774. See also Nos. 23-26 in Formulae Marculfinae aevi Carolini (corresponding to Nos. 14-17 of Marculf, I), *MG.* Formulae, pp. 123-24.

354. Concessions: DDKar., No. 60, Saint-Etienne d'Angers, *ao.* 770; No. 67, Lorsch, *ao.* 772; No. 74, Novalese, *ao.* 773; No. 85, Fulda, *ao.* 774; No. 108, Prüm, *ao.* 775; No. 152, Ansbach, *ao.* 786; No. 163, Saint-Victor of Marseilles, *ao.* 790; No. 173, Aniane, *ao.* 792; No. 194, Charroux, *ais.* 785-800. Confirmations: DDKar., No. 57, Corbie, *ao.* 769; No. 59, Saint-Bertin, *ao.* 769; No. 61, Saint-Maur-des-Fossés, *ao.* 771; No. 62, Saint-Calais, *ao.* 771; No. 64, Murbach, *ao.* 772; No. 66, Trèves, *ao.* 772; No. 68, Saint-Mihiel, *ao.* 772; No. 70, Echternach, *ais.* 771/72; No. 71, Saint-Germain-des-Prés, *ao.* 772; No. 75, Saint-Médard de Soissons, *ais.* 769-74; No. 91, Metz, *ao.* 775; No. 94, Saint-Denis, *ao.* 775; No. 119, Honau, *ao.* 778; No. 120, Saint-Denis, *ao.* 778; No. 123, Saint-Marcel-lez-Chalon, *ao.* 779; No. 125, Novalese, *ao.* 779; No. 128, Saint-Calais, *ao.* 779; No. 141, Saint-Martin de Tours, *ao.* 782; No. 193, Paris, *ais.* 774-800; No. 195, Saint-Martin de Tours, *ao.* 800; No. 210, Ebersheim, *ao.* 810. For the diplomas of concession or of confirmation of immunity, see Tessier, *Diplomatique royale française* (above, n. 347), pp. 63-66, and my study cited in n. 351, pp. 193-98.

355. The only trace of it is the appearance of the formulas 23 and 26 in the Formulae Marculfinae aevi Carolini (corresponding to Marculf, I, Nos. 14, 17), *MG.* Formulae, pp. 123-24; they concern the king's donation of an estate with the privilege of immunity to an *inluster vir.* The privileged status granted in 844 by Charles the Bald to the Spanish refugees in Septimania and in the future Spanish march constitutes an immunity *sui generis: MG.* Capit. II, No. 256, particularly the prooemium (=G. Tessier, *Actes de Charles II le Chauve,* I [Paris, 1943], No. 46). D'Abadal, *Catalunya Carolingia,* II, Pt. 2, Introduction, 399-403, edition, No. V, pp. 422-25, believes that the parts of this capitulary bearing upon this subject come from a lost capitulary of Charlemagne (reconstituted, No. II, pp. 415-16): if this was the case, this immunity *sui generis* in favor of laymen should also be mentioned here.

356. The diplomas cited in n. 354 supply all the necessary examples.

357. See pp. 41-42.

358. See, for example, the diplomas for Saint-Maur-des-Fossés, *ao.* 771;

for Trèves, *ao.* 772; Saint-Médard de Soissons, *ais.* 769–74; Metz, *ao.* 775; Saint-Martin de Tours, *ao.* 782; cited above in n. 354. On this problem see my study cited in n. 351, p. 197, n. 76.

359. The expressions *perennis temporibus, nostris et futuris temporibus* in the diplomas indicate this. When the abbot is mentioned as beneficiary along with his abbey it is said frequently that the favor accorded is also valid for his successors. The renewals do not contradict this statement. They constitute an extra precaution often taken in the Middle Ages.

360. Capitulary of Herstal, *ao.* 779, c. 9, *MG.* Capit. I, No. 20.

361. Capitulare legibus additum, *ao.* 803, c. 2, *MG.* Capit. I, No. 39. The Capitulare de latronibus, *ao.* 804, c. 5, *ibid.*, No. 82, confers to the *missi* powers comparable to those of the counts, but requires imperial authorization for their entry into a territory of immunity.

362. One first meets this fine in some diplomas of immunity granted to a few churches: Saint-Marcel-lez-Chalon, *ao.* 779; Saint-Martin de Tours, *ais.* 782 and 800 (see n. 354). In 803 this appears in c. 2 of the Capitulare legibus additum (see n. 361): . . . *sicut ille qui in emunitatem damnum fecit DC solidos conponere debuit* . . . Louis the Pious limited the scope of this sanction.

363. It is not always easy or even possible in the *notitiae* of judgment to know if one is dealing with an *advocatus ad hoc* or with an *advocatus* who is permanent.

364. Capitula incerti anni, *ais.* 806–13, c. 5 *(a contrario)*, *MG.* Capit. I, No. 86.

365. In the *Capitulare missorum* of these years (*MG.* Capit. I, No. 25) dealing with the swearing of the oath of fidelity, the *advocati* are cited in c. 4 with the *vicarii* and the *centenarii*, which seems to imply a permanent character and an official function.

366. According to the Capitulare missorum Aquisgranense primum, *ao.* 809, c. 22, *MG.* Capit. I, No. 62, the advocates appear to have been named like the *centenarii* and the *scabini* by the count in the presence of the important men (see p. 32 and n. 234); the Programmatic Capitulary of 802, c. 13, *ibid.*, No. 33, supposes an influence exercised by the bishop or abbot having immunity on the nomination of advocates. On the virtues that an advocate ought to have, see in addition to the article of the Programmatic Capitulary: Capitulare missorum of 802, c. 18a (=W. A. Eckhardt, "Capitularia," p. 503, c. 18a and XX); Capitulare Aquisgranense, *ais.* 802/3, c. 14; Capitulare missorum of Thionville, *ao.* 805, c. 12; Capitulare Aquisgranense, *ao.* 809, c. 11; Capitulare missorum Aquisgranense primum, *ao.* 809, c. 22: *MG.* Capit. I, Nos. 34, 77, 44, 61, 62. On the landed estates of the advocates see Capitulare Aquisgranense, *ais.* 802/3, c. 14 (see above).

367. Capitulare missorum, *ao.* 803, c. 3; Capitulare missorum of Thionville, *ao.* 805, c. 12: *MG.* Capit. I, Nos. 40 and 44.

368. It is with them that they are cited in a series of capitularies: Capitulare missorum, *ais.* 792/93, c. 4; Capitulare Aquisgranense, *ao.* 809, c. 11; Capitulare missorum Aquisgranense primum, *ao.* 809, c. 22; see above, nn. 365–66.

369. Capitulare Aquisgranense, *ao.* 809, c. 11, see above, n. 366.

370. These judicial functions explain why it was thought necessary for the advocates to be *legem scientes et iustitiam diligentes . . . iustum semper iudicium in omnibus exercentes* (Programmatic Capitulary of 802, c. 13), that they *habeant voluntatem recte et iuste causas perficere* (Capitulary of Aachen, *ais.* 802/3, c. 14), that they *sciant et velint iuste causas discernere et terminare* (Capitulare missorum of Thionville, *ao.* 805, c. 12); see n. 366.

371. The *audientiae privatae* of the immunists are cited in the diplomas for Trèves and for Metz, DDKar., Nos. 66 and 91.

372. This seems to be implied by the concession of *fredus* to the immunist; if a part of the competence of the *mallus* is never transferred to the court of the immunist, it is impossible to see why the matter of *fredus* would be a question.

373. The assimilation of the advocate with the *vicarii* or *centenarii* (see n. 368), who were not able to preside over the *mallus* when such cases had to be judged, supports this position. See Part III.

374. Capitulare missorum of Thionville, *ao.* 805, c. 12; Capitulare missorum de exercitu promovendo, *ao.* 808, c. 10; Capitula de causis cum episcopis et abbatibus tractandis, *ao.* 811, c. 6: *MG.* Capit. I, Nos. 44, 50, 72.

375. See the important work of H. Mitteis, *Lehnrecht und Staatsgewalt* (Weimar, 1933), or my volume *Qu'est-ce que la féodalité?* (3rd ed.; Brussels, 1957); 2nd German edition trans. by R. and D. Groh, rev. by the author: *Was ist das Lehnswesen?* (Darmstadt, 1967); 3rd English ed. trans. by P. Grierson, rev. by the author: *Feudalism* (London, 1964).

376. See my studies, "Benefice and Vassalage in the Age of Charlemagne," *The Cambridge Historical Journal*, VI (1939); and "Das Lehnswesen im fränkischen Reich. Lehnswesen und Reichsgewalt in karolingischer Zeit," in *Studien zum mittelalterlichen Lehnswesen, Vorträge und Forschungen*, V, ed. Th. Mayer (Lindau and Constance, 1960).

377. This appears, among other places, in the Capitulare missorum of 792/93 regulating the swearing of the oath of fidelity to the king, *MG.* Capit. I, No. 25: while the royal vassals, like the bishops, abbots, and counts, swore the oath with their hands placed between those of the

missi, all the other vassals, like the advocates, *vicarii*, and *centenarii*, swore the oath with their hands between those of the counts.

378. Palace court: *placitum* of 772, DKar., No. 65; it is likely that in the other *placita* preserved from the reign of Charlemagne, the judgment-finders who are cited after the counts, and are not otherwise designated, were royal vassals. Judicial assizes of the *missi: notitia* of a judgment handed down in a plea at Narbonne, *ao.* 782, Devic and Vaissete, *Histoire générale de Languedoc*, ed. Privat, II, Preuves, No. 6 (V), cols. 47–50.

379. Stengel, *Urkundenbuch des Klosters Fulda*, I, No. 83, *ao.* 777.

380. See p. 21 and nn. 118 and 167.

381. Itinerant up to the time when Aachen became the usual residence of Charlemagne; see p. 18.

382. See p. 21 and n. 118.

383. The distinction is already clearly made in the Capitulary of Herstal, *ao.* 779, c. 9, *MG.* Capit. I, No. 20.

384. This is perfectly rendered by an article of a constitution of Louis the Pious for the Spanish refugees of Septimania and the surrounding area, *ao.* 815, which I believe I am justified in using here. In c. 6 it is said: *et si beneficium aliquod quisquam eorum ab eo cui se commendavit fuerit consecutus, sciat se de illo tale obsequium seniori suo exhibere debere, quale nostrates homines de simili beneficio senioribus suis exhibere solent; MG.* Capit. I, No. 132, p. 262 (=d'Abadal [see n. 355], II, Appendix III).

385. For example: in Aquitaine, Astronome, *Vita Hludowici*, c. 3, *MG.* SS. II, p. 608; in Bavaria, Annales Regni Francorum, *ao.* 788, 1st text, p. 80. For the same phenomenon in Italy: P. S. Leicht, "Gasindi e Vassalli," *Rendiconti della Classe di Scienze morali, storiche e filologiche* (R. Accademia Nazionale dei Lincei, 1927); and Leicht, "Il feudo in Italia nell'età carolingia," in *I problemi della civiltà carolingia. Settimane di studio del Centro italiano di studi sull'alto medioevo*, I (Spoleto, 1954), 75–80; E. Hlawitschka, *Franken, Alemannen, Bayern und Burgunder in Oberitalien* (Freiburg im Breisgau, 1960), pp. 32–46.

386. This accounts for the care that he took in instructing the *missi* to make certain that benefices were neither badly cultivated nor despoiled of their inhabitants and of their equipment to the profit of the alodial lands of those who held them; see above, n. 153.

387. By c. 13 of the Capitulary of Herstal of 779 (*MG.* Capit. I, No. 20), Charlemagne uniformly regulated for all the *Regnum* the compensations due to the churches for this type of royal benefice: a rent of recognition and a double tithe; a charter of precarious tenure was intended to maintain the rights of the church. Moreover, those who held such benefices were obliged to assume the burden of support of the churches; this provision had been made for Aquitaine since the reign of

Pepin III, but appears to have been applied for the first time to all the *Regnum* in 794: Pippini Capitulare Aquitanicum, *ao.* 768, c. 1; Breviarium missorum Aquitanicum, *ao.* 789, c. 2; Synodus Franconofurtensis, *ao.* 794, c. 26: *MG.* Capit. I, Nos. 18, 24, 28 (=Werminghoff, *MG.* Concilia, No. 19, G).

388. See p. 21 and n. 119.

389. In the Capitulare episcoporum of 792/93 (*MG.* Capit. I, No. 21), there are cited some *vassi dominici* having lands containing two hundred, one hundred, fifty, or thirty dependent tenures; many of them certainly had less.

390. DKar., No. 177, *ao.* 777; Devic and Vaissete, *Histoire générale de Languedoc*, ed. Privat, II, Preuves, No. 6, *ao.* 782; DKar., No. 154, *ao.* 786; Bitterauf, *Die Traditionen des Hochstifts Freising*, I, No. 166a, p. 163, *ao.* 793.

391. Judgment-finders: Capitulare Aquisgranense, *ao.* 809, c. 5; Capitulare missorum Aquisgranense primum, *ao.* 809, c. 13 (according to the mss. of the group Paris lat. 9654 and Vatic. Palat. 582): *MG.* Capit. I, Nos. 61, 62. Police powers: Capitulare missorum de exercitu promovendo, *ao.* 808, c. 4, *ibid.*, No. 50.

392. This appears to be implied by c. 9 of the Capitulare missorum of Thionville, *ao.* 805, c. 9, *ibid.*, No. 44.

393. Capitulare missorum de exercitu promovendo, *ao.* 808, c. 4; Capitulare Bononiense, *ao.* 811, c. 7; Memoratorium de exercitu in Gallia occidentali praeparando, *ao.* 807, c. 3: *ibid.*, Nos. 50, 74, 48.

394. Capitulare missorum of Thionville, *ao.* 805, c. 6, *ibid.*, No. 44.

395. Capitula de causis diversis, *ao.* 806, c. 3, *ibid.*, No. 49.

396. Capitulare missorum of 802, c. 18a (=W. A. Eckhardt, "Capitularia," p. 503, c. XX: two *missatica* only), *MG.* Capit. I, No. 34.

397. Capitulare Aquisgranense, *ais.* 802/3, c. 20, *ibid.*, No. 77; see the discussion in the first of my studies cited above, n. 376, p. 165, n. 90. The sanction against an individual who did not respond to the appeal was the loss of his benefice.

398. This is to say that we will concern ourselves more with what the German diplomatists call *Akten* than with what they call *Urkunden*.

399. See my study, "Charlemagne et l'usage de l'écrit en matière administrative," *Le Moyen Age*, LVII (1951).

400. For example, Capitula cum primis conferenda, *ao.* 808; Capitula tractanda cum comitibus, episcopis et abbatibus; Capitula de causis cum episcopis et abbatibus tractandis, Capitula de rebus exercitalibus in placito tractanda, *ao.* 811: *MG.* Capit. I, Nos. 51, 71, 72, 73. See p. 23 and nn. 136, 137, as well as my *Recherches sur les capitulaires*, p. 12 (=*Was waren die Kapitularien?*, pp. 25–26).

401. See p. 23.

402. See above, n. 33, and my *Recherches sur les capitulaires*, pp. 18-21 *(=Was waren die Kapitularien?*, pp. 35-40, with a more extensive documentation).

403. This is particularly the case for the *capitularia missorum*, which are here listed according to the order found in Boretius, *MG.* Capit. I, and their date: No. 23, *ao.* 789; No. 24, *ao.* 789; No. 34, *ao.* 802 (better in W. A. Eckhardt, "Capitularia"); No. 40, *ao.* 803; Nos. 43-44, *ao.* 805; No. 53, *ao.* 808; No. 62, *ao.* 809; No. 64, *ao.* 810. See my *Recherches sur les capitulaires*, pp. 47-51 *(=Was waren die Kapitularien?*, pp. 77-82).

404. Capitula per episcopos et comites nota facienda, *ais.* 802-13, *MG.* Capit. I, No. 54.

405. Memoratorium missis datum ad Papam Adrianum legatis, probably *ao.* 785, *MG.* Capit. I, No. 111; instructions to Angilbert sent on a mission to Pope Leo III, *ao.* 796, Alcuini epistolae, No. 92, *MG.* Epp. IV, pp. 135-36.

406. For example: Epistola de litteris colendis, *ais.* 789/800 (copy intended for Baugulf, abbot of Fulda), *MG.* Capit. I, No. 29; older text discovered by P. Lehmann, *Fuldaër Studien*, NF., *Sitzungsberichte der Bayerischen Akademie der Wissenschaften, Philologisch-Historische Klasse* (1927), Abt. 2, excellent edition with commentary by L. Wallach, "Charlemagne's De litteris colendis and Alcuin," *Speculum*, XXVI (1951); for my position see *Recherches sur les capitulaires*, n. 173 *(=Was waren die Kapitularien?*, n. 173).

407. See p. 25 and n. 160. One of these reports has been preserved.

408. Capitulare missorum, *ais.* 792/93, *MG.* Capit. I, No. 25. See p. 13 and n. 67.

409. On these swearings of the oath, see pp. 13-14 and nn. 69-74.

410. Programmatic Capitulary of 802, c. 40, and Capitulare missorum of 803, c. 25, *MG.* Capit. I, Nos. 33 and 40.

411. In addition to the texts cited above, n. 152: Capitula a missis dominicis ad comites directa, *ao.* 806, c. 6; Responsa cuidam misso data, *ais.* 802-13, c. 5: *MG.* Capit. I, Nos. 85 and 58.

412. Capitulare missorum, *ao.* 803, c. 3, *ibid.*, No. 40.

413. The same capitulary, c. 19; *notitia* relating to the execution, apropos the Capitulare legibus additum of 803: *MG.* Capit. I, p. 112, ll. 10-21. See p. 16 and n. 88.

414. See above, n. 153. Among these texts, the most explicit, in regard to what concerns the reports, are: Capitula de causis diversis, *ao.* 806, c. 4; Capitulare de iustitiis faciendis, *ao.* 811, c. 5-7: *MG.* Capit. I, Nos. 49 and 80. One is able to get some idea of these reports from the descriptions of the ancient *fisci* of Annappes, Cysoing, Somain-en-Ostrevant,

and Vitry-en-Artois (which passed into the patrimony of Evrard of Friuli), probably drawn up at the end of Charlemagne's reign or at the beginning of the reign of Louis the Pious, Brevium exempla, *MG*. Capit. I, No. 128; on these see P. Grierson, "The Identity of the Unnamed Fiscs in the Brevium Exempla ad describendas res ecclesiasticas et fiscales," *Revue belge de Philologie et d'Histoire*, XVIII (1939).

415. Capitula per missos cognita facienda, *ais*. 805–13, c. 4, *MG*. Capit. I, No. 67.

416. Capitulare de villis, *ais*. 771–800, c. 28, 44, 55, 62, *ibid.*, No. 32. See on this subject, M. Bloch, "La organización de los dominios reales carolingios y las teorias de Dopsch," *Anuario de historia del derecho español* (1926).

417. See p. 45.

418. Capitulare Aquisgranense, *ais*. 802/3, c. 19, *in fine*, *MG*. Capit. I, No. 77.

419. Annales Regni Francorum, *ao*. 813, p. 138.

420. Capitulare missorum de exercitu promovendo, *ao*. 808, c. 8: one copy *habeat cancellarius noster* (see n. 114); the text of the Capitulary of Herstal (*ao*. 779) was probably kept there, too, without which one could not explain allusions to its dispositions in some later capitularies: *MG*. Capit. I, Nos. 50 and 20.

421. This is implied by the Capitula a missis dominicis ad comites directa, *ao*. 806, prooemium and c. 7, *ibid.*, No. 85.

422. Ansegise, abbot of Saint-Wandrille, who in 827 completed a collection of dispositions contained in the capitularies of Charlemagne, Louis the Pious, and Lothair (as coemperor), appears to have had access to the archives of the palace; but he inspected a number of capitularies obviously inferior to those which have come down to us. Text in *MG*. Capit. I, pp. 382 ff.; see my *Recherches sur les capitulaires*, pp. 69–70 (=*Was waren die Kapitularien?*, pp. 108–11).

Part II

1. In addition to the general works of G. Waitz, H. Brunner and C. von Schwerin, R. Schröder and E. von Künszberg, and H. Conrad described in the preceding part, n. 1, there is a specialized literature of real value that should be cited here: H. Conrad, *Geschichte der deutschen Wehrverfassung*, I (Munich, 1939); H. Delbrück, *Geschichte der*

Kriegskunst im Rahmen der politischen Geschichte, III (2nd ed.; Berlin, 1907); W. Erben, "Zur Geschichte des karolingischen Kriegswesens," *HZ*, CI (1908); F. Lot, *L'art militaire et les armées au moyen âge* (2 vols.; Paris, 1946); J. F. Verbruggen, "L'armée et la stratégie de Charlemagne," in *Karl der Grosse*, I, 420–36. See also my study, "A propos de la cavalerie dans les armées de Charlemagne," *Académie des Inscriptions et Belles Lettres. Comptes Rendus des séances* (1952). For a more extensive bibliography, see H. Conrad, *Deutsche Rechtsgeschichte*, I, 114.

2. There are first of all the narrative sources and above all the Annales, which are often not very explicit; there are the diplomatic sources, which have little information; and there are the archeological and iconographic sources, which should not be neglected. There are especially the capitularies and the documents related to them. They are proportionately more important because they contain, in relation to military institutions, few dispositions general and normative but numerous dispositions more concrete in respect to given situations as, for example, a specific campaign. The capitularies are valuable for information on the manner in which the instructions of the king or the emperor were executed, whether well, tolerably, badly, or not at all. For the capitularies, see the preceding part, n. 3. For the dates of the capitularies differing from those given to them by Boretius and Krause, see the table compiled by A. Verhulst in my *Recherches sur les Capitulaires*, pp. 107 ff. (=*Was waren die Kapitularien?*, pp. 161 ff.).

3. See particularly Capitulare Saxonicum, *ao.* 797, c. 1, *MG. Capit.* I, No. 27: . . . *ut de illis capitulis pro quibus Franci, si regis bannum transgressi sunt solidos sexaginta componunt . . . Hec sunt capitula: . . . et de exercitu nullus super bannum domini regis remanere praesumat.* See also the other enumerations of the six or eight most customary aims of the *bannum* on pp. 11–12 and particularly n. 50.

4. As early as 782 Charlemagne, believing, though mistakenly, that Saxony was subjugated, had gathered some Saxon troops to defend Thuringia and Saxony against the Slavs (Sorbs) from the region between the Elbe and the Saale, but the Saxons revolted against the Franks, who suffered a defeat (Annales Regni Francorum, *h. ao.* [1st text], p. 60). In 787, two years after the first real subjection of Saxony, some Saxon troops participated in the operations against the duke of Bavaria, Tassilo III; in 789, against the Wilzians; and in 791, against the Avars (*ibid., h. ais.*, pp. 78, 84, 88). In 795, two years after a general revolt, Charlemagne called up some troops from elements of the Saxon population presumed to have remained faithful (Annales Laureshamenses, *h. ao., MG. SS.* I, p. 36). In 797 military service was imposed on the Saxons in the same manner as on the Franks (see n. 3).

5. Capitula de causis diversis (=fragment of a capitulary of Nijmegen of March 806; my study, "Observations sur la date de deux documents administratifs émanant de Charlemagne," *Mitteilungen des Instituts für Österreichische Geschichtsforschung*, LXII [1954], 83–87), c. 2, MG. Capit. I, No. 49.

6. A form attested to by the text of the first *Conventus* of Meersen, Adnuntiatio Karoli, *ao.* 847, c. 5, MG. Capit. II, No. 204. The name, as well as the institution, is older.

7. It is implied by c. 18 of the Memoria Olonnae comitibus data, of Lothair I, *ais.* 822/23, MG. Capit. I, No. 158.

8. Capitulare missorum of 792/93, c. 6, MG. Capit. I, No. 25. Programmatic Capitulary of 802, c. 33, No. 33, and Capitulare missorum of the same year, c. 13/XII/XIII, ed. W. A. Eckhardt, "Die capitularia missorum specialia von 802," *DA*, XII (1956), 502 (and MG. Capit. I, No. 34, c. 13). Capitulary of Aachen, 802/3, c. 9, MG. Capit. I, No. 77. The first of these dispositions had been decreed in view of an anticipated expedition against the Avars in 793 (which did not occur); the last, in view of an expedition against the rebellious Avars; Annales Regni Francorum (rev. text), *ao.* 793, p. 93, and Annales Mettenses priores, *ao.* 803, ed. B. von Simson (Hanover, 1905), p. 90. The texts of 802 are probably dispositions of general import.

9. Capitula de causis diversis, *ao.* 806, March, c. 3; Memoratorium de exercitu in Gallia occidentali praeparando, *ao.* 807, c. 1; Capitulare missorum de exercitu promovendo, *ao.* 808, c. 1 and 5; Capitulary of Boulogne, *ao.* 811, October, c. 7; Capitulare missorum of Louis the Pious, *ais.* 818/19, c. 27: MG. Capit. I, Nos. 49, 48, 50, 74, 141. These dispositions were decreed, respectively, for the following occasions: a campaign undertaken against the Sorbs in 806 after various objectives had been considered; a campaign probably planned against the Slavic populations in 807 (a campaign that did not occur); a campaign against the Danes, the Linones, and the *Smeldingi* in 808; perhaps an expedition to be undertaken in 812 against the Wilzians (it seems to me more likely that it concerned a normative general disposition); and finally a campaign against the Bretons, which took place in 818. Annales Regni Francorum, No. 806, p. 121; Chronicon Moissiacense, *ao.* 807, ed. G. H. Pertz, MG. SS. II, p. 258; Annales Regni Francorum, *ao.* 808, pp. 125–26, *ao.* 812, p. 137, *ao.* 818, p. 148.

10. See also p. 52.

11. As Delbrück, *Geschichte der Kriegskunst*, pp. 25–27, wrongly believes.

12. See my work, *Qu'est-ce que la féodalité?*, p. 55, or the German edition: *Was ist das Lehnswesen?*, pp. 36–37 (See Part I, p. 50 and n. 375).

13. Aquitaine: Pippini Capitulare Aquitanicum, *ao*. 768, c. 5 and 9, *MG*. Capit. I, No. 18; Breviarium missorum Aquitanicum, *ao*. 789, c. 6 and 9, *ibid*., No. 24; Astronome, *Vita Hludowici*, c. 3, ed. G. H. Pertz, *MG*. SS. II, p. 608 (=ed. R. Rau, in *Quellen zur karolingischen Reichsgeschichte*, I [Berlin, 1956], 262). Septimania and the so-called Spanish march: E. Mühlbacher, *Diplomata Karolinorum, MG*. Capit. I, No. 179, *ao*. 795 (=R. d'Abadal i de Vinyals, *Catalunya Carolingia*, II, Pt. 2 [Barcelona, 1952], Preceptes per a particulars, No. 1); C. Devic and J. Vaissete, *Histoire générale de Languedoc*, ed. Privat, II (Toulouse, 1875), Preuves, No. 84, *ao*. 814 (=d'Abadal, No. 6), No. 34, *ao*. 815 (=d'Abadal, No. 7); Constitutio de Hispanis prima, *ao*. 815, *MG*. Capit. I, No. 132 (=d'Abadal, II, Pt. 2, Appendix III, pp. 417–19). Bavaria: Annales Regni Francorum, *ao*. 788, p. 80. Italy: P. S. Leicht, "Il feudo in Italia nell'età Carolingia," in *I problemi della civiltà carolingia. Settimane di studio del Centro italiano di studi sull'alto medioevo*, I (Spoleto, 1954), 75 ff.; E. Hlawitschka, *Franken, Alemannen, Bayern und Burgunder in Oberitalien* (Freiburg im Breisgau, 1960), pp. 32 ff. These vassals seem to have been established in groups and to have been obliged to act together and to support each other: Capitulary of Aachen, *ais*. 802/3, c. 20, and Capitulary of Boulogne, *ao*. 811, c. 5, *MG*. Capit. I, Nos. 77 and 74. They often came from a distance: Capitulare missorum, *ais*. 792/93, c. 4, and Capitulare missorum of Louis the Pious, *ao*. 821, c. 4: *MG*. Capit. I, Nos. 25 and 148. See also pp. 51–53 and nn. 384, 396, and 397.

14. Capitula de causis diversis, *MG*. Capit. I, No. 49: c. 1 (Frisia) and c. 2 (Saxony).

15. Memoratorium (see n. 9), c. 2, *MG*. Capit. I, No. 48: two men of two manses—one who joined the army, one helper; three men of one manse—one who joined, two helpers; two men of one manse—one who joined, one helper assisted by one man having a little land; six men of a half manse—one who joined and five helpers; men having only chattels of a certain value—one who joined and five helpers who should give to him, all together, five shillings. Capitulare missorum de exercitu promovendo (see n. 9), c. 1: *MG*. Capit. I, No. 50 (see the text).

16. In 807, between the Seine and the Loire, a greater number of men than usual were called up because of a scarcity that existed in other regions allowing only a small number of men to be called up. In 808 the contingent summoned, probably in a large part of the empire, was less numerous than it had been in 807 between the Seine and the Loire; this was probably a normal situation. It is learned from the dispositions of the Capitulare missorum of 808 that the mobilization of 807 produced serious miscalculations and this was probably the reason why there was no expedition that year (see n. 9).

17. Capitula ab episcopis in placito tractanda, the end of December

828 or the beginning of 829, c. 7, and Capitulare missorum of the beginning of 829, c. 5: *MG.* Capit. II, Nos. 186 and 188.

18. Capitula de expeditione Corsicana of Lothair I, *ao.* 825, c. 3, confirmed by the Capitulare Olonnense mundanum, *ao.* 825, c. 1, *in fine: MG.* Capit. I, Nos. 162 and 165.

19. This resulted from the title of the Memoratorium, which I believe was the original: *MG.* Capit. I, No. 48.

20. Texts indicated in n. 17 and Capitulare pro lege habendum Wormatiense, c. 7, *MG.* Capit. II, No. 193.

21. Annales Mosellani, *ao.* 755, ed. I. M. Lappenberg, *MG.* SS. XVI, p. 495. The date 756 can be defended, L. Oelsner, *Jahrbücher des fränkischen Reiches unter König Pippin* (Leipzig, 1871), p. 448. In opposition, *Regesten,* No. 76i.

22. Annales Alamannici, Annales Guelferbytani, Annales Nazariani, *ao.* 775 (July), *MG.* SS. I, p. 40; Annales Mosellani, *ao.* 777 (June or July), *ao.* 781 (probably July), SS. XVI, pp. 496 and 497. In 790 the assembly *(conventus)* was held at Worms between 9 April and 9 June, but since the army was demobilized there was no *magiscampus,* Annales Lauteshamenses, *ao.* 790, SS. I, p. 34. For the chronology, refer to the *Regesten,* Nos. 190b, 211a, 243b, 305b.

23. A reference to the *Regesten* is sufficient. Pepin III: probably in 756 and 758, in 761, probably in 763, in 764 and 766, *Regesten,* 81a, 86c, 92i and k, 96c and d, 98d (without a campaign), 104a and b. Charlemagne (probabilities): 773, 778, 780, 783, 784, 785, 789, 790, 791, 792, 793, 799, 804, 806, 808, 811, 812, *Regesten,* 158a and b, 214b, 228d, 263a, 266c, 268b, 301b, 305b (without a campaign), 311c, 317b, 320c, 350a, 406f and g, 419b, 431e, as well as 432–35 and 435a, 460b and 463a, 470c and 471a. See what has been said on the assembly, p. 22 and nn. 131–32.

24. Capitulare missorum of 792/93, c. 6 (see n. 8); Programmatic Capitulary of 802, c. 33, and Capitulare missorum of the same year, c. 13/XII/XIII (see n. 8); Capitula per episcopos et comites nota facienda of 806, c. 2 and 3 (campaign of Bavarian, Alamannian, and Burgundian troops against Bohemia, Annales Regni Francorum, *h. ao.,* p. 122); inspection of armament and equipment, Capitulary of Aachen, *ais.* 802/3, c. 9 (see n. 8): *MG.* Capit. I, Nos. 25, 33, Eckhardt, "Capitularia," p. 502 (see n. 8), or *MG.* Capit. I, No. 34, *ibid.,* Nos. 54 and 77.

25. The texts of 792/93, 802, and 806 cited in the preceding note and, in addition, the order given to Fulrad, *ao.* 806 (campaign against the Sorbs); the Memoratorium of 807 (see n. 9), c. 3; the Capitulare missorum de exercitu promovendo of 808 (see n. 9), c. 1; the Capitulary of Boulogne of 811 (see n. 9), c. 7 and 9: *MG.* Capit. I, Nos. 75 (see n. 29), 48, 50, 74.

26. For example, in 806 (letter to Fulrad, see n. 25), state of alert, a

little after 12 April, concentration in the southeast of Saxony, at mid-June; in 807 (Memoratorium, c. 3, see n. 25), state of alert at the beginning of the year, concentration on the Rhine, around Ingelheim, at mid-August (Chronicon Moissiacense, *h. ao.*, *MG.* SS. II, p. 258).

27. There are references to this in the Capitulary of Aachen of 802/3, c. 9 (counts, ecclesiastical lords); Capitula de causis diversis, *ao.* 806, c. 3 (counts); letter to Fulrad, *ao.* 806 (important lords); Capitula per episcopos et comites nota facienda, *ao.* 806, c. 1 and 3 (counts and ecclesiastical lords); Memoratorium, *ao.* 807, c. 3 (important lords); Capitulare missorum de exercitu praeparando, *ao.* 808, c. 1, 3, 4, 5 (counts, ecclesiastical and lay lords); Capitulary of Boulogne, *ao.* 811, c. 7 and 9 (counts and lords): *MG.* Capit. I, Nos. 77, 49, 75, 54, 48, 50, 74.

28. Capitulare missorum of 792/93, c. 6 *(missi, per epistolas)*; Capitula per episcopos et comites nota facienda of 806, c. 3 *(missus aut epistola nostra)*; Capitulare missorum de exercitu praeparando of 808, c. 8 *(missi nostri)*: *MG.* Capit. I, Nos. 25, 54, 50. Formulae imperiales (reign of Louis the Pious), No. 7: . . . *Notum sit vobis quia istos vasallos nostros illos et illos mittimus ad has partes ad exercitum promovendum et heribannum exactandum:* K. Zeumer, *MG.* Formulae, p. 292.

29. *MG.* Capit. I, No. 75. For this text see my work cited in n. 5, pp. 87–91.

30. Two examples for the year 782. Annales Regni Francorum, rev. text: Count Thierry quickly raised troops in Ripuaria to march against Saxony and to combat an insurrection. The same source, the two texts: Charlemagne, learning that some Frankish troops were defeated by the Saxon rebels, marched against them with troops that he had hastily assembled.

31. See p. 26 and n. 174.

32. Letter of Hetti, archbishop of Treves, to his suffragan Frothair, bishop of Toul, *ao.* 817, Frotharii episcopi Tullensis epistolae, ed. K. Hampe, No. 2, *MG.* Epistolae V, pp. 277–78 *(=Recueil des historiens des Gaules et de la France,* VI, No. 25, 395–96). For the satisfactory results with regard to the importance of the effective forces and the rapidity of their mustering, Annales Regni Francorum *h. ao.*, p. 147.

33. Some texts in the narrative sources for the reigns of Pepin III and Charlemagne: *ao.* 766, Annales Regni Francorum; *ao.* 768 *(scaritos),* Continuatio Fredegarii, c. 52 (135), ed. B. Krusch, *MG.* Scriptores Rerum Merowingicarum II, p. 192; *ais.* 773, 774, 776, 778, 782, 784, 785, Annales Regni Francorum; 793, Annales Guelferbytani, *h. ao.*, SS. I, p. 45; 803, Annales Laureshamenses, *h. ao.*, SS. I, p. 39; 812, Chronicon Moissiacense, *h. ao.*, SS. II, p. 259. The character of the light troop of the *scara* is well conveyed by the fact that for the year 785 the revised text of the Annales

Regni Francorum, p. 69, renders the *scaras* sent or led by the king against the Saxons from the first text by the words *cum expedita manu*. The *scarae* are encountered in several capitularies: fragment of a capitulary probably of 803, c. 3; Capitulare Baiwaricum probably of the same year, c. 9; Capitula per episcopos et comites nota facienda, *ao*. 806, c. 2 and 3; Capitulary of Boulogne, *ao*. 811, c. 2: *MG*. Capit. I, Nos. 104, 69, 54, 74. For the *scara*, see particularly Verbruggen, "L'armée et la stratégie de Charlemagne," p. 421.

34. Allusions in the Capitulare missorum de exercitu promovendo, *ao*. 808, c. 9; in the Capitulary of Boulogne, *ao*. 811, c. 7; and for the reign of Louis the Pious, Capitulare missorum of 821, c. 4: *MG*. Capit. I, Nos. 50, 74, and 148.

35. Perhaps Capitulare de villis, *ais*. 771–800, c. 16; Capitulare Baiwaricum, probably of 803, c. 9; Capitula cum primis constituta, *ao*. 808, c. 1, and a list of points to be discussed at the assembly (Capitula cum primis conferenda), c. 9; Capitulary of Boulogne, *ao*. 811, c. 2, and for the reign of Louis the Pious, but valid for that of Charlemagne, the Constitutio de Hispanis prima, *ao*. 815, c. 1: *MG*. Capit. I, Nos. 32, 69, 52 and 51, 74 and 132 (=d'Abadal [see n. 13], II, Pt. 2, Appendix III, pp. 417-18).

36. Karoli Magni Capitulare missorum italicum, *ais*. 802–10, c. 3, 4, 8, *MG*. Capit. I, No. 99.

37. See p. 60 and n. 13.

38. Probably Capitulare missorum of 802, c. 13 b/XIIII; list of points to be discussed at the assembly, *ao*. 808, c. 9; ed. Eckhardt (see n. 8), p. 502, or *MG*. Capit. I, No. 34, *ibid*., No. 51.

39. Capitulare missorum of 802, c. 13 a/XIII; Capitula cum primis conferenda, *ao*. 808, c. 9 and 10; Capitulare missorum Aquisgranense primum, *ao*. 810, c. 16: ed. Eckhardt, p. 502, or *MG*. Capit. I, No. 34, *ibid*., Nos. 51, 64. Annales Regni Francorum, *ao*. 800, p. 110 (inspection and organization of means of defense along the coasts of the North Sea and the English Channel); *ao*. 811, p. 135 (inspections of flotillas at Boulogne-sur-Mer and at Ghent). Astronome, *Vita Hludowici*, c. 15, SS. II, p. 614 (=ed. Rau, p. 278).

40. Capitulary of Boulogne, *ao*. 811, c. 11 (see n. 35).

41. For all that precedes, see the Annales Regni Francorum (the two versions), *passim*. What I call an ethnic group was in reality a Frankish political group composed principally, but not solely, of men belonging to a given Germanic ethnic group.

42. Capitulary of Aachen of 802/3, c. 9: . . . *lanceam, scutum et arcum cum duas cordas, sagittas duodecim*; c. 7; the cudgel, or stick, with which certain warriors armed themselves in addition to the traditional arms was replaced by the bow: *Quod nullus in hoste*

baculum habeat sed arcum. The Capitulare missorum of Thionville, *ao.* 805, c. 6, refers to this article. Capitula per missos cognita facienda, *ais.* 805–13: *scutum et lancea.* The drivers and escorts of the wagons sent to the army by the royal domains (see p. 67 and n. 60) had to have the same armament as that prescribed by the Capitulary of Aachen, Capitulare de villis, c. 64. *MG.* Capit. I, Nos. 77, 44, 67, 32.

43. One finds the principal elements in the likeness of a mounted warrior on a tomb preserved at the museum of Halle that has generally been dated at the beginning of the eighth century, H. Conrad, *Geschichte der deutschen Wehrverfassung* (see n. 1), Plate 3, opposite p. 40.

44. A good example of a long Carolingian sword is that which was found at Strasbourg, Rue des Veaux; it has a total length of 37.2 inches (damascene blade); the short sword found at the same place has a serviceable blade length of 18.9 inches. These weapons are described and reproduced by R. Forrer, *Strasbourg-Argentorate*, I (1927), 233, fig. 157.

45. Capitulare missorum of 792/93, c. 4: . . . *scuto et lancea, spata et senespatio* . . . Letter to Fulrad, *ao.* 806: . . . *scutum et lanceam et spatam et semispatum, arcum et pharetras cum sagittis.*

46. Capitulare missorum of 792/93, c. 4.

47. The Psalterium Aureum of Sankt Gallen (second half of the ninth century) contains some miniatures that, where certain of their data are controllable, reproduce quite faithfully the state of affairs at that time. There, some warriors are wearing the clothing described in the text that is similar to the *brunia* of the tenth and eleventh centuries. This evidence indicates that such was the *brunia* at the time of the Carolingians. See A. Merton, *Die Buchmalerei in Sankt Gallen vom 9. bis zum 11. Jahrhundert* (Leipzig, 1912), plates XXVIII, 2 and XXIX, 1, 2.

48. The *lorica* referred to in the Capitulary of Aachen of 802/3, c. 9 (*MG.* Capit. I, No. 77) is very likely a *brunia*, but it could be a coat of mail or a garment on which had been sewn some metal strips.

49. The helmet is cited in the same article of the Capitulary of Aachen; the leg guards are cited in the Capitulare missorum of 803, c. 7, *MG.* Capit. I, No. 40.

50. According to the rate of conversion of fines furnished by Article 40, 11 (formerly 36, 11), of the *Lex Ribuaria*, ed. F. Beyerle and R. Buchner (*MG.*, in quarto), pp. 94–95 (mss. of class B dating from Charlemagne).

51. The number of cows is calculated on the rate of conversion of the *inferenda* at the time of Charlemagne indicated in the Capitulare missorum Wormatiense, *ao.* 829, c. 15, *MG.* Capit. II, No. 192. For the livestock of the *fiscus* of Annappes: Brevium exempla, No. 25, *MG.* Capit. I, No. 128. For the dimensions of this *fiscus*, P. Grierson, "The

Identity of the Unnamed Fiscs in the Brevium Exempla ad describendas res ecclesiasticas et fiscales," *Revue belge de Philologie et d'Histoire*, XVIII (1939), 452.

52. Capitulare missorum of Thionville, *ao.* 805, c. 6; *MG.* Capit. I, No. 44: . . . *omnis homo de duodecim mansis bruneam habeat; cui vero bruniam habens et secum non tullerit, omne beneficium cum brunia pariter perdat.* See also p. 52 and n. 394.

53. Capitulary of Aachen, *ais.* 802/3, c. 9; Capitulary of Boulogne, *ao.* 811, c. 10: the bishops, abbots, and abbesses were asked to furnish *bruniae* and swords to their vassals: *MG.* Capit. I, Nos. 77 and 74.

54. Capitulary of Herstal, *ao.* 779, c. 20 *(bruniae);* Capitulare missorum of 803, c. 7 *(bruniae* and leg guards); Capitula ecclesiastica ad Salz data, *ao.* 803, c. 8 *(bruniae* and arms); Capitulare missorum of Thionville, *ao.* 805, c. 7 *(bruniae* and arms); Capitulary of Boulogne, *ao.* 811, c. 10 *(bruniae* and swords): *MG.* Capit. I, Nos. 20, 40, 42, 44, 74.

55. The letter to Fulrad makes the same allusion only to the horsemen of his contingent.

56. Capitulare Aquitanicum of Pepin III, *ao.* 768, c. 6; Capitulary of Herstal, *ao.* 779, c. 17; Breviarium missorum Aquitanicum, *ao.* 789, c. 18; letter to Fulrad, *ao.* 806: *MG.* Capit. I., Nos. 18, 20, 24, 75. At the time of a campaign against the Avar rebels in 802 or 803 the counts received the order to put under *defensio*, that is, to reserve for the army, two-thirds of the grass in the counties that the army would cross; Capitulary of Aachen, c. 10, *MG.* Capit. I, No. 77, and for the sense of *defensio* the article cited from the Capitulary of Herstal. It must be noted that the right of requisition of standing grass *(herba)* applied at another time to fodder *(fodrum);* see C. Brühl, "Das fränkische Fodrum," *Zeitschrift der Savigny Stiftung für Rechtsgeschichte*, Germanistische Abt. (1959), and *Fodrum, Gistum, Servitium regis* (Cologne, 1968).

57. For example, the expedition in Saxony, Annales Regni Francorum, *ao.* 782 (rev. text): *Aestatis initio, cum iam propter pabuli copiam exercitus duci poterat.* The fact that the expression is in part taken from Caesar, *De bello gallico*, II, 2, removes nothing from the value of the indication itself.

58. The first campaign against Bohemia under the leadership of Charles the Young in 805, Annales Mettenses priores, *h. ao.*, p. 94: *Et dum nec iam pabula equis aut cibaria exercitui superfuissent . . . exercitus ad propria reversus est.*

59. Capitulary of Aachen, *ais.* 802/3, c. 10; letter to Fulrad, *ao.* 806; Memoratorium, *ao.* 807, c. 3; Capitulary of Boulogne, *ao.* 811, c. 10: *MG.* Capit. I, Nos. 77, 75, 48, 74. The interpretation of these texts and of those which will be cited in n. 60 differs considerably from that which

is usually proposed. The command and the escort of the convoys was frequently furnished by royal vassals, Memoratorium, *ao.* 807, c. 3. See also p. 52 and n. 393. The Capitulary of Aachen (c. 10) anticipated in the reserve of armament some ballista with their munitions and necessary specialized personnel. It also instructed the counts to prepare boats and bridges of good quality. It can be supposed that this means some equipment for a bridge, but what seems more likely is that boats were to be made available and bridges provided or repaired on the route to be followed by the army.

60. The direct or indirect provisions *ad hostem (hostilitium, carnaticum),* which were a burden of the domains, especially ecclesiastical, are well known thanks to the *polyptyques* and analogous documents. As for the provisions to be supplied by the *fisci,* see the Capitulare de villis, c. 30 and 64, *MG.* Capit. I, No. 32.

61. The letter to Fulrad of 806 and the Capitulary of Boulogne of 811, c. 8 *(antiqua consuetudo);* see n. 59.

62. Capitulary of Boulogne, c. 8. The line *(marca)* for those who came from this side of the Rhine and went toward the Loire was the Loire; for those who came from this side of the Loire and went toward the Rhine, the Rhine; for those from beyond the Rhine who marched across Saxony, the Elbe; for those from beyond the Loire who went toward Spain, the Pyrenees. These lines were probably related to the campaigns anticipated for 812 in Spain (which did not occur) and against the Wilzians.

63. Even those of Ferdinand Lot in his book *L'art militaire et les armées au moyen âge,* I, 94, 103; but the author rightly believed in the smallness of the effective troops.

64. See p. 59 and n. 3.

65. Capitulare missorum of Thionville, *ao.* 805, c. 19; Capitulary of Boulogne of 811, c. 2: *MG.* Capit. I, Nos. 44 and 74.

66. Capitulare Saxonicum, *ao.* 797, c. 1; Programmatic Capitulary of 802, c. 7 and 33 (become a case of infidelity; disposition probably not able to be realized); Capitulary of Aachen of 802/3, c. 9; Capitulare missorum of Thionville, *ao.* 805, c. 19 (decreasing rates in relation to the small amount of possessions of the delinquent; does not seem to have been maintained); Capitulare missorum de exercitu promovendo, *ao.* 808, c. 2 and 3, 5 (applied to helpers and to authorities having granted exemptions illegitimately); Capitulare missorum Aquisgranense primum, *ao.* 810, c. 12; Capitulary of Boulogne, *ao.* 811, c. 1 (temporary serfdom for one who was not able to pay), c. 9 (applied to authorities who had given exemptions illegally): *MG.* Capit. I, Nos. 27, 33, 77, 44, 50, 64, 74.

67. Capitulare italicum of 801, c. 2; Karoli Magni capitulare missorum italicum of 802–10, c. 13: *MG*. Capit. I, Nos. 98, 99.

68. Annales Regni Francorum, *ao*. 788, p. 80.

69. Capitulare missorum Aquisgranense primum, *ao*. 810, c. 12; Capitulary of Boulogne of 811, c. 4: *MG*. Capit. I, Nos. 64 and 74.

70. Capitulare italicum of 801, c. 3, *MG*. Capit. I, No. 98.

71. Programmatic Capitulary of 802, c. 7; Capitulare missorum de exercitu promovendo, *ao*. 808, c. 3, 5, 6, 7; Capitula de rebus exercitalibus in placito tractanda, *ao*. 811, c. 2–5: *MG*. Capit. I, Nos. 33, 50, 73.

72. These acts of insubordination became more and more frequent. The mobilization of 807 and that of 810–11 (campaign planned against the Danes) were the occasion for inquests on the subject of these acts and on measures intended to combat them. Capitulare missorum de exercitu promovendo, *ao*. 808, c. 2 and 7; Capitula de rebus exercitalibus in placito tractanda, *ao*. 811, inscriptio, and c. 6–8, 9: *MG*. Capit. I, Nos. 50, 78.

73. The mobilization and the concentration (in August, on the Rhine) of 807 left so much to be desired that the emperor had to renounce the projected campaign, probably against Slavic populations; Capitulare missorum de exercitu promovendo of 808, c. 7, Chronicon Moissiacense, *ao*. 807, SS. II, p. 258, and Annales S. Amandi, *ao*. 807, SS. I, p. 14.

Part III

1. In addition to the works of G. Waitz, H. Brunner, C. von Schwerin, R. Schröder, E. von Künszberg, and H. Conrad noted in n. 1 of Part I, it is necessary to cite here two older works and three others more recent: R. Sohm, *Die fränkische Reichs- und Gerichtsverfassung* (Weimar, 1871), reprinted at Leipzig in 1911 (of remarkable vigor of thought but of excessive systematization); A. Heusler, *Institutionen des deutschen Privatrechts*, 2 vols. (Leipzig, 1885/86); E. Mayer-Homberg, *Die fränkischen Volksrechte im Mittelalter*, I (Weimar, 1912), the same evaluation as for Sohm; R. Hübner, *Grundzüge des deutschen Privatrechts* (5th ed.; Leipzig, 1930); H. Planitz, *Deutsche Rechtsgeschichte*, rev. by K. A. Eckhardt (2nd ed.; Graz and Cologne, 1961). See also my article, "The Impact of Charlemagne on the Institutions of the Frankish Realm," *Speculum*, XL (1965).

2. On the personality of the law see especially Brunner, *Deutsche Rechtsgeschichte*, I (2nd ed.; Leipzig, 1906), 382-99, and L. Stouff, *Etude sur le principe de la personnalité des lois depuis les invasions barbares jusqu'au XIIe siècle* (Paris, 1894), extract from *Revue bourguignonne de l'enseignement supérieur*, IV, Pt. 2.

3. Capitulare missorum, *ais.* 792/93, c. 5, *MG.* Capit. I, No. 25.

4. Capitulatio de partibus Saxoniae, *ao.* 785, c. 33; Capitulare Saxonicum, *ao.* 797, c. 7 and 10; Capitulare de villis, *ais.* 771-800, c. 4; Programmatic Capitulary of 802, c. 1; Capitulare missorum of 802, c. 6 in the text for the missaticum A (for Aquitaine): *MG.* Capit. I, Nos. 26, 27, 32, 33, 34 (=W. A. Eckhardt, "Die capitularia missorum specialia von 802," *DA*, XII [1956], 501); Annales Laureshamenses, *ao.* 802, *MG.* SS. I, p. 39 (diet of October); collection of *capitula* for the *missi* of 806, c. 48, fragment of a capitulary preserved in the collection of Ansegise (for Saxony?), *ais.* 810/11, c. 2, *MG.* Capit. I, Nos. 35 (=W. A. Eckhardt, *Die Kapitulariensammlung Bischof Ghaerbalds von Lüttich. Germanenrechte* NF., *Deutschrechtliches Archiv*, V [Göttingen, 1955], No. LIX, c. xxi-48, p. 85) and 70.

5. Responsa cuidam misso data, *ais.* 802-13, c. 2, *MG.* Capit. I, No. 58. *Notitia* of judgment of 815 at the *mallus* of Autun presided over by the count Thierry, evidence that seems justifiable to use, Prou and Vidier, *Recueil des chartes de ... Saint-Benoît-sur-Loire*, I, No. X, 24-26: ... *Tunc interrogatum fuit iam dicto Maurino sub quale lege vivebat et ipsus sibi a lege salica adnunciabit ...* In the Capitulare missorum of 792/93, c. 5, *in fine* (see above, n. 3), Charlemagne already ordered that in each trial the question relative to the applicable national law might be posed.

6. In principal, the accused; but there were numerous derogations of the rule.

7. Solution adopted in a trial, which is related in Adrevald's *Miracula Sancti Benedicti*, c. 25 (reign of Louis the Pious), ed. Holder-Egger, *MG.* SS. XV, I, pp. 489-90 (=ed. De Certain, I, c. 25, pp. 56-57).

8. A royal *indiculum* obviously ordering a count to execute a judgment of the palace court conforming to the *lex loci vestri* (beginning of the reign of Charlemagne), Cartae Senonicae, No. 26, *MG.* Formulae, p. 196. Judgment of the palace court, *ao.* 812, ordering that a party who had not appeared might be condemned to a fine *sicut lex locis vestre de tale causa docuerit;* DKar., No. 216.

9. This customary and oral character of the major part of the law has been rightly underlined by K. A. Eckhardt in the second revised edition of the *Deutsche Rechtsgeschichte* of Planitz (see n. 1), p. 23.

10. The *Lex Visigothorum* of 654, ed. K. Zeumer (Leges Visigoth-

orum; *MG. Leges nationum Germanicarum* I): applicable to the Visigothic elements of the population living almost exclusively in Septimania, in the counties of the Pyrenees and the trans-Pyrenees.

11. *Lex Saxonum,* ed. K. and K. F. von Richthofen, *MG.* Leges in folio 5, and ed. C. von Schwerin, *Leges Saxonum und Lex Thuringorum, MG.* Fontes iuris Germanici antiqui. I share the opinion of L. Halphen, *Etudes critiques sur l'histoire de Charlemagne* (Paris, 1921), pp. 180–84, on the date of redaction. The revision of 802/3 appears as only a bare possibility: this is the only concession that can be given to those supporting a redaction in 802/3, most notably, M. Lintzel, "Die Entstehung der Lex Saxonum," *Zeitschrift der Savigny-Stiftung für Rechtsgeschichte,* Germanistische Abt. XLVII (1927). *Lex Salica,* Introduction by K. A. Eckhardt in his edition of the text E (second text in 100 titles), *Lex Salica, 100 Titel-Text* (Weimar, 1953), particularly pp. 55–78. *Lex Alamannorum,* Introduction of K. A. Eckhardt in his edition of the *Leges Alamannorum,* II (Witzenhausen, 1962), 8–9. *Lex Baiuvariorum,* K. A. Eckhardt in his re-edition of K. von Amira, *Germanisches Recht,* I (4th ed.; Berlin, 1960), 59.

12. See pp. 7–8. The most important text is the passage of the Annales Laureshamenses, *ao.* 802, *MG.* SS. I, p. 39, which is analyzed in n. 27 of Part I.

13. *Lex Salica,* K. A. Eckhardt, *Lex Salica, 100 Titel-Text,* pp. 70–71, *Pactus Legis Salicae,* I, *Einführung und 80 Titel-Text* (Göttingen, 1954), pp. 218–28; editions by the same scholar, *Pactus Legis Salicae* II, Pt. 2, *Kapitularien und 70 Titel-Text* (Göttingen, 1956), pp. 466 ff., and Pactus Legis Salicae, *MG.* Leges nationum Germanicarum IV, 1, on the bottom of the page (last column). *Lex Ribuaria,* Text B, which K. A. Eckhardt believes to have been established before 803, perhaps at the diet of 802, re-ed. of Von Amira, p. 45, re-ed. of Planitz, p. 74; edition of F. Beyerle and R. Buchner, *Lex Ribuaria, MG.* Leges nationum Germanicarum III, 2, under the text A. *Lex Saxonum,* see above, n. 11. *Lex Alamannorum, ibid.*

14. Hypothetical dating generally accepted with good reason.

15. Lex Angliorum et Werinorum, hoc est Thuringorum; ed. K. F. von Richthofen, *MG.* Leges V, and ed. von Schwerin, see n. 11. Notitia vel commemoratio de illa Euua quae se ad Amorem habet; ed. R. Sohm, *MG.* Leges V. The attribution of this text to the *Francs Chamaves* is traditional but without foundation; I agree with the views of J. F. Niermeyer, "Het midden-Nederlands rivierengebied in de Frankische tijd op grond van de E. q. s. a. A. h.," *Tijdschrift voor Geschiedenis,* LXVI (1953). Lex Frisionum; ed. K. von Richthofen, *MG.* Leges III.

16. *MG.* Capit. I, Nos. 39 and 41. See pp. 7–8.

17. *Ibid.*, No. 68.

18. Capitulare Aquisgranense, prooemium and c. 6 and 7, *ibid.*, No. 77.

19. See p. 8.

20. K. A. Eckhardt, *Lex Salica, 100 Titel-Text*, pp. 59–60, and *Pactus Legis Salicae*, I, Pt. 2, *Systematischer Text* (Göttingen, 1957), prefatory note, pp. 308–9. L. Wallach, *Alcuin and Charlemagne* (Ithaca, 1959), pp. 109–16; I do not believe, despite the remarkable elements collected and grouped by this scholar, that one may argue, as he does, for a tacit reception of *Lex Romana Visigothorum* by Charlemagne (pp. 127–40): such a reception might have been, moreover, utterly useless.

21. This is expressed with special vigor in c. 1 of the Programmatic Capitulary of 802, *MG. Capit.* I, No. 33. This tendency has been justifiably underlined by A. Schmidt-Weigand, *Rechtspflegedelikte in der fränkischen Zeit* (Berlin, 1962), pp. 26 ff.

22. Capitulary of Herstal, *ao.* 779, c. 11; Capitula cum primis constituta, *ao.* 808, c. 2: *ibid.*, Nos. 20 and 52.

23. Capitulare Baiwaricum, probably *ao.* 803, c. 6, *ibid.*, No. 69. The rule introduced was that of the *res porprisa* of the Frankish law, such as it appeared in the *Lex Ribuaria*, c. 78 (75), p. 128.

24. Capitulare Aquisgranense, *ao.* 809, c. 1 and 2, *MG. Capit.* I, No. 61.

25. Capitulare missorum Aquisgranense primum, *ao.* 809, c. 2; Capitula tractanda cum comitibus, episcopis et abbatibus, *ao.* 811, c. 3: *ibid.*, Nos. 62 and 71.

26. Capitulare missorum of 803, c. 9; Capitulare de iustitiis faciendis, *ao.* 811, c. 1 (which, like the disposition of 803, contained the prohibition but also the reservation): *MG. Capit.* I, Nos. 40 and 80. At the council of Reims, *ao.* 813, the fathers demanded the application of this *magnificum capitulum*, c. 43, ed. Werminghoff, *MG. Concilia* II, No. 35, p. 257.

27. I believe it is possible to cite the following *notitiae* of judgment, which date from the beginning of the reign of Louis the Pious: F. Bougaud and J. Garnier, *Chronique de l'abbaye de Saint-Bénigne de Dijon suivie de la chronique de Saint-Pierre de Bèze* (Dijon, 1875), pp. 250–51, *ao.* 815 (=Thévenin, *Textes* [see n. 246 in Part I], No. 115); Pérard, *Recueil* (see n. 147 in Part I), p. 14, *ao.* 815; Prou and Vidier, *Recueil des chartes de ... Saint-Benoît-sur-Loire*, I, No. XVI, *ao.* 818.

28. Capitulare Baiwaricum, probably 803, c. 8, *MG. Capit.* I, No. 69. The rule has the aspect of an instruction given to the *missi*; one is able, however, to suppose that it was also valid for the ordinary courts. In a plea of the *missi* presided over by Arn, archbishop of Salzburg in 802, there is already reference to the acquisition of estates *temporibus domni Pipini regis et Tassiloni ducis;* it is likewise for the time of Tassilo in another plea of the *missi* in 806/7. In a third plea presided over by Arn

in 804, there is reference to a previous possession; but this is because Tassilo and his wife had taken away the estates under litigation from the church of Freising. Bitterauf, *Die Traditionen des Hochstifts Freising*, I, Nos. 184, 232, and 193.

29. See p. 30.

30. Duplex legationis edictum, *ao.* 789, c. 17; Programmatic Capitulary of 802, c. 1; Capitulare missorum of Thionville, *ao.* 805, c. 2; Capitula de causis diversis, *ao.* 806, c. 1: *MG.* Capit. I, Nos. 23, 33, 44, 49; in all these texts the rule is expressed while the following texts imply its existence: Capitulare Baiwaricum, probably 803, c. 3; Capitula a missis dominicis ad comites directa, *ao.* 806; Capitulare missorum Aquisgranense primum, *ao.* 810, c. 20: *ibid.*, Nos. 69, 85, 64. The Capitulary of Mantua, *ao.* 781, c. 1, *ibid.*, No. 90, introduced the rule into Italy: it was thus more ancient in the *Regnum Francorum* than the first reference to it in a capitulary.

31. The *Lex Ribuaria* 36 (32), *de mannire*, ed. Beyerle and Buchner, pp. 87–88, provides for seven summonses with a delay between each of them. C. 6 of the Capitulare legi Ribuariae additum, *MG.* Capit. I, No. 42, reduced the number of summonses to four.

32. This is vigorously expressed in the Programmatic Capitulary of 802, c. 25, *ibid.*, No. 33. But this was an older concern, which was intensified under the empire.

33. Prevention: Capitulare de villis, *ais.* 771–800, c. 53; Capitulare missorum of Thionville, *ao.* 805, c. 16. Repression: Capitulary of Herstal, *ao.* 779, c. 11 and 23; Capitulatio de partibus Saxoniae, *ao.* 785, c. 24; Capitulare de latronibus, *ao.* 804, Capitulare missorum of Thionville, c. 21; Capitula cum primis conferenda et Capitulare cum primis constituta, *ao.* 808, c. 1 and 2, respectively. *MG.* Capit. I, Nos. 32, 44, 20, 26, 82, 44, 51, and 52.

34. See p. 48.

35. Capitulary of Herstal, *ao.* 779, c. 8; Capitulatio de partibus Saxoniae, *ao.* 785, c. 2: *ibid.*, Nos. 20 and 26. C. 3 of the Capitulare legibus addendum of 803, c. 3, *ibid.*, No. 39, is at least, *in terminis*, more favorable to the asylum. The case of the clerk who took refuge in Saint-Martin at Tours, probably in 802, shows that Charlemagne admitted the right of asylum only with many restrictions; see the account with references to the texts in Wallach, *Alcuin and Charlemagne*, pp. 103–40.

36. See on this subject Brunner and von Schwerin (see n. 1, Part I), pp. 639–43. There are not any texts for the *Regnum Francorum* at the time of Charlemagne. But a capitulary of Pepin, *ais.* 782–87, c. 8 (*MG.* Capit. I, No. 91) organized the *Rügeverfahren* in Italy; it appears to be a Frankish institution introduced into the Lombard kingdom.

37. A case where, after homicide, one expected a complaint made by

the count dates from 819; C. Devic and J. Vaissete, *Histoire générale de Languedoc*, ed. Privat, II, Preuves, No. 49 (Toulouse, 1875), cols. 123–24 (=Thévenin, *Textes*, No. 67). The state of affairs that the *notitia* describes is at this time considered normal and certainly ought to be so considered for the last years of Charlemagne.

38. See the excellent and now classic discussions of Brunner and von Schwerin, pp. 296–301, of Schröder and von Künszberg, pp. 179–82, of Conrad, pp. 140–42 (see n. 1, Part I). It is necessary to remember that not all the views of these learned authors are shared by me; the views expressed in this book on the role of free men at certain sessions of the *mallus* differ much from their conclusions.

39. In what concerns the presidency it suffices to refer to the legal texts cited in nn. 40, 41, 43, 45–47, 49, and to the passages relating to the presidency of certain pleas (see pp. 79–80). On the *vicarius*, the *centenarius*, and the *vicecomes*, see pp. 32–34.

40. Formulae Salicae Merkelianae, No. 16, and supplement to No. 28: *MG. Formulae*, pp. 247, 252.

41. Formulae Salicae Bignonianae, No. 13; Formulae Salicae Merkelianae, Nos. 18, supplement to 28, 29; Cartae Senonicae, Nos. 20, 38, 51: *MG. Formulae*, pp. 232–33, 248, 252 (two), 194, 202, 207.

42. See p. 78.

43. In a *notitia* of an assize of the *missi* held at Digne (Provence) in 780 the *scabini* are cited under their proper name *(Scabinas lites, scabinos ipsius civitatis)* and under that of *rachimbourgs (una cum rationesburguis dominicis)*, I. H. Albanès and U. Chevalier, *Gallia Christiana Novissima*, III (Marseilles, Valence, 1899), No. 42, cols. 34–35 (=B. Guérard, *Cartulaire de l'abbaye de Saint-Victor de Marseille*, I [Paris, 1857], No. 31). E. E. Stengel, *Urkundenbuch des Klosters Fulda*, I, II (Marburg, 1958), No. 154, *ais.* 783/84, pp. 230–31 (Franconia). Formulas of Pithou, c. 75; Formulae Senonenses recentiores, Nos. 1 and 6: *MG. Formulae*, pp. 598, 211, and 214.

44. In some texts and notably some *notitiae* of judgment from the south of Gaul contemporary with the reign of Charlemagne but especially posterior to it, the term *iudex* is readily employed to designate regular judgment-finders of the count at the *mallus* or of *missi* at their assizes: Devic and Vaissete, *Histoire générale de Languedoc*, ed. Privat, II, Preuves, No. 6, *ao.* 782, cols. 47–50; No. 57, cols. 134–35, *ao.* 821; No. 39, cols. 287–88, *ao.* 852; No. 150, cols. 306–8, *ao.* 858 (=Thévenin, *Textes*, Nos. 68, 88, 93); Thévenin, *Textes*, No. 71, *ao.* 834. See R. H. Bautier, *L'exercice de la justice publique dans l'empire carolingien*, in *Ecole Nationale des Chartes. Positions des thèses soutenues par les élèves de la promotion de 1943*, pp. 14–15; G. Sicard, "Sur l'organisation judi-

ciaire carolingienne en Languedoc," in *Etudes historiques à la mémoire de Noël Didier* (Paris, 1960), pp. 293–99. Although Bautier considers the *iudices* as different from the *scabini*, Sicard does not take a position on this question. It is my opinion that *iudices* and *scabini* designate the same institution under two different names.

45. The *scabini* and the other judgment-finders grouped together under these names: Formulae Salicae Lindenbrogianae, No. 19; Formulae Senonenses recentiores, Nos. 1, 2, and 3: *MG.* Formulae, pp. 280–81, 211–13. These names reserved for the nonscabinal judgment-finders (*mallus* or assize of the *missi*): Albanès and Chevalier, *Gallia Christiana Novissima*, III (Marseilles), No. 42, *ao.* 780 (see n. 43); *Histoire générale de Languedoc*, ed. Privat, II, Preuves, No. 6, *ao.* 782 (see n. 44), No. 10, *ao.* 791; Bougaud and Garnier (see n. 27), pp. 250–51 (=Thévenin, *Textes*, No. 115), *ao.* 815; Pérard, *Recueil*, p. 14, *ao.* 815; Prou and Vidier (see n. 27), I, No. XII, *ao.* 818.

46. One generally dates the collection of formulas of Bignon from the reign of Charlemagne, before 774; taking into account the traditional character of an important part of the evidence collected in the formularies, I believe "toward" to be more prudent than "before." Formulae Salicae Bignonianae, supplement to No. 7: *Cum resedisset ille vigarius inluster vir illo comite in illo mallo publico una cum ipsis scabinos, qui in ipsum mallum resedebat, ad causas audiendas vel recta iudicia terminanda.* Formulae Salicae Lindenbrogianae (placed later in the eighth century, but originally from the same regions), Nos. 19 and 21. *MG.* Formulae, pp. 230, 280–82.

47. Provence: see above, n. 43. Lower Seine: DKar., No. 138 *(inter Ripheronem comitem vel suos escapinios in pago Tellauo, in mallo publico . . .* ; the *pagus* is the Talou). Franconia: K. Glöckner, *Codex Laureshamensis*, I (Darmstadt, 1933), No. 228, p. 31 (*. . . et scabini et testes . . .* ; further, *. . . missi domni regis . . . cum prefatis scabinis et testibus . . .*). Pagus of the Moselle: DKar., No. 148 (*. . . una cum scabinis et testibus Moslinses*).

48. *Ministerium*: Capitulare Aquisgranense, c. 11, and Capitulare missorum Aquisgranense primum, c. 22, both from 809 (for the second, according to the text of the group Paris lat. 9654 and Vatic. Palat. 582): *MG.* Capit. I, Nos. 61, 62. Functions and duty to be present at sessions: Capitulare missorum of 803, c. 20; Capitulare missorum of Thionville, *ao.* 805, c. 8; Capitulare Aquisgranense, *ao.* 809, c. 5; Capitulare missorum Aquisgranense primum, *ao.* 809, c. 13; Capitulare missorum italicum (whose Italian character appears very dubious; see n. 31 in Part I), *ais.* 802–10, c. 12; Pippini Capitulare italicum (dispositions of Frankish law introduced into Italy), *ais.* 806–10, c. 14: *ibid.*, Nos. 40, 44, 61, 62, 99, 102.

49. See above, n. 47: *Ripheronem comitem vel suos escapinios*. A. de Courson, *Cartulaire de l'abbaye de Redon* (Paris, 1863), No. 191, *ao*. 797: *iudicaverunt scabini Frodaldi comitis* (the count of Vannes?). DKar., No. 204, *ao*. 806: *Gunfridum comitem et suos scabinos* (the count of Chartres). When *scabini* were created by a lord with immunity in order to sit on his *audientia privata*, they were called "his *scabini*": DKar., No. 180, *ao*. 797: the abbot Asoarius of the abbey of Prüm, which had immunity, conformed to what *sui scabini ei iudicaverunt*.

50. Capitulare missorum, *ao*. 803, c. 3; Capitulare Aquisgranense, *ao*. 809, c. 11 (as well as the words appearing in the ms. Paris lat. 4995); Capitulare missorum Aquisgranense primum, *ao*. 809, c. 22 (text from the mss. Paris lat. 9654 and Vatic. Palat. 582): *MG.* Capit. I, Nos. 40, 61, 62. The exclusion of those condemned to death and pardoned: the second and third capitularies cited, c. 1 and 28, respectively. The formula 19 of the collection of Lindenbruch (*MG.* Formulae, p. 280) insists on the fact that the *scabini* are *pagenses loci illius*.

51. Capitula incerti anni, *ais*. 805–13, c. 1 and 2, *MG.* Capit. I, No. 86.

52. Expressions particularly explicit and forceful on this concern: Programmatic Capitulary of 802, c. 1, *ibid.*, No. 33; passage from the Annales Laureshamenses dealing with the mission of *missi* in 802, *MG.* SS. I, p. 38; Capitulare missorum of Thionville, *ao*. 805, c. 16, *MG.* Capit. I, No. 44.

53. Capitulare missorum of 803, c. 20; Capitulare missorum of Thionville, *ao*. 805, c. 16, *in fine*, making allusion to what has been ordered *in alio capitulare*. W. A. Eckhardt, *Kapitulariensammlung*, pp. 19–21, seems to have been right in identifying it with a capitulary of which a fragment was inserted in the collection of Gerbald, bishop of Liège, in 806: *MG.* Capit. I, No. 104, c. 4 (better, the edition of Eckhardt, No. LXII, p. 92). There is in this fragment mention only of *maiores natu* ("men of good birth"), not of *scabini;* the institution of the *scabini* probably was not yet general at this date.

54. Capitulare Aquisgranense, *ao*. 809, c. 5; Capitulare missorum Aquisgranense primum, *ao*. 809, c. 13; Capitulare missorum italicum (?; see above, n. 48), *ais*. 802–10, c. 12. An Italian capitulary of Pepin, *ao*. 810, c. 14, relating to the application of the rule in Italy (with the first mention of the *tria placita quae instituta sunt*) and a *capitulare missorum* of Louis the Pious, belonging to the group of 818/19, c. 14 (with, for the first time, the expression *tria placita generalia*), refer explicitly to the measure decreed by Charlemagne. *MG.* Capit. I, Nos. 61, 62, 99, 102, 141.

55. The *maiores natu*: see above, n. 53. The *vassi* or *vassalli comitum*: Capitulare Aquisgranense, *ao*. 809, c. 5, and Capitulare missorum Aquisgranense primum, *ao*. 809, c. 13 (text of the mss. Paris lat. 9654 and Vatic. Palat. 582).

56. A *notitia* of judgment, No. 40 of the Formulae Augienses B. *MG.* Formulae, p. 362, probably dating from the end of the eighth or from the beginning of the ninth century, cites the *reginburgis nostris*, a term which at that date should designate *scabini*. A *notitia* of judgment of Raetia, Wartmann, *Urkundenbuch der Abtei Sankt Gallen*, I, No. 187, *ao.* 806 (or 807), shows *illos scabinos* in the exercise of their functions as judgment-finders of the count.

57. See above, nn. 48 and 54.

58. Programmatic Capitulary, c. 26, *MG.* Capit. I, No. 33: *Ut iudices secundum scriptam legem iuste iudicant, non secundum arbitrium suum.* Since a very important part of the national laws remained unwritten despite the efforts of Charlemagne, there were always for the judges vast possibilities to make judgments according to their pleasure. E. Kaufmann, *Aequitatis iudicium* (Frankfort on the Main, 1959), p. 57, is inclined to believe that the rule, although formulated for the first time under the reign of Charlemagne, was much older; this is possible, but my learned colleague gives no pertinent arguments in support of his point of view.

59. This is, I believe, the interpretation that should be given to c. 6 of the Capitulare missorum of 802, in regard to the missaticum A (for Aquitaine), *MG.* Capit. I, No. 34 (in the apparatus) and ed. Eckhardt, p. 501 (see above, n. 4): *De legibus mundanis, ut unusquisque sciat qua lege vivat vel iudicat.* The general term *unusquisque* protects at the same time the person judged and the judge. It is the duty of the person judged to know under which law he lives and of the judge to know under what law he will render justice: it ought, besides, to be the same law.

60. Because the texts are difficult to interpret, I quote them. Collection of *capitula* for the *missi* of 806, c. 48: *Ut comites et iudices confiteantur qua lege vivere debeant et secundum ipsam iudicent* (W. A. Eckhardt, *Kapitulariensammlung*, p. 30, believes in a corruption of the text cited in n. 59); Capitula omnibus cognita facienda, *ais.* 802–13, c. 4: *Ut comites et vicarii eorum legem sciant ut ante eos iniuste neminem quis iudicare possit vel ipsam legem mutare;* Capitulare missorum, *ais.* 802–13, c. 3: *Comites quoque et centenarii et ceteri nobiles viri legem suam pleniter discant sicut in alio loco decretum est* (allusion to the text just preceding): *MG.* Capit. I, Nos. 35 (=W. A. Eckhardt, *Kapitulariensammlung*, No. LIX, c. xxi, p. 85), 57, 60. It is likely that when Charlemagne required the counts, their subordinates, and their judgment-finders to have a knowledge of their own law, the emperor and his councilors admitted, wrongly or rightly, that this law was most often also the national law for most of the men subject to their jurisdiction: consequently it was this law whose application by their judgment-

finders they had most often to control. This explanation was favored by Brunner, *Deutsche Rechtsgeschichte*, I (2nd ed.), 388.

61. Capitulare missorum Aquisgranense primum, *ao.* 810, c. 3; Capitulare missorum Aquisgranense secundum, *ao.* 810, c. 15: *MG.* Capit. I, Nos. 64 and 65.

62. It does not appear that the viscount, when there was one, was touched by the prohibition: he was not, in effect, a subordinate of the count but his assistant in all the county (see Part I, pp. 33–34). In any case, there are several *notitiae* posterior to the reign of Charlemagne, of which there are two from the beginning of the reign of Louis the Pious in which the *mallus* sits under the presidency of the viscount, in some cases foreseen by the capitulary of 810: De Monsabert, *Chartes de l'abbaye de Nouaillé* (Poitiers, 1936), No. 10, *ao.* 815; Bougaud and Garnier (see above, n. 27), p. 252, *ais.* 817/18; Devic and Vaissete, *Histoire générale de Languedoc*, ed. Privat, II, Preuves, No. 150, cols. 306–8, *ao.* 858 (=Thévenin, *Textes*, No. 93); E. Germer-Durand, *Cartulaire de l'église Notre-Dame de Nîmes* (Nîmes, 1874), No. 1, *ao.* 876, No. 8, *ao.* 898 (=Thévenin, *Textes*, Nos. 107 and 114); cf. W. Sickel, *Der fränkische Vicecomitat* (n.p., 1907), pp. 53–54, 57–59.

63. To me this seems to have happened from the fact that this same year the capitulary introducing the reform into Italy (see n. 64) mentions *criminales actiones* among the cases that could not be judged by subordinate officials.

64. Pippini Capitulare italicum, c. 14, *MG.* Capit. I, No. 102. Only mentioned explicitly as falling under the stroke of prohibition are *criminales actiones* and trials concerning liberty. I believe, however, that the trials relating to landed property are implicitly included; they certainly were not ranged among the *leviores causae*, which could be judged by the county court presided over by a subordinate official.

65. Capitula de iustitiis faciendis, c. 4, *MG.* Capit. I, No. 80.

66. Posterior to the reign of Charlemagne are some examples of sessions of the *mallus* presided over by subordinate officials judging cases reserved for the count: Adrevald, *Miracula Sancti Benedicti*, c. 24 (see above, n. 7); B. Guérard, *Cartulaire de l'abbaye de Saint-Victor de Marseille*, I (Paris, 1857), No. 26, pp. 32–34, *ao.* 845 (=Thévenin, *Textes*, No. 80); G. Desjardins, "Evêques de Rodez au IXe, au Xe et au XIe siècle," *Bibliothèque de l'Ecole des Chartes*, XXIV (1863), pièces justificatives No. VI, 167, *ao.* 864 (date established by F. Lot, *Fidèles et vassaux* [Paris, 1904], pp. 114, 115, No. 4). It is much more important to point out that the *vicaria* in the west of France and in Burgundy and the *centena* in Lorraine implied in the tenth and eleventh centuries the right to condemn to death. This is hard to explain other than by the fact that

the *vicarii* and *centenarii* had, in reality, preserved the competence that Charlemagne attempted to take away from them. See F. Lot, "La vicaria et le vicarius," *Nouvelle Revue historique de droit français et étranger,* XVII (1893), with an attempt at a different but, it would seem, less satisfactory explanation; C. E. Perrin, "Sur le sens du mot 'centena' dans les chartes lorraines du moyen âge," *Archivum Latinitatis Medii Aevi= Bulletin du Cange,* V (1929/30), 26–30; M. Garaud, "L'organisation administrative du comté de Poitou au Xe siècle et l'avènement des châtelains et des châtellenies," *Bulletin de la Société des Antiquaires de l'Ouest* (1953), pp. 443–47; J. Richard, "Aux origines du Charolais," *Annales de Bourgogne,* XXXV (1963), 88. H. Hirsch believed that the prohibition made by Charlemagne did not apply to the judgment of men arrested in the act; I am inclined to agree with this view, although the argument of my late colleague is weak; *Die Hohe Gerichtsbarkeit im deutschen Mittelalter* (Darmstadt, 1958, reprinted from the edition of 1922), pp. 191–93.

67. Admonitio generalis, *ao.* 789, c. 63; Duplex legationis edictum, c. 22; Programmatic Capitulary of 802, c. 1 (and Annales Laureshamenses, *ao.* 802, *MG.* SS. I, p. 38); Capitulare missorum of 803, c. 15; Capitulare Aquisgranense, *ao.* 809, c. 7; Capitulare missorum Aquisgranense primum, *ao.* 809, c. 17; Capitulare missorum Aquisgranense primum, *ao.* 810, c. 7; Capitulare incerti anni, *ais.* 805–13, c. 1; Capitula de canonibus excerpta, *ao.* 813, c. 10: *MG.* Capit. I, Nos. 22, 23, 33, 40, 61, 62, 64, 86, 79.

68. Programmatic Capitulary of 802, c. 25, and in a certain measure, c. 12; Capitula incerti anni, c. 2. See n. 67.

69. Capitulare Aquisgranense, *ao.* 809, c. 7. See n. 67.

70. Implicitly, most of the texts cited in n. 67. Explicitly, Capitulare Aquisgranense, *ao.* 809, c. 9, and Capitula incerti anni, c. 2.

71. Capitulare missorum, *ao.* 803, c. 15 and 16; Capitulare missorum Aquisgranense primum, *ao.* 809, c. 16; Capitula per missos cognita facienda, *ais.* 805–13, c. 1: *MG.* Capit. I, Nos. 40, 62, 67.

72. C. 9. The text is corrupt, but there is not any doubt concerning its sense.

73. Capitulare legibus additum, *ao.* 803, c. 4; Capitula de missorum officiis, *ao.* 810, c. 5; perhaps implicitly, the Capitulare missorum of Nijmegen, ao. 806, c. 8: *MG.* Capit. I, Nos. 39, 66, 46.

74. Capitulare Aquisgranense, *ais.* 802/3, c. 11; Capitulare Aquisgranense, *ao.* 809, c. 13; Capitulare missorum Aquisgranense primum, *ao.* 809, c. 25 (with the various readings of the mss.): *MG.* Capit. I, Nos. 77, 61, 62.

75. Capitulare legibus additum, *ao.* 803, c. 10; c. 10 of the Capitula a misso cognita facta, *ao.* 802, probably already had the same import,

but lacked the penal sanction giving the disposition of 803 its added weight: *MG.* Capit. I, Nos. 39 and 59.

76. Pepin III: DDKar., Nos. 1 and 12. Charlemagne: DDKar., Nos. 65, 102, 110, 138, 148, 204.

77. The practice goes back to the Merovingian period, but it is found during the reign of Charlemagne: Formulae Turonenses, No. 38; Cartae Senonicae, Nos. 11 and 51; Formulae Salicae Bignonianae, Nos. 8 and 9 (judicial decision); Formulae Lindenbrogianae, No. 19: *MG.* Formulae, pp. 156, 189, 207, 230–31, 280. All these cases concern homicide.

78. Capitulare missorum of Thionville, *ao.* 805, c. 8 (the peculiarities of mss. Paris lat. 9654 and Vatic. Palat. 582 concern only the form). One may ask whether this acquiescence *(adquiescere)* was not the engagement to execute the judgment. This explanation had been discarded by Brunner and von Schwerin, p. 480, n. 52, according to A. Esmein, "La chose jugée dans le droit de la monarchie franque," *Nouvelle Revue historique de droit français et étranger*, XI (1887), 548. They suggested that it concerned an act introduced into the procedure in order to destroy the opposition that the scabinal reform encountered. The explanation is tempting but completely hypothetical. See p. 94.

79. See pp. 23–26.

80. Capitulare missorum Aquisgranense alterum, *ao.* 809, *MG.* Capit. I, No. 63, c. 11: *Quod missos nostros ad vicem nostram mittimus.*

81. See p. 24.

82. Programmatic Capitulary of 802, c. 1, *MG.* Capit. I, No. 33. See above, however, p. 76 and n. 36.

83. Such was the case for the trial relating to the domain of Chaudol before the *missi dominici* sitting at Digne in 780; Albanès and Chevalier, *Gallia Christiana Novissima*, III (Marseilles), No. 42. The mission was confided to the *missi* by Charlemagne after a request made to the king in 779 at the diet of Herstal by the bishop of Marseilles; report by one of the *missi, ibid.*, No. 41.

84. T. Bitterauf, *Die Traditionen des Hochstifts Freising*, I (Munich, 1905), No. 143, *ais.* 791/92, No. 232, *ais.* 806/7.

85. Bishops, abbots, *et ceteri nostri homines*, which means the counts and royal vassals, had to assist with the assizes of the *missi*. The *missi* were instructed to invoke the authority of the royal *bannum* in ordering those who neglected this duty to be present at the assizes; Responsa cuidam misso data, *ais.* 802–13, c. 5, *MG.* Capit. I, No. 58. A count and a lay abbot were present at an assize held by two *missi* at Poitiers in 795; De Monsabert, *Chartes de l'abbaye de Nouaillé*, No. 7.

86. Two *vassi dominici* were present at an assize held by four *missi* at Narbonne in 782; Devic and Vaissete, *Histoire générale de Languedoc*, ed. Privat, II, Preuves, No. 6.

87. Mention of *scabini, rachinburgii, iudices,* or judgment-finders designated in more vague terms *(alii quamplures, boni homines, alii venerabiles)*: Albanès and Chevalier, *Gallia Christiana Novissima,* III, No. 42 (see n. 83); Devic and Vaissete, *Histoire générale de Languedoc,* ed. Privat, II, Preuves, No. 6 (see n. 86); Glöckner, *Codex Laureshamensis,* II, No. 228, p. 31, *ao.* 782; Poupardin, *Recueil des chartes de . . . Saint-Germain-des-Prés,* No. 22, *ao.* 791; *Chartes de l'abbaye de Nouaillé,* No. 7 (see n. 85); Prou and Vidier, *Recueil des chartes de . . . Saint-Benoît-sur-Loire,* I, No. 9, *ao.* 796; Formulae Senonenses recentiores, Nos. 4 and 7, *MG.* Formulae, pp. 213–14; A. Bernard and A. Bruel, *Recueil des chartes de l'abbaye de Cluny,* I (Paris, 1876), No. 3, *ao.* 814 (beginning of the reign of Louis the Pious). See also the *notitia* relating to an assize of the *missi* held at Paris in 803, inserted in a manuscript (Paris lat. 4995) of the Capitulare legibus additum of this year, *MG.* Capit. I, No. 39, p. 112. In Bavaria a *iudex* (that is, a person who had, under Bavarian law, "to find" the judgment) was frequently present. Sometimes there was more than one: Bitterauf, *Traditionen des Hochstifts Freising* (see n. 84), Nos. 142–43, 183–84, 186, 193, 227, 232, 247 (from 791 to 811). In Alamannia where the *iudex* had fulfilled the same role for a long time, one occasionally finds a *iudex* at an assize of the *missi:* Wartmann, *Urkundenbuch der Abtei Sankt Gallen,* I, No. 120, *ao.* 789.

88. Although it concerns the epoch of Louis the Pious (probably a little after 819), one should refer to Adrevald, *Miracula Sancti Benedicti,* c. 25 (see above, n. 7), which is especially instructive on the composition and functioning of an assize of the *missi;* the case concerned the ownership of a group of serfs of an inferior condition *(mancipia),* which was a matter of dispute between Saint-Denis and Saint-Benoît-sur-Loire. The *mancipia* were considered as accessories of the property; Capitulare de iustitiis faciendis, *ao.* 811, c. 4, *MG.* Capit. I, No. 80.

89. This explains why in certain *notitiae* of judgment it is the entire bench of all the judgment-finders that is said to have handed down the judgment.

90. In the account of his mission carried out with Leidrade in the south of Gaul (see nn. 165, 167, and 168 in Part I), Theodulphe always considered the decisions as coming from his colleague and himself.

91. Landed property: the *notitiae* of judgment (except for that of Saint-Benoît-sur-Loire and the formulas), including the Bavarian *notitiae* indicated above, n. 87; also, DKar., No. 165, *ao.* 790. Personal status of a free man: the two formulas and the *notitia* excluded in the preceding reference; also, Formulae Augienses B, No. 23 (end of eighth century), *MG.* Formulae, p. 357; Responsa cuidam misso data, *ais.* 802–13, c. 1, 3, 7, 8, *MG.* Capit. I, No. 58. Brigandage: Capitulare Karoli Magni de latronibus, *ao.* 804, c. 8 and 9, *ibid.,* No. 82.

92. See p. 94 and n. 168.

93. See pp. 79–80 and nn. 61, 64, and 65, Capitulare missorum Aquisgranense primum, *ao.* 810, c. 3: . . . *semper in praesentia missorum imperialium aut in praesentia comitum;* Capitulare de iustitiis faciendis, *ao.* 811, c. 4: . . . *aut in praesentia comitis vel missorum nostrorum.* The same concurrent competence was introduced into Bavaria in what concerned the *res porprisae* (see p. 74 and n. 23), Capitulare Baiwaricum, probably *ao.* 803, c. 6: . . . *ut ante missos et comites seu iudices nostros* . . . : *MG.* Capit. I, Nos. 64, 80, and 69.

94. Capitulare de iustitiis faciendis, *ao.* 811, c. 8, *ibid.,* No. 80.

95. *Ibid.,* c. 12. It would seem that there were similar assizes in Bavaria: Bitterauf, *Traditionen des Hochstifts Freising* (see n. 84), Nos. 251, 258, 288, 299, 327 (from 807 to 814). One meets such assizes under the successors of Charlemagne.

96. Legal records *(placita):* Cartae Senonicae, No. 26, *MG.* Formulae, p. 196; DDKar., Nos. 65, *ao.* 772 (four counts, five royal vassals); No. 102, *ao.* 775 (eight counts, three not identified, one count palatine); No. 110, *ao.* 775 (seven counts, one count palatine); No. 138, *ao.* 781 (three counts, seven not identified, one constable, one count palatine); No. 148, *ais.* 782/83 (three bishops, eleven counts, forty-four *scabini,* one count palatine); No. 204, *ao.* 806 (seven counts, nine abbots, three performing the function of the count palatine); No. 216, *ao.* 812 (seven counts, three not identified, one count palatine).

97. I refer to those that the *placita* indicate by the words *vel reliquis quamplures* or by similar expressions. For the other courts, see p. 77 and n. 45, p. 82 and n. 88.

98. This information comes from Einhard, *Vita Karoli,* c. 24, ed. Holder-Egger, p. 29; Hincmar, *De ordine palatii,* c. 19 and 21, ed. V. Krause in *MG.* Capit. II, pp. 524–25, ed. M. Prou (Paris, 1885), pp. 50–51, 54–57. In the *De ordine palatii* I have used only the most general evidence, which obviously comes from the treatise of Adalard (see nn. 97 and 142 in Part I); as for the more special information, it would be difficult to make a distinction between what comes from this source and the "programmatic" elements derived from Hincmar himself.

99. See the formula of judgment in the *placita: Proinde nos taliter una cum fidelibus nostris, id est . . . et . . . comite palatii nostri vel reliquis quampluribus visi fuimus iudicasse.*

100. Einhard, *Vita Karoli,* and Hincmar, *De ordine palatii,* see n. 98. Capitulare de iustitiis faciendis, *ao.* 811, c. 2, *MG.* Capit. I, No. 80.

101. Annales Laureshamenses, *ao.* 786, *MG.* SS. I, p. 32; Annales Regni Francorum, *ao.* 788, 1st text, p. 80; Astronome, *Vita Hludowici, MG.* SS. II, p. 609 (on the date, *Regesten,* No. 305b); Annales Laureshamenses, *ao.* 792, p. 35.

102. See p. 46.

103. Capitulary issued at the conclusion of the council of Frankfurt, *ao.* 794, c. 6; Capitulare Saxonicum, *ao.* 797, c. 4: *MG.* Capit. I, Nos. 28 and 27.

104. Programmatic Capitulary, c. 34, 15, 17, 19, 24, 31, 32, 33 and 38, 34, 36, 37, *ibid.*, No. 33. For a long time several of these infractions were punishable; what was new was the competence of the palace court.

105. Capitulare Aquisgranense, c. 12, *ibid.*, No. 77. Individual measures were already taken on occasion in this sense (see chiefly Cartae Senonicae, No. 18, *MG.* Formulae, p. 193); but in the present case one is dealing with a normative disposition.

106. Capitulare legibus additum, c. 2, *MG.* Capit. I, No. 39.

107. Capitulare missorum, c. 4 and 18, *ibid.*, No. 40. One can surmise that the dogs of the royal or imperial packs had this characteristic and that men gave the same look to their dogs so that they could hunt in the royal preserves *(forestes)* without being detected.

108. See p. 6.

109. Capitulare Aquisgranense, c. 14, and Capitulare missorum Aquisgranense primum, c. 29, both from 809 (oaths to be sworn at the palace); Capitulare missorum Aquisgranense primum, *ao.* 810, c. 12 and 13 (those refusing to perform military service, and deserters, both under the jurisdiction of the palace court; confirmation of c. 34 of the Programmatic Capitulary of 802: see above, n. 104): *MG.* Capit. I, Nos. 61, 62, 64.

110. All the dispositions that I have analyzed and commented upon speak of sending those presumed guilty *ad palatium, ad regem, ad nostra presentia*, etc. It follows most often from the context that a judgment had to follow, and one is able, I believe, to so generalize. It is nevertheless possible that in certain cases Charlemagne had the intention of settling the case, not by a judgment, but by what we would call today an administrative decision.

111. Capitulare missorum Aquisgranense primum, c. 1, and Capitulare missorum Aquisgranense alterum, c. 8, both from 810, *MG.* Capit. I, Nos. 64 and 65.

112. See p. 84 and n. 100.

113. One notices this in reading c. 4 of the Capitulare missorum of 803; c. 14 and 29, respectively, of the Capitulare Aquisgranense and of the Capitulare missorum Aquisgranense primum of 809; c. 4 of the Responsa cuidam misso data of 802–13: *MG.* Capit. I, Nos. 40, 61–62, 58.

114. Those dealing with the infractions of the military duties of the subjects; see above, nn. 104 (c. 34) and 109; at least if these articles had a general import. Perhaps they only concerned men of elevated rank.

115. The recourses to the palace court after a first judgment will be treated on p. 94.

116. I do not intend to treat here all the aspects of the history of procedure in relation to the action exerted by Charlemagne on the law; I limit myself to four aspects of the subject, which to me seem particularly important: the proofs, the execution of the judgment, the recourse after judgment, and the procedure in case of apprehension in the act. For the proofs see my treatment of the subject, "La preuve dans le droit franc," *Recueils de la Société Jean Bodin*: XVII, *La preuve II. Moyen Age et Temps Modernes* (Brussels, 1965), 71–98.

117. The very just appreciation of E. Kaufmann, *Die Erfolgshaftung* (Frankfort on the Main, 1958), p. 51. On the ordeals see H. Nottarp, *Gottesurteilstudien* (Munich, 1956), and on their origins, A. Erler, "Der Ursprung der Gottesurteile," *Paideuma. Mitteilungen zur Kulturkunde*, II (1941). The pagan origin is not valid for the proof of the cross (see pp. 88–89).

118. In the same way as Kaufmann, *Erfolgshaftung*, pp. 49 and 52–53, with good reason, has strongly underlined it.

119. I follow U. Stutz, "Die Beweisrolle im altdeutschen Rechtsgang," *Zeitschrift der Savigny-Stiftung für Rechtsgeschichte*, Germanistische Abt. XLIX (1929).

120. It suffices to refer to F. Beyerle, *Das Entwicklungsproblem im germanischen Rechtsgang*, I (Heidelberg, 1915), 383–96.

121. Cartae Senonicae, Nos. 21 and 22; Formulae Salicae Merkelianae, Nos. 27, 28, and 30; Formulae Salicae Lindenbrogianae, No. 21: *MG. Formulae*, pp. 194, 251–53, 282; Synodus Franconofurtensis, *ao.* 794, c. 9, *MG*. Capit. I, No. 28; Formulae Senonenses recentiores, Nos. 2 and 5, *MG*. Formulae, pp. 210–11, 213–14.

122. Capitulare legi Ribuariae additum, *ao.* 803, c. 4: he who is accused of having robbed a flock will have the right of clearing himself by an oath with twelve oath-helpers (modification of title 18 of text B of the *Lex Ribuaria*=text A, 19 [18], I, ed. Beyerle and Buchner, p. 81: the proof could be made by an oath along with seventy-two oath-helpers). Capitulare Karoli Magni de latronibus, *ao.* 804, c. 3: he who is accused of brigandage is able to clear himself by an oath with some oath-helpers. Capitula Karoli Magni apud Ansegisum servata, c. 1: he who, accused of having attacked a *missus dominicus* with arms and in a band, desires to free himself by proving that he did not know the position of the person attacked can do so by an oath with twelve oath-helpers; c. 5 (fragment of a capitulary for Saxony): if a Saxon accuses a man of having robbed him of an object or of having caused him damage, and if the accused refuses the judicial duel or the proof of the cross, he can clear himself by an oath with oath-helpers. Capitulare missorum Aquisgranense primum, *ao.* 809, c. 28: a person condemned to death and hav-

ing obtained pardon could not clear himself by oath but only by the judgment of God: *MG.* Capit. I, Nos. 41, 82, 70, 62.

123. Capitulare legi Ribuariae additum, *ao.* 803, c. 11 (adjunct to title 68 of text B of the *Lex Ribuaria*=text A, 69 [66], I, ed. Beyerle and Buchner, pp. 119–20); Capitulatio de partibus Saxoniae, *ao.* 785, c. 32 (implicitly): *MG.* Capit. I, Nos. 41 and 26.

124. In more than one case the texts refer to a *iudicium Dei* with no more information than this. In such cases it is impossible to know which judgment of God was involved; for example: Synodus Franconofurtensis, *ao.* 794, c. 9, and Capitulare missorum Aquisgranense primum, *ao.* 809, c. 28: *MG.* Capit. I, Nos. 28 and 62; DKar., No. 181, *ao.* 797.

125. The Pactus Legis Salicae, 56, §1, 2, and 3 mention the *inium* or another kind of proof (ed. K. A. Eckhardt, II, Pt. 1, 324–27=ed. *MG.* Leges nationum Germanicarum of the same, pp. 210–11). The *Lex Salica Karolina*, 59 (ed. K. A. Eckhardt, II, Pt. 2, 521–22=ed. *MG.* Leges nationum Germanicarum of the same, p. 211) has dropped the *inium* in what corresponds there to §1 (the core of the matter) and to §2; if the word is maintained in what corresponds to §3, it is without doubt the result of the negligence of a scribe.

126. Capitulare legibus additum, *ao.* 803, c. 5, *MG.* Capit. I, No. 39. This type of crime, particularly odious and, it seems, difficult to combat, continued to preoccupy Charlemagne; see Capitula de rebus exercitalibus in placito tractanda, *ao.* 811, c. 10, *ibid.,* No. 73.

127. Capitula de Iudaeis (if this capitulary is not of Louis the Pious), c. 6, *ibid.,* No. 131. The mode of proof foreseen in the first place was the testimonial proof.

128. I persist in considering the judicial duel a means of proof, whatever may have been its original import. It is pleasing to be in agreement on this point with H. Nottarp, *Gottesurteilstudien* (see n. 117), pp. 118–19 and 269–70.

129. As justly observed by F. Beyerle (above, n. 120), pp. 411–16.

130. (*1*) Capitulare legi Ribuariae additum, *ao.* 803, c. 4: in the case of robbery of a flock, if the plaintiff objects to the accused freeing himself by an oath with oath-helpers, a duel will be substituted (see above, n. 122). (*2*) *ibid.,* c. 7: *intertiatio,* that is, the procedure to follow when one discovered his own property, which had been stolen, in the hands of another (*Lex Ribuaria,* text B, 35=text A, 37 [33], 3, ed. Beyerle and Buchner, p. 90); if that one in whose house the stolen object had been found pointed out the person from whom he had received the object and this person had appeared but had refused to take the object, thus denying ever having had it, there would be a duel between the two. (*3*) Capitulare Karoli Magni de latronibus, *ao.* 804, c. 3: in case of accu-

sation of brigandage, if the plaintiff objects to the accused freeing himself by an oath with oath-helpers, there will be a duel (see above, n. 122). (*4*) Capitulare Aquisgranense, *ao*. 809, c. 1: if someone declares that the oath sworn in execution of a judgment by an accused already condemned to death and pardoned will be false, there will be a duel between them. (*5*) Capitula Karoli Magni apud Ansegisum servata, c. 5 (probably a fragment of a capitulary for Saxony): someone is arrested by a Saxon and accused of having stolen from him an object or of having caused damage to him, and unless the accused had the stolen object on his person, which would have constituted an apprehended crime, there will be a duel: *MG*. Capit. I, Nos. 41, 82, 61, 70. The second explanation proposed for this policy would find support in a fragment of an Italian capitulary, if this capitulary was really from Charlemagne, which is not at all certain; Capitula italica, c. 8, *ibid*., No. 105: . . . *melius est ut in campo cum fustibus pariter contendant quam periurium perpetrent.*

131. (*1*) *scuto et fuste*; (*3*) *cum fustibus*; (*4*) *cum arma*; the texts (*2*) and (*5*) only say *campo.*

132. (*1*) Subsidiary to the oath with oath-helpers, alternative with the proof of the cross; (*2*) alternative with the proof of the cross; (*3*) subsidiary to the oath with oath-helpers; (*4*) preliminary statement that an oath was false; (*5*) alternative with the proof of the cross or with an oath with oath-helpers.

133. See my study, "L'épreuve de la croix dans le droit de la monarchie franque," *Studi e materiali di storia delle religioni*, XXXVIII (Rome, 1967).

134. Landed property: Formulae Salicae Bignonianae, No. 13, Formulae Salicae Merkelianae, No. 42: *MG*. Formulae, pp. 232–33, 257; DKar., No. 102, *ao*. 775. The law of marriage: Bavarian synod of Salzburg, presided over by Arn, *ao*. 800, c. 46, in Statuta Rhispacensia, Frisingensia, Salisburgensia, *MG*. Capit. I, No. 112, and *MG*. Concilia II, No. 24A, pp. 212–13 (very obscure).

135. See nn. 130 and 132, Nos. 1, 2, and 5. Suppression by Louis the Pious: Capitulare ecclesiasticum, *ais*. 818/19, c. 27, *MG*. Capit. I, No. 138.

136. Kaufmann (see above, n. 117), p. 50, has very justly written about the formalism affecting all the trial.

137. This explains the prohibition to submit someone to the judgment of God without a judicial suit; Capitulare missorum, *ao*. 803, c. 11, *MG*. Capit. I, No. 40.

138. Capitulare missorum Aquisgranense primum, *ao*. 809, c. 20, *ibid*., No. 62: *Ut omnes iuditium Dei credant sine dubitatione.* This prescription would not be included if some doubts had not been expressed.

139. DDKar., No. 138, *ao.* 781, and No. 148, *ais.* 782/83 (palace court); Devic and Vaissete, *Histoire générale de Languedoc*, ed. Privat, II, Preuves, No. 6, *ao.* 782 *(missi)*, and No. 10, *ao.* 791 *(mallus)*; Poupardin, *Recueil des chartes de . . . Saint-Germain-des-Prés*, I, No. 22, *ao.* 791 *(missi)*; De Courson, *Cartulaire de . . . Redon*, No. 191, *ao.* 797 (=Thévenin, *Textes*, No. 191) *(mallus)*; Formulae Senonenses recentiores, No. 3, *MG.* Formulae, pp. 212–13 *(mallus)*; Bougaud and Garnier, *Chronique de . . . Saint-Bénigne de Dijon, suivie de la chronique de Saint-Pierre de Bèze*, pp. 250–51 (=Thévenin, *Textes*, No. 115), *ao.* 815 *(mallus)*; Pérard, *Recueil*, p. 14, *ao.* 815 *(mallus)*; Prou and Vidier, *Recueil des chartes de . . . Saint-Benoît-sur-Loire*, I, No. 10, *ao.* 815, and No. 11, *ao.* 817 *(mallus)*; Bougaud and Garnier, p. 252, *ais.* 817/18 *(mallus)*; Prou and Vidier, No. 12, *ao.* 818, and No. 16, *ao.* 819 *(mallus)*. Reform of Louis the Pious: Capitula legi addita, *ao.* 816, c. 1 (2 texts), and Capitula legibus addenda, *ais.* 818/19, c. 10: *MG.* Capit. I, Nos. 134–35 and 139.

140. Capitulare legibus additum, *ao.* 803, c. 11, reiterated and precisely stated by the Capitulare missorum of Thionville, *ao.* 805, c. 11: *MG.* Capit. I, Nos. 39 and 44.

141. Witnesses presumed suspect and disqualified: Capitulare legibus addendum, *ao.* 803, c. 11; Capitulare missorum, *ao.* 803, c. 21; Capitulare Aquisgranense, *ao.* 809, c. 1. Examination of the witnesses before their deposition under oath and, in such a case, individual interrogation: Capitulare missorum of Thionville, *ao.* 805, c. 11; Capitulare Aquisgranense, *ao.* 809, c. 6. Several of these dispositions and notably those of c. 11 of the Capitulare missorum of Thionville were introduced into Italy; Pippini Capitulare italicum, *ao.* 810, c. 12: *MG.* Capit. I, Nos. 39, 40, 61, 44, 61, 102.

142. All legal records cited above, n. 139, dealt with trials of this sort.

143. DDKar., No. 65, *ao.* 772, No. 110, *ao.* 775; Bernard and Bruel, *Recueil des chartes de . . . Cluny*, I, No. 3, *ao.* 814.

144. De Monsabert, *Chartes de . . . Nouaillé*, No. 50, *ao.* 780 (after examination of the written evidence, postponement of the case, obviously in order to permit the use of witnesses); DKar., No. 102, *ao.* 775; Pérard, *Recueil*, p. 14, *ao.* 815.

145. *Lex Ribuaria*, 62 (59), ed. Beyerle and Buchner, pp. 114–16.

146. Capitulare missorum, *ao.* 803, c. 3; ecclesiastical Capitulare missorum of Thionville, *ao.* 805, c. 4 (text of the ms. Guelferbytanus inter Blankenburgenses 130.52): *MG.* Capit. I, Nos. 40 and 43. *Notarius* in these two texts corresponds to *cancellarius* in the others. See also the text cited in the following note.

147. One notes this in reading a fragment of a capitulary, probably dating from Charlemagne, that favors the authority of a charter of manu-

mission established by a *cancellarius* but admits that it may be contested; Capitula francica, c. 7, *MG.* Capit. I, No. 104.

148. DKar., No. 138, *ao.* 781.

149. See p. 76 and n. 36.

150. In more of the legal records (indicated below, n. 151), see the Capitulare de iustitiis faciendis, *ao.* 811, c. 3, *MG.* Capit. I, No. 80: *a misso nostro et comite . . . eligantur.* This article contains some dispositions on the choice of witnesses worthy of confidence. The dispositions relative to the requisite qualities of witnesses at the testimonial proof (see above, n. 141) were evidently applicable to witnesses at the inquest.

151. (*1*) E. E. Stengel, *Urkundenbuch des Klosters Fulda*, I, No. 83, *ao.* 777 (=DKar., No. 116, Appendix) *(missi).* (*2*) Albanès and Chevalier, *Gallia Christiana Novissima*, III (Marseilles), No. 42, *ao.* 780 (=B. Guérard, *Cartulaire de . . . Saint-Victor de Marseille*, I, No. 31) *(missi).* (*3*) Glöckner, *Codex Laureshamensis*, II, No. 228, *ao.* 782 *(missi).* (*4-5*) Formulae Augienses B, No. 22 *(missi)* and probably No. 40 *(mallus),* end of eighth or beginning of ninth century, *MG.* Formulae, pp. 357 and 362. (*6-11*) Bitterauf, *Die Traditionen des Hochstifts Freising*, I, Nos. 184 and 185, 193, 247 *(missi),* 237, and probably 251 and 258 (assizes held by several counts, bishops, or abbots; substitute for the assizes of the *missi;* see pp. 82-83 and n. 95), *ais.* 802, 804, 806-11, 814, and 807. (*12*) Wartmann, *Urkundenbuch der Abtei Sankt Gallen*, I, No. 187, *ais.* 806/7 *(mallus).*

152. Only texts (*5*) and (*12*) treated the *mallus;* the first is perhaps later than 802; and the last certainly is.

153. The rule was only formulated under Louis the Pious, Capitula de iustitiis faciendis, *ca. am.* 820, c. 1. But it is the foundation of c. 2 of the Capitulare missorum of 818/19; in this case one is dealing with a traditional rule that goes back to the beginnings of the institution, early in the reign of Charlemagne: *MG.* Capit. I, Nos. 144 and 141.

154. See n. 151. Texts (*1*), (*2*), (*3*), (*6-11*), (*12*) deal with suits concerned with real property where churches were involved; in the first three cases these lands were ancient royal domains; text (*5*) reports on a suit over real property in which the parties were individuals.

155. The diet of October concerned itself with the possibility of establishing the ownership of private churches *(Eigenkirchen)* of which the peaceful possession for thirty years could not be proved; Capitula a sacerdotibus proposita, c. 17, *MG.* Capit. I, No. 36.

156. At least according to text (*4*); see p. 94 and n. 168. But texts (*4*) and (*5*) are corrupt in certain places and are very difficult to understand.

157. Formulae Salicae Bignonianae, No. 7 (serfdom), No. 27 (landed

property); Formulae Salicae Merkelianae, No. 29 (burglary); Formulae Salicae Lindenbrogianae, No. 19 (homicide): *MG.* Formulae, pp. 230, 237, 252, 280.

158. Assizes of *missi:* Albanès and Chevalier, *Gallia Christiana Novissima,* III (Marseilles), No. 42, *ao.* 780; Devic and Vaissete, *Histoire générale de Languedoc,* ed. Privat, II, Preuves, No. 6, *ao.* 782; Bernard and Bruel, *Recueil des chartes de l'abbaye de Cluny,* I, No. 3, *ao.* 814; (in the three cases, landed property). *Mallus:* Cartae Senonicae, No. 11 (murder), No. 20 (colonate), No. 51 (murder); Formulae Salicae Bignonianae, No. 8 (homicide), No. 9 (homicide), No. 13 (landed property); Formulae Salicae Lindenbrogianae, No. 21 (serfdom); Formulae Senonenses recentiores, No. 5 (colonate), No. 6 (serfdom), No. 7 (landed property): *MG.* Formulae, pp. 189, 194, 207, 230–31, 232–33, 282, 213–14.

159. My opinion hardly agrees with that of Brunner and von Schwerin, *Deutsche Rechtsgeschichte,* I (2nd ed.), 484–85, for whom the differences between the two series of texts are purely formal.

160. Formulae Senonenses recentiores, No. 1 (colonate), No. 3 (serfdom), No. 6 (serfdom), *MG.* Formulae, pp. 211, 213, 214.

161. Bavaria and Alamannia: see Part I, p. 33 and n. 239. Septimania: Devic and Vaissete, *Histoire générale de Languedoc,* ed. Privat, II, Preuves, No. 6, *ao.* 782.

162. Except for the first, the texts to which I refer envisage other cases in which this method of constraint was used. Capitulatio de partibus Saxoniae, *ao.* 785, c. 27; Capitulare legi Ribuariae additum, *ao.* 803, c. 6; Capitulare Aquisgranense, *ais.* 802/3, c. 13; Capitulare Aquisgranense, *ao.* 809, c. 3 and 4; Capitulare missorum Aquisgranense primum, *ao.* 809, c. 11: *MG.* Capit. I, Nos. 26, 41, 77, 61, 62.

163. Such as it was for military service, Capitula de rebus exercitalibus in placito tractanda, *ao.* 811, c. 6, *ibid.,* No. 73.

164. I give here a summary of the classic views on the subject as they are expressed by Brunner and von Schwerin, pp. 472–79. On the whole they appear justified.

165. Capitulare missorum of Thionville, *ao.* 805, c. 8, *MG.* Capit. I, No. 44. See p. 81 and n. 78.

166. Pippini regis capitulare, *ais.* 751–55, c. 7, *ibid.,* No. 13.

167. What is said is based on the evidence furnished by the capitulary of Pepin and on the capitularies of Charlemagne (see nn. 165 and 169); this summary agrees on the whole with the views of Brunner and von Schwerin, pp. 479–81.

168. This is what appears to have been the case in Formulae Augienses B, No. 22, *MG.* Formulae, p. 357; see above, nn. 151, 156.

169. Capitulare Saxonicum, *ao.* 797, c. 4; Capitulare Baiwaricum, probably *ao.* 803, c. 7: *MG.* Capit. I, Nos. 26 and 69.

170. Capitulare missorum of Thionville, c. 8, *in fine;* see n. 165.

171. There are some discussions of this procedure in several of the works cited in n. 1; that of Brunner and von Schwerin on pp. 626–36 is preferred. See also my article, "Note sur la preuve dans la procédure en cas de flagrant délit en droit franc," *Miscellanea mediaevalia in memoriam J. F. Niermeyer* (Groningen, 1967).

172. Capitulary of Herstal, *ao.* 779, c. 11, whereas c. 23 seems to relate to brigands not arrested in the act; probably, also, Capitulare missorum Aquisgranense primum, *ao.* 810, c. 11: *MG.* Capit. I, Nos. 20 and 64.

173. Capitulare Karoli Magni de latronibus, *ao.* 804, c. 2, *ibid.,* No. 82: *Si latro de liberis personis fuerit ortus, postquam reprobatus fuerit inventus secundum antiquam consuetudinem iudicetur. Si vero dictus fuerit latro et non fuerit conpraehensus, qui eum conprobare voluerit secundum legem adprobare faciat.* It would appear that c. 21 of the Capitulare missorum of Thionville, *ao.* 805, *ibid.,* No. 44, confirms this disposition.

174. See p. 75.

175. On *faida* it suffices to refer to Brunner and von Schwerin, pp. 692 ff. The study of J. M. Wallace-Hadrill, "The Bloodfeud of the Franks," in his collection *The Long-haired Kings* (London, 1962), pp. 121 ff., is limited to the Merovingian period, but it constitutes a useful introduction to the problem as it was at the time of Charlemagne. F. Beyerle (see above, n. 120), pp. 242–59, gives a list of cases of *faida* that one may consider as recognized in most of the Germanic laws; it is with reason that he presents this list only under reservations expressed a number of times. The Burgundian law and the Visigothic law did not exclude *faida,* but they severely limited it; see A. von Halban, *Das römische Recht in den germanischen Volksstaaten,* I (Breslau, 1899), 220, 222, 288, 289.

176. Capitulary of Herstal, c. 20, *MG.* Capit. I, No. 20.

177. C. 67, *ibid.,* No. 22. It is naturally to other means that the royal *iudices* had to have recourse when homicide had not been committed *causa ultionis,* but *causa avaritiae* or *latrocinandi.*

178. Capitulatio de partibus Saxoniae, *ao.* 785, c. 31: the king left to each count the right of prohibiting *faida,* if he judged it useful, under pain of a fine of sixty shillings; Capitulare Saxonicum, *ao.* 797, c. 9: the king reserved to himself the right of issuing "with the *consensus* of the Franks and of the faithful Saxons," dispositions prohibiting *faida* under pain of a doubled fine (two times sixty shillings); it would appear that

the remainder of the article concerns the *maiores causae: MG.* Capit. I, Nos. 26 and 27.

179. See p. 6.

180. Programmatic Capitulary of 802; c. 22, *MG.* Capit. I, No. 33.

181. Capitulare missorum of Thionville, c. 5, *ibid.,* No. 44. Prohibition against carrying a *brunia,* a lance, and a shield in the interior of the country.

182. The same article.

183. End of the same article.

184. Allusions to Article 5 of the Capitulary of Thionville, in the Capitulare missorum of 808, c. 1, and Capitulare missorum Aquisgranense primum, *ao.* 810, c. 10: *MG.* Capit. I, Nos. 53 and 64.

185. See, among others, a fragment of a *Capitulare missorum* from the very end of the reign of Charlemagne or from the reign of Louis the Pious, Capitula originis incertae, c. 2, *ibid.,* No. 79. Here, one is enjoined to proceed against troubles provoked by *faidosi homines.*

186. It is probable that *faida* had also been practiced by men living under the Burgundian, Visigothic, or Roman law.

INDEX

Index

This index is concerned primarily with technical terms and with political, legal, and military institutions. Since the entire book concerns Charlemagne, his name does not appear as an entry. Other proper names are listed only when they are related to political, legal, and military institutions.

Date Due